MADELEINE

Introduction to the 1919 Edition by Judge Ben B. Lindsey

New Introduction by Marcia Carlisle

First published in 1919, this life story of a prostitute was the subject of a famous law case involving issues of obscenity, freedom of speech, and "white slavery." Self-educated and successful, Madeleine offers an eloquent, vivid account of brothel life in the 1890s, in the city (St. Louis and Chicago), in the Western boom town (Butte, Montana), and on the Canadian frontier. She describes the daily workings of both "high" and "low" class houses, her relationships with other women, the Madames, the customers, and with members of the "legitimate" society in which prostitution flourished. Perhaps most importantly, *Madeleine* offers a glimpse into the emotional perils a prostitute faced and shatters many illusions about her feelings toward herself, her work, her family, and others.

Marcia Carlisle is an historian of nineteenth century America who has written on prostitution.

MADELEINE

An Autobiography

Introduction to the 1919 Edition
by Judge Ben B. Lindsey

New Introduction by Marcia Carlisle

PERSEA BOOKS
New York

Introduction © 1986 by Marcia Carlisle

This edition published in 1986 by Persea Books. Originally
published in 1919 by Harper & Brothers.

For information, address the publisher:

Persea Books, Inc.
225 Lafayette Street
New York, New York 10012

Library of Congress Cataloging-in-Publication Data

Madeleine : an autobiography.

   Originally published: New York : Harper & Brothers, 1919.
   Bibliography: p.
   1. Prostitutes—United States—Biography.
   2. United States—Moral conditions—Case studies.
HQ144.M3 1986   306.7'42'0924   [B]   86-4924
ISBN 0-89255-108-9 (pbk.)

Printed in the United States of America.

INTRODUCTION

O that thou wouldst hide me in the grave
That thou wouldst keep me secret
Until thy wrath be past,
That then wouldst appoint me a set time
And remember

Job's Lament, as Madeleine remembered it

Madeleine: An Autobiography is the story of a woman's career as a prostitute in late nineteenth-century America. When it was published in 1919, it achieved a short-lived notoriety because of efforts to suppress it. Descriptions of sexual transactions between prostitutes and their customers did not alarm censors, for there are few; *Madeleine* is not a document of the demi-monde. Instead, it was the author's failure to be humbled by her experiences and her critical attitude toward Christian reformers that offended. Since then, *Madeleine* has gone largely unnoticed. Occasionally historians have examined the text as a document from which to pull details of brothel prostitution in the 1890s. They have done so with the assurance that, although it was published anonymously, the information offered is accurate.

But is *Madeleine* a prostitute's autobiography written

INTRODUCTION

in her own words? Was the writing done by a prostitute, or is it her story as told to or reported by someone else? The question will be valid as long as the identity of the author remains unknown. Yet there is sufficient reason to assume that the text is authentic.

Undoubtedly, there were (and are) prostitutes literate enough to have written a text as polished as *Madeleine*. Some "fallen women" were educated in their early years and continued to educate themselves as they grew older. A career in prostitution did not prevent women from developing intellectual interests and abilities, and none of the original reviews of *Madeleine* raised the issue of authorship. There were those who wanted to discredit the book, but no one suggested that the book was a fraud. Harper and Brothers might have defended itself in the lawsuit that followed publication by revealing that the book was written by a reformer, for example. Instead, the publisher stood by the book as a prostitute's autobiography and protected the author's identity when it might have been advantageous to reveal it.

Perhaps the most convincing argument for authorship lies within the text itself. The coherence of content, structure, and style grows directly out of the life described. The flat, even quality of the narrative is consistent with the wealth of household and "female" details that are included along with the matter-of-fact descriptions of dealings with the other brothel inmates and the police. There is little sensationalism to arouse the reader, but there is sentimentalism aimed at a female audience. The narrative is driven by self-interest and not by social concern. It is the image of the woman as legitimate social

INTRODUCTION

actor, not the woman as victim, that emerges from the story. Given what we are learning about "voice" and autobiography, it is unlikely that the material could come from Madeleine's life but have been written in the words of another person. The voice is too clear and too consistent to have been imposed on the material by a collaborator, who would not have been a part of the world and the events described.

Thus, *Madeleine* is valuable beyond its informative nature. It stands as a consciously crafted record of the material and emotional perils faced by prostitutes of the period as they lived a life of precarious independence outside the traditional structures of support. As the reviewer in *The Nation* noted at the time, "the oldest profession" had never before yielded "a personal document of any significance." In this respect, *Madeleine* was a first when it was released in 1919.[1]

As autobiography, *Madeleine* affirms some patterns discerned by scholars in women's written self-portraits, and it challenges others. As a cultural document of the Progressive Era, it stands in marked contrast to both the dramatic white slave narratives and the fact-filled but moralizing vice commission reports. The account of one woman's attempt to achieve independence, it can be read as a feminist narrative, and, certainly, as a companion volume to other works that focus on the same theme and time period, such as Stephen Crane's "Maggie: A Girl of the Streets" (1893). Like the more recently issued *Maimie Papers* (the letters of an American prostitute to her reformer, 1910–1922), Madeleine's account of her life shatters many illusions about the feelings of a harlot toward herself, her work, and those around her.

The autobiography is divided into three books and an epilogue. Book I encompasses Madeleine's earliest years, her move into prostitution and her final break from her family. Here, she describes the circumstances which brought about her "social bankruptcy" and those which made possible her spiritual renewal. Book II covers her career as a prostitute in brothels in St. Louis, Kansas City, and Chicago, and her erratic involvement with Paul, her lover. It concludes when Madeleine realizes that she and Paul cannot break down the wall of mistrust between them and build a life together. Book III treats her years as a madame in a frontier city in Canada, her alcoholism, and her final rejection of prostitution. It ends when Madeleine acknowledges that from then on she can and must walk alone. The epilogue is a bitter attack on Progressive reformers who worry about "white slavery," the abduction of young women into a life of prostitution, a phenomenon Madeleine insists did not exist.

In the work, two clear structures (two texts) are developed. One is the history of Madeleine's career, the chronicle of her climb from a young streetwalker to a sophisticated madame. The other is the literary self-portrait of a woman who struggled to achieve independence and self-knowledge. The latter text, the more intriguing of the two, is, at times, an appeal to the reader to understand her—a complex, wronged but proud woman. At other times, this text is contrived, false, an attempt to create a fictional life more conventional, more proper than the one actually lived. The tension between

INTRODUCTION

the two structures, one common to autobiographies, forces the reader to acknowledge the ambiguities characteristic of the presentation of self in any genre.

. . .

Finding herself unmarried and pregnant at seventeen (circa 1887), Madeleine turned to the self-sufficiency prostitution offered rather than follow what were considered to be the morally appropriate courses of action: confinement in shame in a Magdalen home for fallen women or suicide. "I, an attractive, young girl, homeless, defenseless, hungry and in a few months to become a mother, had no choice between the course I took and the Mississippi River," she wrote. The content of her autobiography from this point on confirms conclusions found in recent research on prostitution during that time period. Prostitution was a business operated primarily by madames who were as diverse as the women they employed. Houses of prostitution catered to a hierarchy of clientele, and a hierarchy existed among the prostitutes themselves. The houses were ranked both by the women who entertained there and the men who frequented them. Working class men visited low-cost, low-class houses which were filled with the daughters of immigrants dressed in common wrappers, establishments like Madame C–s, a house in Chicago in which Madeleine lived for a short time. High-cost, high-class houses (like Miss Allen's "Ice Palace" where Madeleine was "Miss Blair"), where white collar working men, politicians, and the rich went, were filled with women who wore luxurious gowns and had impeccable manners. In all houses, there were rules that assured the madame her

INTRODUCTION

profit and protected the reputation of the house as one free of disease. Daily schedules were maintained. At certain hours, the women slept. During the afternoons, they attended to the ordinary concerns of life (shopping, grooming, etc.). In the evening, guests were met and entertained.[2]

The women lived in isolation from "respectable" society, about which they were often openly cynical. Madeleine claimed that women "in the life" were working women who paid a high price in order to pursue their profession, a claim made by some of today's historians of prostitution and by women in today's sex industry. But, she asserted, such women did not cheat in the delivery of the merchandise for which they were paid. On the contrary, the women who sold themselves into what she called "loathsome" marriages were guilty of the sin for which the scarlet women paid. Such claims were also made at the turn of the century by feminists concerned with women's status and prostitution.

The complicated meshing of the values of respectable society with those of the world of prostitution is evident in one of the most painful sequences (and one of the few sexual encounters) Madeleine described: the evening with the "beast." The "beast" was a guest in Miss Allen's house. He was a man who moved in high society, accompanied by a proper wife. When Madeleine met him, he was on a spree. A fellow prostitute had been with him all night and by the next afternoon was on the verge of killing him, so anxious was she to escape his pawing hands. House rules dictated that a customer could not be left alone, so Madeleine became the object of his seemingly endless caresses. "My soul revolted at the task," she wrote, "but I was anxious to make money." And she did.

Madeleine worked in collusion with another more experienced woman, and together they sold the man the same bottle of liquor many times over (although neither of them drank) and in various ways encouraged his drunken generosity. They worked the man, and he in turn "exacted his pound of flesh" from them. When it was over, the two women divided the money they made, giving Miss Allen only the fixed price of the house for the time the guest had been there and the income from the sale of the one bottle of liquor they actually had used. Although Madeleine was concerned about the dishonesty involved, it was cheating Miss Allen, not the male customer, that rankled. For the "beast" and the hypocrisy he represented to her, she had only contempt. When he finally left, she lay there questioning her Creator. Why had He made beasts like that? "Surely His wisdom had not decreed that one set of women should live in degradation and in the end should perish that others might live in security, preserve their frapeed chastity, and in the end be saved." But as there was no answer forthcoming, she aired her room, soaked in a hot tub, and washed her skin with rubbing alcohol to remove the traces of the day. Then she left the house and took a rejuvenating walk by the lake. She tried to cleanse her mind by substituting thoughts from the pens of great men whom she idealized for thoughts of the "beast" and the brothel.

Throughout the book there are similar references to

INTRODUCTION

Madeleine's efforts at self-education. She draws and paints, reads poetry and essays—all in an attempt to complete the education she would have had if her own father had not "fallen" into alcoholism and deserted the family. She treasures that education, the impulse to learn about great works, as a mark of distinction in a world in which such achievements were believed to be rare. She offers the reader the image of herself as a thwarted Renaissance woman as if to balance the stronger image of the working prostitute.

Madeleine's attempt to separate herself from her work and from others in the trade is an important part of her defense against the stigma of being a prostitute. She presents herself as educated, reserved, unwilling to force herself on a customer. Maimie Pinzer, of the *Maimie Papers*, a Philadelphia prostitute, also tried to elevate herself above other prostitutes. She proudly portrays herself as a woman who chose to date selected men—to be a high class call girl, in today's terminology—and who had never lowered herself to become a brothel prostitute. Both Maimie and Madeleine take special pride in personal appearance, clothing, tidiness. Both admit (with a tone of defiance) that they are not beautiful. Instead, they emphasize their style and refinement, attributes each believes are attractive to the men they know. They are ladies, equal in their own estimation to women outside the trade whom society recognizes as ladies.

Madeleine's initiation into prostitution is familiar. She began to experiment with sex as a curious, young teenager, then became a prostitute in her late teens. Like others in documented cases, she came from a family

INTRODUCTION

from which one parent was missing. In many cases, the parent was dead; in others, as in Madeleine's, the parent was absent, a result of alcoholism or other illness. Once in the trade, a young woman typically moved from brothel to brothel as Madeleine did. But, unlike Madeleine, few had patrons who offered to help them leave the trade. Reformers believed that all prostitutes died young; today's historians find that many just disappear from public records and are hard to trace. What information exists, however, suggests that some changed occupations or married. Some women moved in and out of prostitution, finding that virtue did not pay as well as vice. Madeleine herself was bitter that such a good woman as her mother was dying in poverty, unable to accept the financial benefits of Madeleine's "fall."

Once a prostitute became a mother, the pressure to remain in the life increased (for financial reasons), but the desire to get out increased, too. Census records show that children lived in many of the disorderly boarding houses in the working class neighborhoods of cities such as Philadelphia and New York. These residences, in which prostitutes mixed with other women, were the subject of concern among moral reformers in the 1880s, and they often attempted to remove children from what they deemed improper surroundings. When faced with the loss of their children, some prostitutes struggled against the courts, the church, their neighbors, and other family members in order to keep custody of children they loved. Some agreed to allow the child to live in another house at their expense. Others didn't fight and gave up their children. Feelings and circumstances varied.[3]

INTRODUCTION

Madeleine's account of her feelings for her son provides a very rare glimpse into her dilemma of motherhood and strongly contradicts the reformer's belief that a career in prostitution destroys maternal love. Madeleine loved her son, worked to support him, to keep him healthy and happy and living with her. When the boy died, the description of his death (written in the style of the best Victorian sentimental fiction) and Madeleine's anguish at her inability to save him, are heart-wrenching. Madeleine's feelings ran deep, as deep as the feelings of any mother toward her child. Her hostility was increasingly for men, "the mere sowers of seed" who father children irresponsibly. When she found herself pregnant again, she risked a dangerous abortion rather than bring another child into a world with which she was increasingly at war.

Madeleine treasured her personal independence although the direction of that independence was determined by default. Her break with her family (and her consequent entry into the profession) was forced upon her by her self-righteous, alcoholic father, a man who abandoned his family, leaving them to face certain poverty. Her break with her lover, Paul, requires more consideration. Paul and Madeleine met in a brothel. They fell in love, and over the years Paul patiently supported Madeleine as she struggled in and out of trouble. According to Madeleine, Paul wanted to marry her, but she could not bring herself to trust him, to believe that he would not try to remake her to fill his own needs. In particular, she could not bear the idea of being dependent on him. But her account of this relationship is suspect.

INTRODUCTION

For instance, Madeleine insists that, no matter what she did, Paul always saw her as a worthy mate. Perhaps she was unwilling to admit that she felt unworthy of him and therefore could not allow herself to accept him; or perhaps Paul was actually less willing to accept her as she was. In any case, she does not give us a realistic portrait of him or the relationship. Instead, she uses him to legitimatize her projected self-image as a desirable woman who was not trapped by her profession but free to do as she pleased. As she would have us believe, her failure to establish a life with Paul was not a failure but a positive and deliberate step toward an independent life.

Madeleine saw her deepening involvement in prostitution as another aspect of her commitment to independence. She began as an inexperienced streetwalker and, in her twenties, became a member of Chicago's finest brothel establishment and then the madame of a successful brothel in Canada. The direction of her life contradicted the popular myth (still in fashion) that a harlot's way was downward to ruin. In fact, she had worked her way up the ladder to success. What seems contradictory in her account of her growing independence is that while she defied the ideals of a Victorian lady, she also cherished them. Her struggle to be what fate forced upon her (a prostitute) did not diminish her desire to be what was consequently beyond her reach (a Victorian lady). But she believed that Victorian ladies were allowed their lifestyle primarily through hypocrisy. Rather than accept either that hypocrisy or the degradation of society, she fought for what she perceived as her only salvation:

independence. This paradox is what makes *Madeleine* an exceptional autobiography. It is what makes its author come alive as a complex human being.

. . .

According to Estelle Jelinek in an essay on tradition in autobiography, few autobiographies achieve the ideal of self-revelation that many associate with the genre. Neither men nor women open up the whole of their emotional lives to the reader. Detailed examinations of certain subjects close to the heart are routinely avoided. One's romantic attachments, husbands, wives, siblings are discussed only incidentally. The reasons for this reticence and the methods of detachment used may vary but are linked to the purposes in writing the autobiography.[4]

Typically, men who write autobiographies do so as representative actors in a given time period. Their stories are often success stories—linear, orderly chronicles of achievement. Confident of their personal worth and the value of their words, men tell life histories that contain the kind of advice an older man of the world might pass on to a younger generation of men. Women, less confident of their social worth, attempt to convince readers (most often, other women) of the value of their lives. Their autobiographies lack the grounding in traditional history, are less orderly and more likely to be a kind of sorting through of events and people aimed at authenticating a particular self-image.

It was a common practice in the writing of these autobiographies for the author to reshape his/her past. These liberties taken with fact were meant to achieve a special

INTRODUCTION

effect. For instance, a series of less dramatic events might be recast as one significant event that emerges as a turning point in the author's life story. Such was the case in Margaret Sanger's autobiographical account of her decision to focus on birth control. Authors sometimes compromised the truth in the interest of retrospectively designating sign-posts in their development. At other times, events and people were simply left out to achieve a coherent self-image. Self-interest and the message of the text (not absolute truth) were the guidelines for the genre.

The movement of women into the public sphere, into careers outside the home, allowed them to begin to develop the kind of self-consciousness that an autobiography demands. They began to think of themselves as individuals, not as relative creatures. During the Progressive Era (1900–1914), autobiographies of women began to be written and published in increasing numbers in the United States. These life stories were often accounts of their author's activities as leaders in one of the many reform efforts for which that era is known. Frances Willard (Women's Christian Temperance Union), Margaret Sanger (the birth control movement), Elizabeth Cady Stanton (the women's movement), and Ida Barnett Wells (the anti-lynching movement) all wrote autobiographies in their lifetimes. The reform effort is the central theme in each, and events in their private lives are recorded only as they relate to this public work. These autobiographies are transitional. Personal conflicts and confusion remain hidden behind their records of achievement in public works. Only later would women achieve a self-identity separate enough to include intro-

INTRODUCTION

spection about feelings as part of their written texts. But Madeleine's position outside the security of family and respectable work enabled her to develop a strong self-identity before other women of her generation. She was forced to be conscious of her self and more aware of her feelings, and she was, therefore, willing to write about them. Because she was denied the privilege of being a relative creature she was able to find a "voice" and anticipate the kind of autobiographical writing that was to come.

.   .   .

For many students of American history, the year 1919–1920 was a year of disgrace. Post-war America became the battleground for a war on progressive forces that had shaped the early years of the new century. Radicals, reformers, and romantics faced censure from "patriotic" Americans who increasingly viewed their efforts to achieve social justice as alien-inspired. A wave of strikes, initiated in response to spiraling inflation and low wages, was seen as evidence of Bolshevik influence in the labor movement. A series of bombings directed at public officials was seen as proof that the Russian Revolution was making its way to American soil. Throughout the nation, native-born Americans harassed immigrant Americans and attempted to enforce a consensus that the American way of life was above criticism. Radical publications were silenced. Offices of radical organizations (broadly defined) were illegally searched and destroyed. "Soviet Arks," ships carrying those considered undesirable aliens, left New York harbor amid cheers. To the degree that the Red Scare of 1919, as it is called, was an attempt to restore an illusory consensus, to return to a vision of America not marred by the conspicuous criticism of the problems wrought by industrial development, the events were a reaction to reform efforts in preceding years.

The Progressive Era, roughly defined as the years between 1900 (when Theodore Roosevelt came to the White House) and 1914 (when World War I broke out in Europe), was the time when the concern for the shape of industrial America moved many young, educated men and women to examine the landscape of large urban areas with the methods of the new social sciences. A new breed of reformer, the settlement house worker, lived in and made surveys of neighborhoods in the crowded centers of cities; roving journalists investigated the workings of state and local governments. As their results became known, a call for social justice was heard in the sanctuaries of churches, in the meeting halls of reform organizations and legislative bodies. It was a call heard with some apprehension by those who feared the success of efforts to alter a status quo by which they profited handsomely.

The published results of this "muckraking" shocked many good citizens. For some, there could be only one explanation for abundant abuse buried beneath great wealth: The Christian soul of the nation was corrupt. The forces of greed and lust had conspired to weaken the very moral fiber of young and old. For such people, nothing was more disturbing than the vice commission reports that documented the extent of prostitution in American cities. From 1911 to 1916, there were vice investigations in twenty-seven cities and three states.[5]

In *The Response to Prostitution in the Progressive Era*, historian Mark Connelly analyzes the most significant of these reports, "The Social Evil in Chicago." When it was published in 1911, Connelly argues, it began "what might be termed a collective act of ritual humiliation by urban America." The four hundred pages of facts and figures described prostitution as part of a network of other social ills on which it fed and which fed it: the saloon, police corruption, urban political machines, and family "pathology." In addition to the disturbing scope of the nefarious trade (it seemed to be everywhere), there was a good deal of evidence about the organization of a whole vice industry that suggested to the researchers that prostitution had become "commercialized." Brothels were operated as businesses, managed and controlled to produce profits. The entrepreneurial spirit of which Chicago city fathers had boasted had itself been "prostituted." The growth of the city had come about "dollar for dollar with moral decay."[6]

The publication of all the vice commission reports did not lead to the ultimate ideal of the absolute annihilation of prostitution. Instead, as Ruth Rosen argues in *The Lost Sisterhood: Prostitution in America, 1900-1918*, the main effort to eliminate prostitution, the closing down of the most notorious red-light districts in a few cities, did little except promote a reorganization of the trade outside the brothels. The publication of the reports, however, did bring about a great deal of soul-searching and public discussion of prostitution, although that, too, in the end, proved fruitless.

Among those Progressive Era intellectuals who grap-

INTRODUCTION

pled with the problem of prostitution were Emma Goldman, Jane Addams, Theodore Roosevelt, Lincoln Stef-
fans, and Walter Lippmann. Countless others, less
famous but equally concerned, wrote poems and plays
and stories about prostitutes and their lives. Floyd Dell,
in 1914, was forced to tell a would-be contributor that
The Masses, a journal dedicated to art and politics for
the masses, could not use his poem. "We get about eight
poems about prostitutes every day," he wrote, "and we
are convinced that it is an overworked subject."[7]

Still, radicals and conservatives alike argued the old
questions in a new language. Was prostitution a necessary evil? Were the women who became prostitutes vic-
timized by the double standard, by economic exploitation, or by both? What were the sources of the problem?
Were they physiological: Was it male lust and female
passivity? Were they psychological: Were prostitutes
feeble-minded or maladjusted? Or were the sources en-
vironmental, the result of a culture of poverty? Was the
fallen woman a victim or a heroine? Was her life sad
testimony to the injustice of poverty or the noble resistance to it? And what was to be done?

Few new solutions arose out of all the formulations.
What answers were proposed were often as simplistic
as the analyses that spawned them: a minimum wage
for women workers, sexual purity for men, tougher city
ordinances to control the profits of prostitution. The
new social realism, like the vice commission reports
themselves, was burdened by old myths and ideals. It
was not possible, as some hoped, to formulate a new
conscience for an ancient evil.

The strength of the fascination about prostitution was

INTRODUCTION

evident in the many white slave narratives that were published at the same time as the vice commission reports. Between 1909 and 1914, twenty-two such tracts appeared. One of the most famous of these, Reginald Kaufman's *The House of Bondage*, went through fourteen editions within two years of its publication in 1910. The central concern of the narratives was the young country girl (symbol of innocence) who was lured to the city. Far away from the wholesome influence of family, she fell victim to one of the thousands of procurers, the white slavers, who were thought to lurk there. The young woman was then drugged, dragged into prostitution, enslaved, and ruined for life. The more mundane reasons for the proliferation of prostitution cited by the vice commission reports were quickly forgotten as the readers of the white slave narratives vicariously walked the streets of the forbidden underworld with the helpless young creature. They were terrorized and titillated at the same time. Indeed, there were more lurid details in these fictional accounts of prostitution than in Madeleine's own story. But in fiction, it was death, and not success, that awaited the heroine.[8]

It was in the fading shadow of the white slave scare and in the bright lights of the Red Scare that *Madeleine: An Autobiography* appeared. Within weeks of its appearance in October, 1919, an agent for the Society for the Prevention of Vice filed a complaint against C. T. Brainard, president of Harper and Brothers, the publishing house. The complaint was made on the basis of a section of the New York State Penal Code which stated that it was a misdemeanor to sell, lend, or give away any

INTRODUCTION

obscene, lewd, lascivious, filthy, indecent, or disgusting book, magazine, newspaper, or picture.[9]

Censorship because of "obscenity" was not a new practice in the United States. The Vice (anti-vice) Societies had emerged in the post-Civil-War period as protectors of a genteel literary tradition and advocates of a new "social purity." The name most often associated with the important events in the history of censorship up to that time was Anthony Comstock. Comstock's legislation was responsible for barring the distribution of Theodore Dreiser's *Sister Carrie* (1900) and Margaret Sanger's "Family Limitation," a 1914 birth control pamphlet. By 1919, "Comstockery" was somewhat out of style, but social purity advocates still wielded enough power to be heard.[10]

As historians have suggested, the older social purity forces and the new progressive vice commissions were both part of one conservative reform establishment. However, the progressive style of presentation (documenting the hard facts about vice and making them available for public discussion) was in conflict with the older tradition which called for suppression of such information, unless packaged with proper humility and regret.

John Sumner and Ben B. Lindsey, two men who represented this conflict, came together in the dispute over the publication of *Madeleine*. Sumner was an attorney who became Comstock's successor as the agent of the Society for the Prevention of Vice. Lindsey was, at the time, the controversial judge of the Denver Juvenile Court, itself a product of progressive reform efforts. He

INTRODUCTION

had also written, in 1910, a book entitled *The Beast,* an attack on an unjust economic system (the beast) nurtured by powerful special interests at the expense of those without power. Lindsey believed the system was the root cause of a variety of social ills, prostitution among them. Thus, he claims in his introduction to *Madeleine* that the author had done "a great public service" by bringing the facts of her life to print. Facts, to Lindsey and other progressive reformers, were powerful tools in bringing about social change.[11]

To men of Sumner's persuasion, the "facts" of prostitution must not be presented to the public because they encouraged a misguided discussion of what was better left in silence. The only education the public needed about prostitution was that it was an absolute evil. To suggest that there were legitimate reasons why a woman might turn to prostitution was to paint in shades of gray an issue that was black and white. A similar argument took place earlier when the social purity forces blocked attempts by "enlightened" reformers to initiate the (state) regulation of prostitution in the interests of protecting public health. The regulation of prostitution was seen as a recognition of prostitution as a persistent reality instead of an evil to be eradicated.

C. T. Brainard did not side with Lindsey and the progressive forces. Instead, he defended himself by disclaiming direct responsibility for the book's publication. According to his testimony, the book was accepted for publication by Harper's Literary Conference, which as a general rule operated without his intervention. That group, after receiving the manuscript from an anony-

INTRODUCTION

mous author, submitted it for review to Judge Lindsey and to four other reviewers: a judge of a Domestic Relations Court in Ohio, a librarian, a minister, and the Chief Medical Officer of the Federal Medical Service in Chicago. Harper's attorney, John Larkin, reported that "all of these persons replied that the book should be published by all means, which the company did." Brainard reported that he did not read the book until after the summons was served.[12]

Brainard believed the action was brought against him because of his position on an Extraordinary Grand Jury which had recently investigated corruption in New York City government. To substantiate this, he testified that the District Attorney conducted a cross-examination of him that extended to questions about his life and career "from the time I was ten years old, but most of it was a tissue of falsehoods, with just a thread of truth running here and there." In addition, Brainard claimed he was treated like a "desperate criminal" by police authorities who went so far as to fingerprint him, actions he believed were meant to humiliate him.[13]

The treatment Brainard received, however, was typical of the investigative style that predominated during the Red Scare. At the same time the complaint was filed against him, the pages of *The New York Times* were filled with articles about the arrests and trials of suspected Communist sympathizers and outspoken intellectuals. Most of these individuals were charged under the new criminal anarchy statutes which were often as loosely worded as the section of the penal code under which Brainard was charged. Compared to many of his con-

INTRODUCTION

temporaries, Brainard was lucky. The Municipal Court found him guilty as charged and fined him $1000. The decision was later overturned on an appeal that successfully argued the reformist intent of the book. But the fate of *Madeleine* was sealed. Harper's apparently withdrew the book from circulation in spite of the decision of the Appeals Court.[14]

Reviews of the work at the time of publication varied. *The New Republic* called it "the story of a prostitute who had been driven to it by economic reasons." The reviewer was skeptical about the literary merits of the book but concluded by saying that "under her romantic draperies is a pathetic and hideous reality, and if the sight of it suffices to crack at least one suburban complacency, the publication of *Madeleine* is justified." *The New York Times* found no reason for the book to be in print as it added little to what the public already knew. To them, *Madeleine* was the story of a woman who was "simply choosing, all the time... the easiest way to make money." *The Nation* understood more of what Madeleine had tried to project in her autobiography. The reviewer commented on the literary merits of the text and marveled that Madeleine had written with "dignified restraint" of a life in the underworld; he recognized that she had achieved a kind of self-knowledge that was admirable.[15]

All told, the reviews in 1919 suggest a range of opinion about prostitutes and their life stories that is reflected today. There is still resistance to viewing prostitutes as working women; there is still concern that the essence of prostitution is sin, a woman's sin; there is still a debate

INTRODUCTION

about the victimization of prostitutes, particularly whether young women come to the city and fall prey to unscrupulous procurers. There is still a mystique about prostitutes that is evident in the numerous television programs, plays, movies, and novels about prostitutes and their world. And there is still the possibility that *Madeleine* (under proposed anti-pornography legislation) could be deemed unfit for the reading public.

What Madeleine did not include in her autobiography—her life after she left prostitution and was restored to a decent (if hidden) place in society—would have been an important addition to our knowledge about prostitution, then and now. Her angry epilogue against the men and women involved in the attack on white slavery suggests that it was this that had prompted her to tell her story. But who she was and where she was at the time of the book's writing remain a mystery. What she left us is an important addition to the developing tradition in women's autobiography and a clear record of a painful but important part of women's history.

Marcia Carlisle
September, 1985

NOTES

1. *The Nation,* November 22, 1919. The problem of collaboration is a difficult but not obscure issue for social historians. It is raised as an issue in authenticating slave narratives, workers' autobiographies, and memoirs of various kinds. The debates around the precise authorship are lively and crucial to our understanding of narrative voice in historical documents. No claim is made on behalf of *Madeleine* that an editor did not clean up the text. The aid of such a person, however, should not raise questions about the value of the text as an original. Most historians, too, rely heavily on editorial aid from friends and colleagues as the testimonials in the prefaces to their books indicate.

2. The literature on the history of prostitution is booming. For a reasonable introduction, one that includes information from which my text is drawn, see: Ruth Rosen. *The Lost Sisterhood: Prostitution in America, 1900–1918* (Baltimore: Johns Hopkins University Press, 1982); Marion S. Goldman. *Gold Diggers and Silver Miners: Prostitution and Social Life on the Comstock Lode* (Ann Arbor: The University of Michigan Press, 1981); Marcia Carlisle. "Prostitutes and Their Reformers in Nineteenth Century Philadelphia" (Dissertation, Rutgers University, 1982); Lucie Cheng Hirata. "Free, Indentured, Enslaved: Chinese Prostitution in Nineteenth Century America," *Signs* (Autumn, 1979), 3–29; Paula Petrik. "Prostitution in Helena, Montana, 1865–1900," *Montana: The Magazine of Western History* 31 (1981), 28–41; Joel Best. "Careers in Brothel Prostitution, St. Paul, 1865–1883," *Journal of Interdisciplinary History* (Spring, 1982) 597–619; Ruth Rosen and Sue Davidson, Eds. *The Maimie Papers* (Old Westbury, NY: The Feminist Press, 1977). The first and most important study (although it is not about American prostitution) remains Judith Walkowitz's *Prostitution and Victorian Society: Women, Class, and the State* (Cambridge: Cambridge University Press, 1980).

3. See Carlisle, "Prostitutes and Their Reformers."

4. Estelle C. Jelinek, Ed. *Women's Autobiography: Essays in Criticism* (Bloomington: Indiana University Press, 1980). In particular, see Jelinek's own essay, "Women's Autobiography and the Male Tradition," 1–20, which informs the discussion of general patterns and traditions.

5. Mark Connelly. *The Response to Prostitution in the Progressive Era* (Chapel Hill: University of North Carolina Press, 1980), 15.

6. *Ibid,* 92–113.

7. Letter, Floyd Dell to "Mr. Harris," dated June 25, 1914.

8. Connelly, Chapter 6, 114–135.

9. *New York Times,* February 15, 1920.

10. Paul Boyer. *Purity in Print* (New York: Charles Scribner's Sons, 1968), 49–52.

11. Charles Larsen. *The Good Fight: The Life and Times of Ben B. Lindsey* (Chicago: Quadrangle Books, 1972).

12. *New York Times,* January 31, 1920.

13. *New York Times,* January 24, 1920.

14. Boyer, p. 50. See also Eugene Exman. *The House of Harper* (New York: Harper and Row, 1967).

15. *The New Republic,* December 24, 1919. *The New York Times,* November 16, 1919. *The Nation,* November 22, 1919.

INTRODUCTION TO THE
1919 EDITION

I WRITE this introduction to *Madeleine* because
it is a book that may be misunderstood by many and
it deserves to be read without prejudice—with an
open mind. And I commend warmly the courageous
frankness of the author in writing it and of the
publishers in bringing it out.

I will soon begin my twentieth year on the bench
of a court in a city of about three hundred thousand
people. It is a good, average city—certainly no
worse and I sometimes think a little better than
other cities of its size. But the problems of one
city are much the same as those of all cities. During
this time as a judge I have dealt mostly with human
problems that some people look upon altogether as
moral problems. For seven or eight years I tried
most of the divorce cases in such a city, with a record
of having divorced some five thousand people in
that time. And then for many years it has become
my duty to preside in those delicate affairs known to
the officers as "sex cases." At first they concerned
mostly the protection of society against prostitution.
Then they turned gradually to the *protection of
women against society*. These cases are often con-

ducted regardless of the technicalities of law. We cease to be a court; we become, rather, a place of adjustment of human frailties and difficulties. In a word, we now deal with people and the causes of bad things. We no longer deal merely with the things. We no longer use vengeance, violence, stupidity, and ignorance as the only remedy for these things. In this experience I was forced to the conclusion that there are no good people and no bad people—only good things and bad things. It gives me a great charity and a great sympathy— not for sin, but for sinners. It teaches me that while it is difficult at times to know how to fight sin without fighting sinners, in the end it is the better policy to conquer the sin and save the people. For sinners are only people. We do not fight sick children—we fight the *disease*. People are only children grown up.

Thus it is that I have an intense appreciation of *Madeleine*. It ought to be read and pondered over. It is *true*. The Madeleines are right in your midst.

Not that I may not have some criticisms and that I may not differ in some conclusions. . . . But the author has told us the facts—as fine, as splendid, and as sordid and as human as some of them are. And facts are the most powerful factors in reforms.

In dealing with the cases of hundreds of young girls I have cried out in an agony of hopelessness at times that not one of them could rise up to throw the facts in great bloody chunks into the faces of people, a people asleep that needed to be shocked—

aroused. This Madeleine has done, and I congratulate her and thank her for it. It is a great public service. She has followed all the tortuous, trying paths of a young girl gone wrong, but not "ruined" necessarily, as the conventional lie would have us believe.

Never in history so much as now, facing mighty changes, after upheavals of war, have we needed more the truth about our smug society and the things we are responsible for that make for the "sins" we denounce, the sins that we will not lift one little finger to alleviate except by methods generally so narrow and absurd that they merely add to infamies they are intended to suppress.

I agree in the main with the conclusions of Madeleine, including most that she says about the white-slave traffic and the utter lack of real humanity in a great many of our so-called welfare workers. And most of the real social workers who are human workers will also agree with Madeleine.

I stand for purity and decency in the home and the maintenance of those institutions that are dear and necessary to our civilization, but is it not high time that society changed the relative values it sets upon "sin"—especially those sins for which it is in a large measure so much to blame? By numerous acts it encourages prostitution. For its *own* victims the remedy has been ostracism and jails. Such is its cry: "Stone her! Stone her!" Is there not even more reason now than in His time for society to change its attitude? Not that we wish to justify sin, but that we wish to do justice and in the end learn how to fight evil more and women less.

Of course *Madeleine* can hardly be recommended to youth of tender years, but neither could some portions of Shakespeare or the Bible. It would be a very good thing for girls having reached a reasonable maturity to really know more of our "Madeleines." I believe we should teach children—wisely and properly, of course—what evil is. We should tell them where it lurks and where and how it strikes.

If we take alone the smug and contented moral rather than the just and eternal human attitude, then, indeed, and only then, shall the "Madeleines" be numbered among the "ruined" and the "lost."

BEN B. LINDSEY.

JUVENILE COURT OF DENVER,
September, 1919.

BOOK I

MADELEINE

An Autobiography

CHAPTER I

IF I dwell at some length on the story of my ancestry and my childhood it is for the purpose of setting forth the elements of weakness and of strength which were inherent in my character and which, combined with the circumstance of my life, brought about my social bankruptcy and made possible my spiritual redintegration.

A few years after the close of the Civil War my parents came from their birthplace near the Atlantic seaboard and settled in a thriving town of the Middle West. I was born in this place and grew into young womanhood without ever having been more than twenty-five miles from my native town.

This community was new and crude, and its inhabitants were for the greater part persons of little education and few aspirations. If they had ever possessed ideals they must have left most of them behind them in the older communities from which they came.

3

MADELEINE

My parents had many traditions of race, of class, of education, and of religion; they were looked upon as being rather peculiar in the principles which they sought to instil into the minds of their children. Even as a small child I received much religious instruction, which, singularly enough, I wove around the personality of my great-grandfather. I had learned to read at an unusually early age, and possessed rather a remarkable faculty for the English language. Sonorous words appealed to me and soon found a place in my memory. The two questions most often found on my tongue were: "How do you pronounce this word, father?" and, "What does it mean?" So that when I read in a very old newspaper, a cherished possession of my mother's, an account of the death of my great-grandfather, together with an account of his life, his virtues, and his piety, I retained a clear recollection of one paragraph because there were many new words in it that fell musically upon my ear. It read: "He represented the highest type of a Christian gentleman, this venerable citizen, this grand old patriarch, who as a young man left his native land to found a home on the virgin soil of free America that he might worship God according to the dictates of his own conscience."

My mother had a portrait of him which showed a benignant-looking old gentleman, clothed in the stately garments of his day; and he was to me a very real person, though he had died many years before I was born. My mother often spoke of him in terms of great reverence, referring especially to his piety and his kindliness. He was often quick to anger, she said, but he was also quick to repentance, and if he had offended relative or friend he asked his pardon and the pardon of God before he slept.

I was brought up in a strict heaven-and-hell belief. If I were a good child and pleasing in the sight of God I would go to heaven, but if I were a naughty girl then hell would be my portion throughout all eternity. Great-grandfather C—— came, in my mind, to take the place of God. While I prayed to God it was really Great-grandfather C—— whom I wanted to please and stand well with. I could imagine him walking, majestically, through the gold-and-jasper streets, and I wanted to go up there and walk beside him. When I was wilful I grieved, not because I had lost God, but because I had lost Great-grandfather C——. Now, confused as these childish ideas were in my mind, it is clear to me that almost my first outlook on life held the thoughts of a Supreme Being and a future punishment for sin.

My early companionship with my father was a very happy one, for I not only loved him better than any one else in the world, but I was very proud of him. He was of distinguished bearing, handsome, brilliant, and possessed of that personal magnetism which makes for leadership. In the social, political, and business life of our town and county he was a conspicuous figure.

We were a large family; our friends were always telling us that we were a mighty fortunate one, and no doubt we were. We were exceptionally healthy children who never seemed to have any of the common ailments that prevailed in other homes. We had some means and a beautiful home. Both of our parents possessed a high degree of intelligence and sane religious beliefs. No children could have begun life under more auspicious conditions.

My mother seemed to have been created for the expressed purpose of being a mother, for poise and common sense were her distinguishing characteristics. My father was the mainspring of our pleasant home life. Mother was the balance-wheel.

We heard much of the beauties of literature and had access to many good books. My eldest brother and myself had this one common love, though we were diametrically opposite in many other things. He had a reserved manner and was thought to be very proud. He preferred the companionship of boys much older than himself and he did not see any sense in playing with girls, but he would read with me or to me for hours at a time.

Our laundress had a little son about my own age, and I often played with him, though father frowned upon my doing so, for he held rigid ideas of caste. One day when I was about eleven I was playing in the hayloft with this little companion when my father called me to dinner. His voice was unnaturally harsh and sounded as if he were angry. Without knowing what was wrong, I feared to answer him. He called again, his voice more angry than at first, and in fear and trembling I answered.

6

A few minutes later he came up into the hayloft where we two little ones crouched in fear. His face was purple with rage as he seized my little playmate and began shaking him until the little fellow screamed in terror. I thought he meant to kill the child, but at length he threw him back on the hay and, putting me across his shoulder, went down the ladder.

Without a word to me father started for the house, but on his way seemed to change his mind, and set me down, while he cut a switch from a near-by tree, and then and there administered such a terrible beating that for weeks my body was a mass of bruises. It was years before my nervous system recovered from the shock.

My screams brought the cook, the laundress, and my mother to the scene. When mother saw the cause of my terror she ran forward and grasped father's arm. None of the subsequent horrors of my life ever blotted out the memory of that moment as he raised his arm to strike her. She was white, but not a muscle of her face moved as she waited for the blow to fall. Father glared at her a moment, his handsome face distorted by a demoniacal grimace, then, still in that inarticulate rage, he threw the switch from him and went into the house. I did not see him again that day.

Mother was very silent as she undressed me and put me to bed, but Aunt Jennie, our old negro cook, who had come into the household before I was born, was not so discreet. After mother had gone Aunt

Jennie came to me with soothing words, denunciation for my father, and my long delayed dinner.

Then I learned that my beloved father was "jest plain crazy drunk." Aunt Jennie went on to tell me that he had been drinking for two years, and that she and mother had resorted to every device to keep his weakness hidden alike from his friends and his children, but she, for one, refused to hide his shame if he was "goin' to take to killin' little children."

This was but the first of many inexplicable beatings that I received. He never struck mother; he seldom whipped one of the other children. If any one crossed him when he was drunk I made vicarious atonement. When he was sober I was his favorite child. When he was drunk I was the one who suffered most. For many years I was seldom without the marks of his brutality.

Not long after the whipping episode father sold his business and went away. Mother said he was in poor health and needed a change. He was gone for several months, but his letters came at regular intervals. After I became a woman I read those beautiful letters. Each one was a literary gem; each one replete with expressions of undying love for his family, and filled with high resolve for the conquest of the enemy and his return to his own place in the world. Yet much of this time he was drinking heavily and spending money like a drunken sailor.

After his return our home was sold under mortgage,

AN AUTOBIOGRAPHY

but we did not immediately move out. Father gave his pledge to mother, and for a time all was well. He started in on a salary to retrieve his fallen fortunes. He planned to move to a farm which he still owned, after he should have saved some money. He and the boys would lead a splendid outdoor life, mother would be always at his side to keep him in the path of duty, we girls should be sent away to a good school when we were old enough.

It was a beautiful picture, wonderfully drawn by a man who was a master of English, but it never materialized. Instead, the pledge was broken, the farm was sold, the family never saw a dollar of the proceeds, and we went to live in a small house in a poor neighborhood.

Father soon lost his position and went away to seek work. My eldest brother, who was fifteen, left school to assume the burden which his father had laid down. All the following winter he sat up nights in the bitter cold in a vain endeavor to keep abreast of his class, striving, fighting, praying for the education that was being denied him.

I was thirteen that fall, but I could in no way assist in the family finances. There was no demand for child labor in our town; neither could I go to school, for there was no money to buy books and clothes. In the midst of all this trouble a new baby was added to our already large family.

Words are feeble things with which to convey any idea of the horrors of that winter which followed my thirteenth birthday. One may become inured to

suffering without becoming indurated by it. Many
black and bitter waters of hunger and humiliation,
of shame and sorrow, of unmerited punishment and
social injustice, of physical suffering and spiritual
despair have passed over my head since that time.
Above the roar and swirl and buffeting of these many
waters the memory of that winter has always stood
out conspicuously.

My brother did a man's work, but he did not draw
a man's pay. My little brothers and sisters often
cried for food when there was no food to give them.
The baby wailed incessantly because mother was
insufficiently fed, and we stayed in bed as much
as possible, trying to keep warm.

At irregular intervals father came home, drunk
and demoniacal, to sober up, repent, and become
again the courteous gentleman, the kindly parent,
the loving husband of his brief sober periods.

Mother never failed him. We children heard no
word of reproach for the man who had wrecked her
life and ours. She met poverty and shame, as she
had met prosperity and honor, with a poise and
a dignity that I have never seen equaled.

She was powerless to change conditions. She
was powerless to change him, but she could meet
any fate with a calm exterior. This man had been
the playmate of her childhood. He was the lover of
her youth and the husband of her choice. She had
not taken him for fair weather only; she had chosen
him for life. It never entered her mind to abandon
him.

In the spring we moved again, this time to the worst neighborhood in the town. On either side of us, and across the street, the houses were occupied by prostitutes. All of them had other, ostensible means of support. The attitude of the town was too puritanical to permit wide-open, publicly recognized houses of ill fame. They were boarding-houses, dressmaking-shops, hand-laundries, and the homes of working-men whose wives added to the family finances by occasional prostitution.

Thus disguised, these resorts flourished, and they were a far greater menace to the youth of the neighborhood than any wide-open places would have been. These women assumed the virtuous air that deceived none but the very young; even they heard whispers which aroused prurient curiosity and quickened the cosmic urge.

Neither my brother nor I ever went to school again, and I developed into young womanhood in this noxious environment. I was strictly forbidden to visit these neighbors. I was in no sense a delinquent child, but I *was* a growing girl to whom a good meal was a rarity. These people had good things to eat, served on nice china. They had clean table-cloths; we had none at all. Their houses were palaces compared with the wretched place that I called home. Needless to say, I visited them whenever I had an opportunity, and I heard many suggestions and learned many things that it is not well for a girl to know.

I liked nice clothes, but my love for them was not

inordinate, which was well, for I never had decent clothes, to say nothing of pretty ones. Amusements, or recreation of any sort, were unknown to me, except as something to long for and to dream about, especially after meeting some group of nicely gowned girls who had been my playmates in childhood, girls of the circle in which I rightfully belonged.

My early childhood had been spent in an atmosphere of good literature, and my love of books was stronger than my love for recreation. As a child I had heard the masters of prose and poetry discussed at great length. I had a most tenacious memory, and knew by name the great writers as distinguished from the mediocre. Neither were within my reach.

My intellect was not satisfied by *Goldie Rivers, the Beautiful Cloakmaker*, nor by *Léontine, the Pirate's Daughter*, but, this being the only class of books obtainable, I devoured them eagerly. Our neighbors had an abundant supply of this drivel, and I borrowed freely, along with other books which were far less harmful.

One would have to live through it to realize the agony a high-spirited, sensitive girl may endure when she is the town drunkard's daughter, especially when that town drunkard had once been one of the leading citizens.

I was never permitted to forget that this was my position. I had no girl companions—my sisters were too small. Instead of girl friends, I made clandestine visits to ignorant, corrupt women who wore a scanty garb of respectability, and whose influence was far more pernicious than a public prostitute's would have been. I had no boy friends. Our home was far too squalid to invite them to, even if there had been any boys who would have gone with me openly. I was fair game for any predacious male who might be attracted by my youthful face or my well-developed figure.

Men who had been my father's friends made open or tentative advances to me. To one man who insulted me I made indignant threats to tell my father. He laughed contemptuously and answered: "That would not help you. He would only get drunk and beat you."

He had struck at the tap-root of the matter. I had not only lost my father's support in material matters; I had lost his protection as well. My mother was tied hand and foot by ill health, poverty, a sickly baby, and the care of a large family. I needed both my parents; I had neither. The mating instinct was developing strongly and I had no legitimate outlet of study, amusement, companionship, or recreation.

I made a terrific effort to keep above the level of my environment and that of my forbidden companions. My mother's training and example, and my own inherent sense of decency, fought for the right. My environment and social isolation fought against it. The result was inevitable; I lost the battle.

When I was seventeen the family affairs seemed to have reached their lowest possible level. Dirt,

MADELEINE

squalor, ignorance, vitiated standards, sin, all the horrible concomitants of poverty engulfed me. But I still retained many traces of the earlier condition to which I had been born. The most notable example was my retention of the English spoken in my home, which was not only different from that used by our present neighbors, but notably better than that spoken by the "first families."

I cannot refrain from speaking of this, because it played such a large part in my life, both for sorrow and for joy. It always made me a marked woman in an environment where no standards of English prevailed. It brought me into much conflict with those who considered me "stuck-up, when she hain't got nothing to be stuck-up about." And it brought me much notice and consideration that I would not otherwise have received.

Shortly after my seventeenth birthday there came to my mother a letter from a former servant who was married and living in St. Louis. She offered to send money for my expenses to the city, and to care for me after my arrival there. She suggested factory work as offering the best opening for untrained workers, as well as involving the least expenditure for clothes.

At this time we had not heard from father for nearly a year, but we knew that he would never consent to the plan, even if we could consult him. Mother and I decided that it was the only chance I would ever have to work out my own life, and she accepted it for me, with many secret tears and

14

prayers. She made it plain to me that my fate was in my own hands, that the temptations were many and the opportunities few; but she believed that I had a high degree of intelligence, and that I would make opportunities for myself if I were given a chance. Above all, she believed that I would have a chance to study when I should have access to books; and she laid many injunctions on me to use the public library at every spare moment.

And then came the more intimate conversation in which she tried to tell about things of which, to my shame, I knew more than she. I could only listen in silence and resolve in my heart that this thing that had come into my life should be cast out forever, and that, God helping me, I would become all that she expected of me, working always with the view of lightening her burdens and helping her to shield the younger girls. My two little sisters were rarely beautiful children, and I knew that they would need every safeguard that could be thrown around them. In my heart I said, "My darling mother, I have deceived you, and I am not worthy to be your daughter nor a sister to your children; but with every effort that a girl can make I will strive to become worthy."

Want and misery had been our portion through several years, but love and the ties of blood had not become lessened, and the thought that one of us must go out alone into the world was a grief almost too great to be endured. My oldest brother, who was my mother's counterpart in mind and

countenance, possessed the same dignity and forti-
tude, and shared her pride of birth. He had taken
his father's place, not only as the breadwinner, but
as counselor and guide for the other children. The
younger ones gave him the same obedience and
respect that they gave mother, and all of them had
for him a passionate love, though they stood somewhat in awe of him. I was too near his own age
to obey him, though I valued his good opinion very
highly and stood in awe of the disapproving frown
he would always bestow upon me after he had learned
of one of my visits to our questionable neighbors.

He bore his burden without complaint; he could
do a man's work and carry a man's responsibilities,
though he was but a slender boy. But no amount
of social isolation would have driven him to association with people whose social, educational, or
moral standards were not those of his own mother;
and he could not understand that I was of different
mold. I loved the things that he loved, but I did
not possess his fineness of temperament nor his
isolation of spirit.

I was thankful that a way of escape from my hate-
ful surroundings had been opened to me, and I felt
a lightening of the burden of fear that I had carried
for several months—the fear of my brother's scorn
if he should learn of my sin and the greater fear of
my mother's heartache. Father was still the adored
one, and we mourned for him during his long silence
as sincerely as if he had been the most devoted
parent in the world. Since mother did not criticize

him to us, it was but natural that we children should not criticize him to her nor to one another; we looked upon him as one who suffered from a horrible malady, and always referred to the happier days as the time "when father was himself."

On the day of my leaving mother, my brother and myself were very silent, but the younger children, who adored Sister—as they always called me—wept loud and long and would not be comforted. At the station our good-bys were few, because they had already been said. I almost broke down at the last moment, but was enabled to restrain my feelings because I knew that my mother would consider it unseemly if I made a public display of my grief.

But when the train had pulled out of the station my grief broke through the barriers I had built up, and I wept all the way to the city, without any thought of the unseemliness of publicly displaying my emotion. I was only a little girl and I did not in the least want to work in a factory, nor live with our former servant, nor leave my home and my little brothers and sisters, nor the cuddling baby brother who was my especial care. He was old enough to talk by this time, and as night shut down I tried to peer through the darkness and picture him crying for Sister, and my own tears poured forth afresh. And I still weep when I think of the little chap who, as he grew older, always said, when he saw an attractive young woman, "Mother, she looks like Sister, but I do not think she looks so nice."

CHAPTER II

IT was eleven o'clock at night when I arrived in
St. Louis, and as I had never before been out of
bed at that hour, I was somewhat frightened and
bewildered by the clamor and the crowd until I
heard a cheery voice at my elbow exclaiming:
"My, but you have grown! And you look just like
your ma; I would have known you anywhere."
And thereupon I was gathered to an ample bosom
on which I proceeded to pour out my homesick tears.

After I had been petted and soothed by a hand
that had soothed me in childhood, and my tears
dried on her own handkerchief, my one-time nurse
turned to the quiet-looking man who accompanied
her, and introduced her husband, asking me if I
remembered Fred James, who used to deliver groceries at our house when she was a nurse there.

I remembered him well, and after the exchange of
greetings his first remark was an echo of his wife's
greetings, "You certainly look like your ma."

Mrs. James added the little sting with which
every one always qualified this compliment, "She
does and she don't; she will never be as good-looking
as her ma."

On the street-car, however, she sought to divert

my thoughts from home by telling me about the position she had held open for me, in the factory in which she was forewoman. I was to be a check-girl, whose duties would consist in checking out bundles of work to the machine-workers and in checking in the finished product. It sounded very complicated to me, but she assured me that I could do it, that she would be at my elbow for the first week; after that I could "go it alone."

The pay would be five dollars a week, out of which I was to pay her two dollars for board, and a room which I should share with two older girls, a younger sister of Mrs. James, and a cousin who lived with them. Both girls worked at the factory, as also did Mr. James. They all made good wages and were laying up money. Mrs. James was a woman of keen judgment, straightforward and industrious; she was clearly the head of the household. My mother had thought highly of her integrity and intelligence, and I knew that I was in capable hands.

Just as I fell asleep, or so it seemed, I was awakened by Mrs. James at the door of the bedroom, her brisk voice calling, "Come, girls, it's four-thirty; time to get up."

Why any one should get up at four-thirty was a mystery to me, but I followed the example of my bedfellows and reluctantly dragged myself out of bed. I had always understood that Missourians were lazy, but if an entire household arose at four-thirty, the climate could not be as enervating as I had supposed.

MADELEINE

Both the girls were frankly curious about me, and discussed me quite freely in my presence, but without the least thought of giving offense. Being wage-earners who had supported themselves for several years, they looked upon me as a green little country girl, to be patronized and instructed in the ways of the city.

It did not require much time to discover the reason for the early rising; there was plenty of work to be done, in which all took a part; there was breakfast to be got, and the house to be set in order before leaving for the factory. The house wore a spick-and-span appearance that would have put to shame many housewives who spent the day dawdling over their tasks. The women made their own clothes, snatching the time whenever they could; and in good weather they walked to and from work, although the distance was more than two miles.

After the first week at the factory I experienced no difficulty with my work, the chief requisites being alertness and attention, qualities that I possessed, together with a fair chirography, and a quickness at figures which pleased Mrs. James, though it did not surprise her; for, as she remarked, "Your pa and ma are the smartest persons I ever knew; you would have no excuse for being a blockhead." And for the next ten minutes she held forth about the blockheads with whom circumstances compelled her to deal.

Although I had few difficulties with my work, I never grew accustomed to the noise made by eighty power-machines running at top speed, each one of them making twice as much noise as an ordinary sewing-machine. After listening to their deafening racket all day I dreamed of it at night. This and the various sounds from the city's streets at length began to "get on my nerves."

I wiped away many a secret tear, for I was homesick and unutterably lonely. I envied the machine-girls who laughed and sang at their work and carried on their communication by their own peculiar sign code, for no human voice could be heard above the roar of the machines.

I never became intimate with any of my fellow-workers, for I had a certain shyness which I could not overcome, and I spoke a different language which made those around me declare that I was "stuck-up, an' tryin' to talk stylish." No girl enjoys being set apart from her fellows, and, being a perfectly normal girl, I was no exception to this rule. I went to the extent of trying to speak their language in my effort to be one of them; but the only result was to offend my own ears and bring forth a sharp reprimand from Mrs. James to the effect that I need not try to talk like a Missourian.

On Saturday nights my two roommates often went to a show or a dance with their "fellows," but when they brought along a young man to act as escort for me Mrs. James promptly vetoed my going to a dance or having young-men callers. As I did not demur, that settled the matter to her entire satisfaction. Accordingly, she wrote to my mother that

MADELEINE

I was a good girl and an obedient one; however, the obedience caused me little effort, since I had never learned to dance and the young man did not interest me.

On Sunday mornings, when I would gladly have lain in bed to rest, she sent me to church, although no other member of the household attended. In her time our own household had been a church-going one, although the custom had been abandoned in recent years for lack of decent clothes to wear; but Mrs. James felt that her duty to my mother included religious guidance for me, which she was quite willing should come through others.

After I had been in the city for about two months my health, which had always been perfect, notwithstanding the hardships and poor food of our home, began to fail. I lost my appetite, had frequent attacks of vomiting, and did not sleep well. I managed to get through my work at the factory with great effort, but the walks home were one long-drawn-out torture. At the end of three months Mrs. James was seriously alarmed; at first she had attributed my failing health to the hot weather, but it was autumn now and the air was an elixir; still I did not improve. I cried at the slightest provocation, and seemed to be all nerves. As I had never before been sick, I made sure that I was going to die. Then my mother would never know that I had been a wicked girl, nor that I had tried to redeem my unspoken promise to her when I had whispered to myself that I would become worthy to be her daughter.

Another month went by, and the women's faces around me grew grave when they spoke of me. One night I heard the girls talking about my illness, "She is not fit for work; she ought to go home." I only sighed wearily. Perhaps my mother would know what to do for me, but I did not want to go home; I had taken great pride in the fact that I was making good on the task assigned to me. On the morning after this conversation Mrs. James came to me before I was up and said that she and I would not work that day, because she had decided to take me to a physician, all home remedies having failed.

After the doctor had announced the result of his diagnosis I could only stare at him in dumb amazement. It seemed to me that he must be speaking of some other girl, not of me. Mrs. James sat with face blanched and lips trembling before the words came to them; then she burst forth: "It cannot be true, Doctor. I promised her mother to guard her; she has never gone out alone since she came to St. Louis; and she does not know a young man in the city."

My sense of justice came to the relief of my stiffened tongue and impelled me to tell them that it had happened in my home town; beyond that I could say nothing, shame had made me speechless.

By the time we had returned to the house Mrs. James had threshed the matter out in her own mind and decided that at all costs my mother must not know the truth; with her usual perspicacity she added: "If your father had been himself, this would never have happened. There is not a man in B—— County that would have dared bring shame to him if he were the man he was ten years ago."

I knew that she spoke the truth. I knew, moreover, young as I was, that I would never have dared, either, had he "been himself." I, too, had taken advantage of his disability and struck him in his most vulnerable spot, the honor of his womankind; indeed, the honor of all womankind, for whatever his other failings, he had never been known to impugn the character of any woman; and he looked with loathing upon men who spoke lightly of feminine virtue. It was his most reverent assertion that no woman of his own or my mother's name had ever borne the breath of reproach. In my hour of bitterness and shame I almost forgot the gentle woman whose heart would break if she knew, in my grief for the proud man whom insidious foes, without and within, had brought so low.

"I will not say anything to the girls until I can think what is best to do," said Mrs. James, as she went into the kitchen to prepare our lunch.

I stood in the sitting-room, still wearing my street clothes, while her remark kept ringing in my ears; the conviction that finally penetrated to my consciousness was that the girls must know. I, who in my secret heart had felt so superior to these illiterate working-girls, must become a byword to them, because, despite my better birth and breeding,

I had lost that jewel of virtue which they still retained; yes, and I must bring shame into the home of this kindly woman, who, out of reverence and love for my mother and a lingering respect for my father, had treated me as if I were of different clay.

A sudden resolution came to me; I must go away. Where, I had not the least idea, but I must get away from these humble friends and bear my disgrace alone. I went into my room and took from my trunk the small sum of money I had saved—fifty cents a week, for four months; for I had promised my mother that I would spend Christmas at home; and I had resolutely resisted all temptation to buy girlish finery, that I might keep that promise.

Twelve dollars; it seemed a large sum as I carefully tucked it into my bosom and stood irresolutely looking into my trunk. No, I could take nothing else, I decided; and then I saw a small photograph of my mother, which had been taken in the heyday of her matronly beauty when I was a child of ten. I wrapped it carefully in a clean handkerchief and, putting it with the twelve dollars, I went forth to hide myself from the only friends I had in St. Louis.

Although I was not at that time aware of it, it was from myself that I was trying to hide. I hailed the first passing car, and as I was utterly unfamiliar with the city and had no objective point in view, I rode to the end of the line. Leaving the car, I found myself in a suburb of the modest sort, where I wandered aimlessly up and down the blocks and across vacant lots, until I had lost all sense of direction. My mind and soul were in such torment that I only vaguely sensed fatigue and hunger; until at length I dully realized that it was growing dark and that I had never before been on the streets at night alone. The thought of suicide obtruded itself into my consciousness, but I rejected it, because I firmly believed in the old-fashioned hell; and I had no desire to precipitate myself into that abode of the lost, although I entertained no doubt as to its being my ultimate destination. With the thought of suicide there had come to me a sense of the anxiety which Mrs. James would suffer on account of my absence; perhaps she would telegraph to my mother; that contingency must be averted at once. I walked on and on until at last I came to a drug-store, and, going in, purchased stationery and a stamp. I asked the man in charge if I might write a letter; he handed me a fountain-pen and, pointing to a table in the rear of the store, invited me to make myself at home. There were no customers in the place at this time, and I was not interrupted as I wrote my incoherent letter to Mrs. James. I could not restrain my tears as I made my plea that she would not tell my mother that I was not with her; I knew perfectly well that she would not tell her of my condition.

When I had finished my letter I thanked the man for his kindness and asked him where I would find the nearest post-box. He came up close to me, a middle-aged creature, oleaginous in person and unctuous in manner, and putting his hand on my arm inquired, "Are you in trouble, little girl?" and then answering his own question, he continued: "I know you are. Can I help you?"

It had not been necessary for me to come to a great city to meet men of his stamp; I had seen them in my own country town. Men who had known me since my babyhood had not spared me their insults, and I was in no doubt as to this man's meaning. But protest was useless and I was inexpressibly tired, so I thanked him for his solicitude, told him there was nothing wrong, and started to go out of the store, whereupon he barred my way, and, again putting his repulsive hand on my arm, made a proposal so offensive that high above shame and grief and weariness my anger arose and I lashed him with the fury of my contempt until he stood aside and let me pass.

I was still shaking with anger when I reached the street; but clearly in my mind the resolution formed itself that, although I was an outcast from my friends and my family, I would never become the prey of such creatures as he.

Although I did not then realize it, I had that night found a weapon of defense—one with which I often wounded myself, but one which served me in good stead in many conflicts with creatures who wore the guise of men, and on whom diplomacy, or womanly sweetness, or an appeal to chivalry would have been worse than wasted; moral cowards who would take to flight before the white heat of a woman's scorn—to attack her later from ambush if they could.

Hailing an approaching street-car, I boarded it, neither knowing nor caring where it should take me. Every inch of me ached from the long hours of wandering and of mental anguish, and I was grateful for the rest which the car afforded me. I sank into a half-sleep, in which I seemed to be forever frantically walking toward a given point, to find, when I reached it, that I was facing a high, impenetrable stone wall, but when I would have turned to retrace my steps there was no pathway leading backward.

From this stupor I was awakened by the jostling of many persons leaving the car; I followed the crowd and found myself in front of the Union Station; on entering the waiting-room I saw by the large clock facing me that it was nine-thirty. I had left Mrs. James's house before noon, and in my wanderings must have covered many miles. I had eaten nothing since early morning; and then, because neither grief nor shame can kill and because I was very young, hunger was the sensation uppermost for the time being; I went in search of food.

After eating supper life appeared a little brighter to me; I left the station with the intention of finding a room for the night. The conventions had been strongly impressed upon me, and so, notwithstanding the fact that by breaking the moral code I had become an outcast, it did not seem to me respectable that a young girl should be on the street alone at ten o'clock at night.

The clamoring hotel-runners and expressmen and hack-drivers confused me, and after three successively insolent hackmen had touched my arm and leered up into my face with their "Hack, miss?" I became frightened and retreated to the safe shelter of the waiting-room. Almost as soon as I had sat down I fell into a troubled sleep, from which I was awakened by a touch on my arm, and I screamed in terror at the thought that men were to go on forever touching my arm; but I was reassured when I saw the kindly face that was bending over me. At once I knew that there was no evil design therein.

"You were sleeping pretty soundly, all right. I hope I didn't scare you, ma'am," said the man, who wore a cap marked "Depot Master."

"No, sir," I answered, "or at least you do not frighten me now; you did when you touched me."

"For a long time I have been watching you sleep, and I was afraid you would miss your train, so I woke you up to ask what train you are taking."

In consternation I glanced up at the clock and saw that it was after one. The waiting-room was almost deserted. What in the world should I say? I turned to the official in great trepidation. "I—I—I was not going anywhere," I faltered.

The man looked puzzled. "Then what are you doing here at this time of night?" he asked. Then, a light seeming to dawn on him, he sternly inquired: "See here, young lady, I know that you are a country-town girl. Are you running away from home?   You had better tell me all about it; perhaps I can help you."

That was what the vile man in the drug-store wanted to do—to "help" me.   I looked sharply at this man, with eyes that were beginning to have a prescience of masculine designs, but there was nothing but kindly interest in his face.   Still, I could say nothing; at all hazards I must guard my secret; wild horses could not drag it from me so long as I was able to conceal it; and then, as if in mocking derision of my efforts at concealment, the first ominous movement of the newly created life took place inside my body.

In speechless fright I sank back in my seat and looked at the man in dumb agony.   Visions of the reform school, of the House of the Good Shepherd— places that I had heard the girls at the factory refer to as punitive refuges for wicked young girls—swam before my tortured imagination.   Public disgrace; my proud father's daughter, my beautiful mother's little girl, my splendid brother's sister in one of these institutions with a public brand of infamy upon her.   It was too much; my soul rose in revolt against a punishment that was out of all proportion to my offense.   Still I could not speak.

The depot-master, sensing something of my suffering, gave my arm a pat which contained nothing but reassurance.   "Well, well, young lady," he said, "you can't stay here all night.   Think it over, and if you can't tell me, I will see what I can do, anyway."

At the end of half an hour he returned with a cheery, "Feel any better now, my child?"

"You are very good to me, sir," I stammered, "and I am thankful, because I *am* in deep trouble; I cannot talk to you about it. But I am not running away from home; although I am a country-town girl, I came here, with my mother's consent, to work in a factory."

"Where have you been living?" he asked.

I told him the name of the street, but not the number; I added that I had left my boarding-house only that day. I hastily assured him that I had some money; only, I did not know where to go.

"Well, well, you look like a good girl," he said, kindly. "I had a notion to call a policeman and have him question you, but I am glad now I didn't. There is a hotel up the street kept by decent people that I know well. I shall take you up there. They would think it strange for a nice girl to be out at this time of night, so I shall tell them that you missed your train. You can get a room somewhere else to-morrow; this is no neighborhood for a girl to be in alone."

In the presence of the night clerk at the hotel he assumed a very brisk manner to cover up his kindness. "John," he said, "here is a young lady who has missed her train and does not know where to go, as she is a stranger in the city; give her a quiet room and let her sleep late, for she is pretty tired." Turning to me, he drowned my tremulous thanks in a brusk: "You are all right here, little girl. Good night."

CHAPTER III

MY long, dreamless sleep of exhaustion was not disturbed until the twelve-o'clock whistles awakened me. I sat up in bed and looked around the unfamiliar room; then I remembered all the horrid events of the day before, and jumped out of bed in alarm. I must not stay here. The depot-master had said I should only remain in that hotel overnight. It did not enter my mind to disobey him. I wondered if he had girls of his own. If he had, I thought, they must be proud to have such a nice man for a father.

When I went to put on my stockings I discovered a blister on each heel, and I had great difficulty in getting my swollen feet into the shoes that had been large enough for them the day before. As I put on my clothes I tried to formulate some plan of action, but no plan presented itself to my sorely harassed mind. Being of a naturally buoyant disposition, however, I felt that something must happen; surely my fate could not be so black as my fancy had painted it the day before.

The approaching motherhood, in itself, meant nothing to me. The thought of a child had but one meaning—disgrace, which carried with it the penalty of separation from my loved ones and disability for the work which would enable me to sustain life. At home I had often known hunger, and now I made no vague, abstract speculations about it; I knew it only too well, and the very prospect of it made me heartsick.

But if I could not work, I must starve. Yet, with the ready optimism of my nature, I felt that there must be work which I could do, something which would not prove so arduous as my task at the factory had grown to be.

Moreover, my twelve dollars did not now seem so large a sum as it had seemed the day before. Already I had spent one dollar, and it was but little more than twenty-four hours since I had left Mrs. James. I had not yet bought breakfast.

My heavy hair was with great difficulty brought into a state of order, without the aid of comb or brush, and I made a mental note of the fact that I should have to spend at least twenty-five cents for a comb.

There were many factories in the city other than the one in which I had worked, but my fear that Mrs. James would find me, together with the certainty that I could not much longer do the work required, made me hesitate to try the factories. Without influence I could not hope to get another position "checking," and I had had no experience in the machine-work. I knew that inexperienced operators could not, at best, earn more than a dollar and a half a week for the first few weeks. Indeed, I had checked the work of beginners that

came to only sixty cents a week after ten hours a
day of grilling toil.

With no wardrobe other than the clothes on my
back, I could not expect to get a position in a
department store; the only other possibility was
housework. I had little training in that, for one
does not learn much about housework in a
wretched hovel of three rooms almost destitute of
furniture, nor does one acquire culinary skill when
the food to be prepared consists of soup-meat and
potatoes (seldom enough of that) and corn-bread,
made without either eggs or "shortening."

In the restaurant where I ate breakfast I picked
up a copy of *The Globe-Democrat* and looked over
the "Help Wanted" advertisements, selecting two
which specified that young girls were in demand. I
went out to look for employment at domestic service.

My utter ignorance of the city made it difficult for
me to find the first address I sought. The depot-
master's remark about having a policeman question
me made me fear to seek knowledge from that
source, and I was too bashful to ask the passers-by.
At length I hit upon the expedient of boarding a
street-car and asking the conductor as I paid my
fare. In this way I got the desired information,
but at the cost of a precious nickel.

When at length I reached the house the haughty
dame who answered the bell shut the door in my
face, with the curt information that she did not
interview prospective servants in the afternoon.

If ladies did not interview applicants in the afternoon, there was no use in my trying the other address. I decided the only thing to do was to get a room and wait until morning.

Nor was I destined to find a position next day, nor any of the following days. My unsophisticated air made me appear even younger than I was, and I had neither references nor experience to aid me in my search. While I was shabbily dressed, I had not the manner nor appearance of the Southern servant-girl of that period, who was usually recruited from the class that Missourians called "trash." My speech also was against me, and was the cause of invidious remark by many of the women to whom I applied for work—hopefully at first, and at last in frantic despair as my small sum of money decreased to the vanishing-point.

The car fare made heavy inroads on my purse, for I seemed to be always taking the wrong car and paying an extra fare; and while in the beginning of my pregnancy I had no appetite, now I was always hungry. In my search for work I was much out of doors in the crisp October air that was like a tonic and increased my appetite to alarming proportions. The life within my own likewise called constantly for "Food! food! food!"

In St. Louis, which is the central market for one of the earth's garden spots, food was very cheap at that time; but, cheaply as it could be bought, the day was not long in coming when I could no longer buy it nor pay for a room to shelter me from the streets.

MADELEINE

I, an attractive young girl, homeless, defenseless, hungry, and in a few months to become a mother, had no choice between the course I took and the Mississippi River.

And the well-dressed man with whom I spent the night, after I was shelterless, left me, with a derisive laugh, when I timidly asked him for money next morning.

It was a raw day, and the wind tearing through my thin clothes chilled me to the marrow as I left the lodging-house where I had spent the night. I went down-town and into one of the big department stores; in the rest-room I wrote two letters, for. I still had a few stamps in my purse. One was to Mrs. James saying I had found work and was all right, and asking her to send my mail to General Delivery.

The other letter was to my mother. I wrote as if nothing had happened, explaining that I had missed my usual letter on the previous week because I had not found time to write. I wrote that I was well and getting along nicely, although at that moment hunger was cutting me like a knife and I had no place to go when I should be forced to leave the warm rest-room.

There was an inner rest-room in which patrons were permitted to eat lunch, and from well-filled boxes many suburban shoppers were partaking of their midday meal. As I hungrily watched them eat and then toss their scraps into a large waste-basket in the corner, my heart filled with bitterness

36

that these women should have food to throw away while I starved.

When at length the rest-room was deserted I dived eagerly into the basket and, bringing forth all the scraps I could find, sat down and greedily devoured them.

At eleven o'clock that night, as I stood on a quiet street corner shivering from cold and hunger, a well-dressed negro came up to me in a deferential manner and hesitatingly accosted me. "Excuse me, miss," he said, "but I done been watchin' you stand on this corner like you was lost, and I 'lowed maybe you was out to make money and findin' it hard to brace up to a man. If I's you I'd be keerful, 'cause the police in this man's town am mighty stric' and you is liable to get pinched; you done been standin' here for a right smart while."

"Thank you," I gratefully answered, and, turning up a side-street, made haste to get out of that neighborhood. When I had gone about a block I heard hasty steps behind me in the quiet street, and my heart almost choked me. That it was a policeman I did not doubt. Being "pinched" meant nothing to me in the sense the negro had intended to convey. It meant a policeman who would question me about my home, discover my condition, and send me to the reform school. I was ready to break into a run when the negro who had spoken to me came up beside me.

"Now, missie, hain't no use you being so skeered; they's no policeman in this block, and I want to

MADELEINE

tell you where they's a rich white man 'at would
give a lot of money to git aholt of a pretty girl
like you. He'd be mighty good to you, too. I
works for him, and he don't live very far from here.
If yore out to make money, you better go where you
can git it, 'cause yore too bashful to ever make it
on the street. You shore needs lots of brass for
that, an' you hain't got it. You just follow me and
I'll take you to that white man."

His manner was as deferential as his argument was
irrefutable. If I wanted to make money, the place
to go was where I could get it. It took "brass," and
I had none. After a brief hesitation, I gave a nod
of consent and followed him down the street. He
walked on for several blocks, from time to time
looking backward to see if I still followed. We
were getting into a shabby neighborhood, and I was
beginning to doubt that any man with so much
money lived in this street, when he stopped before
a small cottage and waited for me to come up to
him.

I did not doubt about the white man, but I
questioned about the money. My experience of the
night before had shown men to me in a new light.
I knew that they shirked their moral responsibilities,
but I did not doubt that they were willing to pay,
in cash, for the soft white body of a girl. Now I
had learned that they were as ready to cheat in a
monetary transaction with her as they were to
shirk their moral obligations.

When the negro saw my hesitation he came up

beside me, his manner changing from the courteously logical one he had at first employed to one of passionate pleading.

"Don't you be skeered now. He shore am a mighty fine man, and he'll suttenly treat you right; he's got lots of money," and as if to prove it, he took from his own pocket a large roll of bills.

"Hain't nothing he wouldn't do for a nice white girl like you," he went on, but now his passionate pleading frightened me; I knew it was he who wanted "the nice white girl."

Every "fine, protesting fiber" of mind and body arose in revolt against the fate which had overtaken me. I had not chosen to become an outcast from my family; I had not chosen to be a lost creature of the streets; I did not want to be cold and hungry and in the streets at midnight, with a panting negro offering me money for my aching body; I did not want that within me which was making my own frame a burden to drag around on my throbbing, weary feet. My God! had I come to this in payment for a moment's sin? And in my misery I shrieked aloud my protest: "I hate you! I hate you!" But it was not the negro at whom I shrieked.

A cab turned the corner as I screamed aloud my agony of defiance and despair. The driver pulled up sharply at the curb, and as the passenger inside opened the door to discover the cause of the commotion the negro took to his heels.

I did not stop my incoherent protest against the world, against an unjust fate, against my Maker, until the man from the cab had seized me by the shoulders and vigorously shaken me. "For Heaven's sake," he exclaimed, "stop that yelling and tell us what the trouble is. Don't you see that we want to help you?"

I stopped screaming, but I could not yet talk coherently. The cab-driver gave his version of the affair. "As I turned the corner there," he said, "I heard this girl screaming like mad; there was a big coon with her, but he ran away when I pulled up."

"Did the brute hurt you?" inquired the man who had shaken me.

I shook my head. "He only frightened me and made me angry," I answered.

He smiled quizzically at me. "Well, that scream was a mighty good weapon; I would not lose it if I were you; it is handy to have around. It is a good thing we came along when we did; and now you must let me take you home."

"I have no home. I am a bad girl," I answered. "That negro told me that the man he works for would give me lots of money; but he told a lie, because he wanted me for himself."

The man tapped his foot thoughtfully on the sidewalk for a moment. "Even bad girls," he said, "usually have homes of some sort. You don't look very bad; but if you want to make some money, perhaps you had better come with me."

My teeth were chattering with the cold, but my mind was growing numb with the numbness of despair as I preceded him into the cab. He gave a direction to the driver before entering, and explained to me: "We are going down to Tony Faust's and get something to warm you up while we talk it over. You poor little kid, you are half frozen!"

I leaned against soft cushions without speaking, and he respected my silence as we drove on.

Arriving at Faust's, where he seemed to be well known to the waiters, we were shown into a private room. "A hot toddy, Fritz," he ordered, "for the lady, and see that it is hot and strong; and something soft for me, as I am on the water-wagon."

After the drinks were served he gave the order for supper, and told me to drink my toddy while it was hot. I recalled a pledge I had taken in early childhood, and pushed the glass away. "I can't take that," I said. "I belong to the Band of Hope."

"Poor little girl, you belong to the Band of the Hopeless right now; and that absolves you from the pledge. You will have more hope after you have something hot inside you. Drink it," he said, peremptorily, and I obeyed.

After I had swallowed the last drop a warm glow permeated mind and body. I reflected that I should have to go to hell, anyway, so breaking my childhood's pledge did not seem such a heinous offense as it would have otherwise.

When the thick, rare beefsteak, with mushrooms, was brought in I eyed it greedily; when my host served me with a dainty portion I wanted to take it in my teeth and rend it. "As free from ceremony's sway as famished wolf that rends its prey."

An almost forgotten incident of childhood came to mind, putting me at once on my good behavior. At a large family dinner-party, where several mothers wrestled with unruly children, it was remarked by many of them, in my hearing, that, although my mother was not present to keep me in order, I was a very polite child and had the best manners of any little girl in town.

I did not want my kind host to think me a savage, even though he had found me screaming in the streets, so I ate as daintily as I had on that day when I had been so proud to be called "the best-mannered little girl in town."

A noted actor was playing "Richelieu" in the city, and my host entertained me with a description of the man, contrasting him with another great actor he had seen in the same character.

His courtliness to a starving girl whom he had picked up in the streets caused my mind to revert to the well-dressed man who had laughed derisively when I timidly asked him for money. I added another item to my rapidly increasing store of knowledge of the ways of men. A man with a true heart of a gentleman does not change his attitude of courtesy toward women because the woman in question chances to be one of the fallen sisters. That is a conclusion I have never found reason to alter.

After supper he took me to his rooms, where he anticipated my every need with a gentleness that was balm to my aching heart; giving me his own dressing-gown and slippers, and laying out a clean nightshirt for me, after he had first turned on the bath.

When I came from the bath, with the long robe trailing under my feet and the slippers falling off at every step, he laughed indulgently and I tried to join him, but the muscles of my mouth refused their office.

"It is after three," he said, "and I have to see a man at 'The Planter's' at nine-thirty. I will go down there now and get a room for the night. You sleep as long as you like. I will be up about one, and we will have lunch together. The maid who takes care of my rooms comes about ten, but you need not let her in."

He gave me a friendly handshake and was about to open the door when he seemed to think of something else. "I had better leave you some change for breakfast," he continued, "in case I am detained." He picked up my shabby purse, and, after putting something into it, again bade me good night and went out.

4

CHAPTER IV

THE nourishing supper which my host had served me, followed by the inestimable boon of a hot bath, a beautiful warm room, and a comfortable bed; the glow of gratitude in my heart for this man who had shown me such kindness, with the additional delicacy of leaving me, all conduced to the relaxation of my outraged nerves and my exhausted body.

After a prolonged sleep I had entirely recovered from the effects of my protracted fast, which but for the waste-basket scraps had been unbroken for forty-eight hours.

My host did not come in until one-thirty, but I had slept so long that I had just finished dressing when he entered the apartment. I busied myself in setting things to rights, while he walked about, expatiating on the pleasure it gave him to find some one at home waiting for him. When the lunch, which he had ordered from a near-by restaurant, was brought we laughed over his attempt to help arrange the table, and he made the discovery that I could laugh; he proposed that I should remain with him for a few days until I had other plans.

It was quite evident that he did not consider me a

AN AUTOBIOGRAPHY

bad girl in the sense I meant when I had announced that fact to him the night before. He knew that there was much behind the scene that I was making when he had met me, and he was obviously expecting to be taken into my confidence; but much as I longed to have him understand, I could not tell him the truth. It did not occur to me to tell him a lie.

The process of education in the oldest profession in the world is like any other educational process, in that it requires time and effort and patience; it can only be acquired by taking one step at a time, though the steps become accelerated after the first few.

I had yet to learn that lying was a part of the profession and was included in the curriculum; that it was employed, not only as a means of advertising and arousing interest, but also as a measure of self-defense against impertinent inquirers. And I had yet to learn that every man's vanity, regardless of how casual his intercourse with "one of the girls" may be, leads him to expect that she shall take *him* into her confidence, and tell *him* the truth about her family affairs, and her private life, and her "right name," and why she is adventuring in the primrose way, though he is quite ready to concede her right to "conceal hersel', as weel's she can, frae critical dissection" on the part of others.

Since I was utterly ignorant of these facts pertaining to the profession which had been thrust upon me, I could only maintain a painful silence in answer to the delicately veiled hints of my host that I tell him all about it.

45

MADELEINE

After lunch he again put money into my purse, remarking as he did so that perhaps I would like to do a little shopping, and suggesting the places where one could buy to the best advantage; he added that I would better have dinner before I returned, as he might be detained until too late to dine with me.

My first purchases were in the underwear department; after that I bought stockings and shoes, and was trying to decide what would be the most sensible way to spend the remainder of the money when I was suddenly seized with a panic, because of new and disquieting movements from the life that was within my own life. My long rest of the night before had been so complete and the arrival of my host had been so early that for many hours I had forgotten this other part of my existence.

Hurriedly leaving the store with my parcels, I hastened back to the apartment and, tearing off the clothing which was now suffocating me, I threw myself on the bed and gave way to angry, frantic, futile tears. However, the movement inside of me ceased, and gradually I grew calm again. I counted the money which remained from my shopping expedition, and decided that I would not even buy my dinner; I had spent too much already.

There was no use quarreling with myself about what could not be undone, and I had sorely needed the articles I had bought. I prepared the bath, and afterward, when I had put on the new garments, I would not have been a woman had I failed

46

to feel the glow of satisfaction which came over me as I felt the touch of clean, dainty linen.

At six-thirty my appetite got the better of my would-be prudence and I went out for dinner, which I ate with all the more relish because I felt that I should not have bought it. My host came in a few moments after my return and I put aside my anxiety in an effort to be agreeable to this man who had shown me so much kindness.

He was a brilliant conversationalist, and my shyness made me a good listener; he spoke on many subjects of which I had no knowledge; but with a habit which had been formed in early childhood I laid them away in my capacious memory for reference at the first opportunity.

After a while he told me something about himself and his personal affairs. At his father's death he had inherited a comfortable fortune and a large share of his father's business. He said, regretfully, that he had neglected his business and had spent a great deal of money in reckless living. For the past year he had been drinking steadily; until about five weeks before his meeting with me, when he had contracted a disease which made it imperative for him to stop. He mentioned the name of the disease; but the only idea that was conveyed to my mind was that it could not be a very bad thing if it had caused him to stop drinking; moreover, he did not seem to be suffering much pain.

When I mentioned this he said that he had suffered considerably at first, but the doctor now considered him cured; however, he was not taking any chances, and was earnestly trying not to drink again.

He went on to say that my presence would be a godsend to him, for he disliked being alone in his rooms; and he had a great struggle to leave liquor alone when he was with his friends, who were a pretty rapid lot.

My heart went out to him in his struggle with the enemy that had wrecked our own home; I rejoiced that I could be of service to him, in return for his kindness to me. Eleven o'clock came very quickly, and after he had taken his departure from his own rooms, that I might have undisputed possession for the night, I felt sorry that he was so old—he must have been at least twenty-eight. But perhaps it was all for the best, I reflected; if he were younger, perhaps I should fall in love with him.

At two o'clock the following afternoon he came bounding in like a school-boy and insisted on taking me shopping, though, to be sure, I was not loath to go. He bought me a hat and a coat, and a gown with silk lining and the various accessories, waving aside my shocked objection to his spending so much money.

I remained in the department store while the needful alterations were made in the gown; afterward I donned my new garments in the fitting-room, preparatory to keeping a dinner engagement with my benefactor, who had left me after making the purchase of my new wardrobe.

Conscious that I was looking well in my new

clothes, I felt a natural glow of elation when I met him; but was somewhat disconcerted when he suggested that I should go into a hair-dresser's and have my hair "done up," as we were going to the theater. Evidently I was not looking so nice as I had supposed. Seeing my disappointment at his lack of approbation, he hastened to assure me that I looked all right; he explained, smilingly, that the reason for his suggestion was my "pigtail," which made me look so young that he feared he might be arrested for cradle-robbing.

That explanation served to soothe my newly discovered vanity, because I disliked the pigtail very much; but I had to wear it because I had not yet learned to dress my hair in any other way.

That night, after our return from the theater, he appeared reluctant to leave, and it must be confessed that I did not find him so entertaining as on the night before. I had enjoyed the evening, but now I was very tired; my tight clothing was causing me excruciating pain, and I longed to be alone.

When at length he had gone I sat down to brush my hair and prepare for bed. As I brushed I pondered over this man's generosity in giving so much and asking nothing in return. Surely the world could not be so heartless as I had thought. I had just received proof that chivalry had not entirely died out of men's hearts.

As I got into bed I heard his key in the door. As soon as he had entered the room he began making profuse apologies; he would stay only a minute;

he had felt impelled to come back and tell me how much he had enjoyed my society; how my refinement had appealed to the best that was within him; how adorable and altogether charming he had found me to be. The flattery, which would have been pleasing to my unaccustomed ears a few hours earlier, only wearied me now. But with true masculine density he could not see that I was bored; with true masculine vanity he appeared to think I was as loath to have him go as he was reluctant to leave.

Then I made the discovery that the reason for his continence was not, as I had supposed, his exceeding great virtue, but the illness from which he had recently suffered. When he saw that I did not in the least understand what he was talking about he explained in detail. He had contracted a venereal disease which, if properly treated, was no worse than a severe cold. His physician had pronounced him cured, but he would not ask me to expose myself unless I fully understood that there was an element of risk. At worst it was not a virulent disease, and the risk was slight, but it would make no difference in our friendship if I should refuse to run that risk. Much of his explanation was Greek to me: I understood thoroughly, although he made no intimation of it, that this man had found me starving in the streets; that he had fed and sheltered and clothed me; and that he did not demand payment. Nevertheless he did expect it, and pleaded for it. . . . I paid.

I had learned another of the lessons of the oldest profession, "Man gets his price for what man gives us."

In the morning he was worried and not so sure of there being no risk. He hovered over me as I put on the garments that had been so beautiful the day before, when I had thought them a free-will offering; now that I had paid the price for them they were to me merely a covering for the body, a means of protection from the cold. He wearied me with his attentions, and I was glad when he had gone.

I was not at all apprehensive about the disease, partly because I had never heard of it before, and he did not seem to have suffered much from it; partly because I had none of that haunting fear of contagion by which so many persons are made miserable. Exposure to smallpox, a disease that at the time of which I write was looked upon as most deadly, would not have frightened me at all; this disorder of which I had just heard had no terrors for me. The thing which I most feared in the world was hunger. That was something of which I had personal knowledge.

After I was alone I went down to the post-office and found two letters awaiting me there. One was from Mrs. James, in which she implored me to write home every week, even if I would not let her know my whereabouts. She told me to continue having my mail sent to her, and that she would forward it

to General Delivery; she said she would help me
to keep the truth from mother, and believed she
was serving God in so doing. There was no word
of reproach for me. She begged me to let her
know when my time came, that she might be with
me.

The other letter was from my mother. She had
not worried at my not writing, because of a letter
from Mrs. James in which she had written as if
nothing had happened.

As soon as I returned to the apartments I answered
both letters. In the one I told the truth as to my
present movements, but not of the happenings before
I had reached this haven of refuge. I did not give
my address. In the other I wrote as if I were still
at the factory, and made no reference to having
left Mrs. James.

A few days after the events of which I write
business matters called my host to Kansas City,
and I accompanied him. When we had been a week
in Kansas City the disease to which I had been
exposed made its appearance and I could not return
with him to St. Louis. He was filled with regret
that I had contracted the disease; though he felt
but little remorse for the act that had made it possible. He was most solicitous for my recovery, and,
as the physician who was called in advised the hospital, he left me well provided with money, and after
securing my promise of forgiveness begged me to
return to him when I had recovered.

If the physician who attended me or the nurses

discovered my pregnancy they took no cognizance of it. I was given a room with another girl who was suffering from the same disease, and we received scant courtesy from the nurses, though the physician was very kind, especially to me. He said I would be all right in a couple of weeks; he explained that there were no after-results to women from this disease, though men frequently suffered for a long time.

The girl with whom I found myself was from a house of ill fame on Fourth Street, and, far from being ashamed of it, she proceeded to tell me all about it. As I had the disease, she accepted me into the fellowship, though in a rather contemptuous way, referring to me as a "titbit." She decided at once from my verdancy that I had not come from a house, and she deduced from the dainty clothes with which my friend had liberally provided me that I was a kept woman with a "live one on the string."

Mamie, as she called herself, nad no reserve whatever; she told me all she knew of evil, and whatever she did not know, she drew on her imagination for and told for good measure. Her English and her manners, or, rather, her lack of them, shocked me almost as much as her frank discussion of everything pertaining to sex, including her own illness. She looked upon the disease as a matter for jesting; that she, an old-timer of six years' standing, should have been caught napping struck her as being a huge joke on herself.

MADELEINE

It was an unbearable recital and filled me with heartsick loathing for her and for all of her kind. I felt sure that human degradation could go no farther; when she took a box of cigarettes from under her pillow and offered me one I was speechless with indignation. She refused to be snubbed, however, and in the dark days of suffering which followed, Mamie's spontaneous good nature finally won my grudging admiration, though she did not succeed in inducing me to join her in a cigarette; indeed, the shock she gave to my sense of decency at that time prevented me from ever even trying to smoke them.

She had quite recovered from her illness, and was importuning the physician at every visit to give her a certificate, so she could go about her business; she would have gone without it, but for the reason that her landlady would not let her make money unless she had the desired document. Mamie advised me, when I should have the misfortune to lose "my man," to go into a house. She said that a girl who got into the right kind of a house had good food, a beautiful room, and was cared for if she got sick; she was not preyed upon by the class of men who wanted something for which they were not willing to pay. She was protected by the police, and, what was still more important, she was protected from the police.

When she had received her certificate she was as happy as a high-school girl who has just been handed her diploma.

"Don't ever be fool enough to go into the streets," was her parting advice, and she shuddered, as if at some horrible recollection. I, too, shuddered at the hideous memory her words had conjured up. With an invitation to come and see her, and a good-by to the nurses, as cordial as if they had been unfailingly considerate of her, she was gone.

Long letters came to me every day from the man in St. Louis; and I answered in letters which, if they were not so long nor so loving as his, seemed to satisfy him. I had a very tender spot in my heart for him, for I knew that he had really grown fond of me and that he had not intended to harm me. I appreciated his many fine qualities, even if he were no longer on a pedestal.

When I was ready to leave the hospital at the end of three weeks I had great difficulty in getting into my corset and my clothes, and as soon as I had reached the hotel to which the doctor had directed me I at once removed them and sat down to ponder over the situation. The doctor had advised me to remain in Kansas City for a while until all danger of renewed infection, on either side, should be over. He thought the best way to avoid temptation was to keep away from it. He had said this to my friend when he was called in for consultation, and we were agreed as to his wisdom.

I now realized that I could not hope to keep my secret from my friend much longer. I did not answer his latest letter, because there was nothing to write except the truth. I could not tell him that; I must let him pass out of my life, thinking whatever he would of me.

During the following week I tasted every variety of homesickness, of loneliness, and of despair. I ripped open my coat and sewed fifty dollars into the lining. That should be for my confinement; I would not touch it though I starved. After putting this sum away I had money enough to keep me for a week longer; there would then remain more than three months until the event. There was nothing for it but to send for Mamie and consult her. If I brooded much longer, I was sure I should lose my mind.

When Mamie came, in response to my message, and I had told her of my resolve not to return to St. Louis because of my condition, she promptly told me that I was a little fool, pointing out many ways in which I could deceive my friend while I "pulled his leg" for enough to carry me through my coming trial. She attempted to show me how I could still hold him, by lying about the city in which my home was located, and pretending to go home. After it was all over I could return to him and he would never know. I rejected the scheme at once; I had one person to lie to now, my mother. I did not find the task so easy that I cared to embark on another sea of lies. I wanted to shriek the truth from the house-tops, I was so burdened from concealing it.

Mamie still maintained that I was a fool, but of course it was my own business. She would see her landlady and ask her to take me, though she bluntly told me that a girl in my condition would not be considered a drawing-card; still, as I showed it very little, I should be able to make money for a little while yet. She left me with the assurance that I would hear from her in a little while. I had not told her about the fifty dollars.

In a couple of hours a note came saying that Miss Laura, her landlady, would take me and that I was to come down at once. After I had packed my bag my courage failed me. It was impossible; I could not go.

After two days of struggle with myself I made the attempt, but when I reached Fifth and Broadway a drunken man was being ejected from a saloon by an irate bartender, and the air was sulphurous with the oaths they were exchanging. In soul-sick terror at the thought of proximity to such conditions of life I turned and fled back to the hotel.

At the expiration of another two days I took down my coat and tentatively fingered the spot where I had hidden the money. I did not take it out and I knew that I would not touch it until my time came. I had no vague ideas of the horrors of being moneyless; I knew this monster which is called poverty, in all its soul-destroying aspects; I knew that if I used the money it was only postponing the evil day. . . . I went to see Mamie.

When I turned into Fourth Street my courage again failed me, and I was about to beat a retreat when Mamie came out of a restaurant across the street and warmly greeted me. The porter, who came to the door in response to our ring, said that Miss Laura was in her room, and we were shown in. I saw a woman comely and middle-aged, who bore no resemblance to the horrible creature of my imagination. She greeted me in a soft, well-bred voice, and everything about her so eloquently spoke of her potentialities for motherhood that instinctively I looked around for the children who should have been clinging to her skirts.

Her first question was about my age. She thought I looked older than my seventeen years, and no doubt I did. The condition I was in, the anxiety and illness which I had just suffered, gave me an air of maturity which would have seemed impossible to any one who had known me a few weeks earlier.

"Does your family live in Kansas City?" was her next question. "And will they make trouble when they find you here?" I told her that my family did not live there, did not know of my presence in the city, and that she need fear no trouble from them. In response to her question, "Do you understand what this life means?" I succinctly answered, "Yes, it means food and shelter."

"It means more than that, my dear." She smiled, rather sadly. "But we must take it as we find it and make the best of it."

When she asked me if I had ever known a man I was surprised, because I thought Mamie had told her all about me. I discovered in the course of our conversation that Mamie had told her little, and that that little was misleading. With her customary mendacity, Mamie had not told her one word of the truth concerning my condition. She had not concealed it through any desire to shield me, but through sheer inability to tell the truth.

We had a few minutes' conversation on other topics; then she rang for the housekeeper to take me in charge, giving her instructions to have the "house doctor" see me before I was permitted to "come into the parlor."

The housekeeper shattered another preconceived idea. She was a stately-looking woman somewhat over thirty, and perfectly fulfilled my ideal of a Southern aristocrat, in which girlishly romantic conclusion I happened to be correct. She looked at me rather sadly and asked me where in the world I had met Mamie. It was evident from her tone that Mamie did not stand very high in her estimation.

I explained that I had met Mamie at the hospital, and she asked me no further questions. One of the first things impressed upon me by her was that I should never ask questions about the private affairs of other girls; conversely, none would be asked about mine.

She looked approvingly at my street clothes and regretted that I had nothing suitable for the house. "I will borrow a wrapper and a parlor dress for you from one of the other girls," she said. "You will not want to go in debt the first thing."

She went out, to return in a few moments with a girl whom she called Bessie, explaining to her my

need of proper clothes for the house. Bessie was a
Jewess, no longer very young, who still bore the
traces of a beauty which had been marred by her
protest against life rather than by time. She looked
inexpressibly tired and disillusioned with life. After
a little conversation, in which she was at first rather
inclined to be cold and distant, she took me to her
own room and placed her ample wardrobe at my
disposal, selecting for me a red robe of Grecian
design which left my arms bare and exposed much
of my chest and shoulders, but relieved me of the
necessity of wearing a corset.

She took down my abundant hair and dressed it
in a Greek knot with bands, and had started to
"make-up" my face when I interposed an objection
which all of her arguments were unable to overcome. I would not have my face painted, and that
settled it! Not only for that day, but for all of the
succeeding days in which I remained in the business.
I had to draw a line somewhere. Doubtless cigarettes and paint were the least harmful of the concomitants of prostitution (having at this late date
been admitted into good society), but they were offensive to me, and I drew the line at them.

As Bessie worked she kept up a running fire of
comment on the life I was about to enter, telling
me that if I had any sense I would find some other
kind of a job, no matter how menial, rather than
enter upon a path from which there was no turning
back. When I told her of my condition she became
very gentle in her manner to me, but she continued

to protest against the life. Some of her sayings kept ringing in my mind for many days; indeed, at intervals, for many years.

"You are young now. Men will swarm about you if you learn how to please them. It lies with you whether they show you much consideration or not. It is in your power to make them do so. But as you grow older you will find them losing consideration for you. Men who have known us for five years are always ready to swear that they have known us for ten. Those who have known us for ten years refer to us as 'grandmothers,' 'old women,' 'has-beens,' and call us other names even less complimentary.

"Most women who have been ten years in the business are still under thirty and retain much of their youthful charm; many of them have improved in appearance; but if they stay in the place where they are known, they become 'old-timers' to the men and do not receive the consideration shown to younger women. The one consolation is that they usually make more money than the beginners."

I told her that my friend in St. Louis had said that prostitutes never lived over seven years; that they usually died earlier than that. Bessie laughed, but her laugh contained no mirth. "There is no such luck," she said. "I am twenty-eight and I have been in the business since I was eighteen. I am a long way from being dead. There are eleven girls in this house, exclusive of you. Five of us have been here, at intervals, for over ten years.

MADELEINE

One of the five has been here at various times for
fifteen years. Two have been here steadily for
over six years. The others are comparatively new
in the business. Miss Laura has kept house in
Kansas City for nearly twenty years. She herself
was a boarder in St. Louis at the close of the Civil
War. She does not look like a candidate for the
graveyard, does she?"

Two of the other girls dropped in about this time,
and when Bessie attempted to introduce me it was
discovered that I was nameless. Each of these
girls had a favorite name to propose, Bessie had
still another; none of them pleased me, and the discussion waxed warm until one of the girls suggested
that we go down and let Miss Laura decide.

Miss Laura suggested Hazel, which brought forth
a discussion of "lucky" names; superstition enters
largely into the lives of these people, and even Miss
Laura and the housekeeper, both women of superior
intelligence, were not exempt from the taint of it.

The essential requisite of a name seemed to be
that some "lucky" girl had borne it. I suggested
the name Miriam, which was instantly rejected because several girls bearing that name had been
notably unfortunate; consequently no one who bore
it could hope to "have luck." At length I hit upon
the name "Madeleine," and as none of them had ever
known any one by that name, lucky or otherwise,
it was decided that I should take a chance with it;
finally, and for "good luck," Bessie gave me the
surname of Blair.

CHAPTER V

AT that time the moral conditions in Kansas City were abominable. The restricted district extended for several blocks on Third and Fourth streets, but segregation was a name only, not a fact.

Vice flourished in all parts of the city, but especially in the rooming-house districts; wine-rooms were wide 'open for any one having the price of a drink; private houses and assignation - houses abounded throughout the residential parts of the city; and the roadhouses ran full blast for twenty-four hours a day.

Besides the local product of the city itself, many of the small towns of Missouri, Kansas, and Texas sent their quota of the raw material of prostitution into Kansas City; and Kansas City, not to be outdone in courtesy, returned a finished product to the houses of the smaller cities in these states. But an overplus still remained, with the result of a glutted market and poor business.

There were three first-class places, of which Miss Laura's was one. That is, these houses maintained a high price, regardless of the condition of business or of the keenness of competition, and they harbored a better class of women.

Table-board was five dollars a week, which meant that the girl must make ten in order to pay her board; after that was settled half the money she made was her own. The girls were supposed to turn in half of the standard price of the house, but if a man gave them more, it was their own. In many houses the landladies claimed half of whatever the girls received, regardless of the regulation fee.

This led the girls into a labyrinth of lies, which they justified on the plea of self-defense.

In many of the houses there was a system of fines by which the girls paid two dollars and a half for any infraction of the rules. One place was particularly notorious for this practice. One of the girls was calling at Miss Laura's one day when I asked her what percentage the girls paid her landlady. "Oh, the first ten dollars you make, and all the rest," she laconically replied.

In the house where I lived there was no attempt to take from the girls anything but half of the standard price. If the girl received a gift of money from a man she was not constrained to conceal the fact through the certainty of having to share it with the landlady. This not only led to a better spirit, but gave the girl the opportunity to spend the money more judiciously.

When girls were compelled to lie about the amount of money they had received they were much more likely to buy liquor with it, and "blow it in with the gang," than to employ it for their actual needs.

AN AUTOBIOGRAPHY

Neither was there a system of fines at Miss Laura's except for a failure to be in the house during "parlor hours," which were from 8 P.M. until 4 A.M. Even this rule was not an inflexible one, a reasonable excuse being accepted unless the girl was obviously under the influence of liquor.

Most of the customers were of a rather staid sort, for Miss Laura kept too many "old-timers" to be popular with a very fast crowd. The other houses referred to her place as the "Old Ladies' Home," although none of the women were old in the matter of years.

Miss Laura always smiled indulgently when she heard of this name, for it was to her a far more important matter that the girls should look upon the place as "home" than that she should make a great deal of money. Her mail was a heavy one, containing letters from girls in all parts of the country, who remembered her and her house with gratitude when they had contrasted it with other places where they made more money, but from which the vital touch of kindliness was absent.

This woman, whom God and nature had designed for a beautiful motherhood and whom circumstance had cheated of her birthright, was endeavoring, so far as lay in her power, to live up to the standards which had been laid down for her in early youth. Her father, who was a slaveholder in Missouri at the outbreak of the Civil War, was killed in one of the early battles. Marauding bands had driven off their stock and burned their home, and her

MADELEINE

mother, who was in a delicate condition, had been tortured before her eyes in an effort to make her reveal the whereabouts of valuables that the marauders believed she had hidden.

The death of her mother following the birth of twins had left four children: Miss Laura, at that time a girl of sixteen, a sister eighteen months older, and the two infant sons, who afterward proved to be feeble-minded, possibly as a result of the horrors their mother had endured previous to their birth.

A noted Union general had offered "protection" to the girls and a safe-conduct to St. Louis. They paid for the protection and the safe-conduct in the manner in which men often claim payment from defenseless women, and later they entered a house of ill fame in St. Louis. Afterward they came to Kansas City. They had prospered in the business, and after the war they gathered up some of their old house slaves, who were still with them at the time of which I write. The cook, the waitress, and the porter in Miss Laura's house were all former slaves of her father.

Never once had these sisters faltered in their obligation toward their unfortunate brothers. They had a private home in the city, with a housekeeper and a teacher for the "boys," who were queer-looking little men, with excellent manners and the mentality of children of eight.

Every business of this kind reflects, to a large degree, the personality of the keeper, and the spirit of the house is largely the spirit of the woman who presides over it. Because this woman was broad-gaged and kindly, there was a spirit of tolerance and fellowship in her establishment such as I have seldom seen elsewhere. Competition was keen among the girls, as it must be in this profession, but there was an unwritten law that girls must not compete by unfair methods.

Miss Laura's great desire was to make the girls comfortable. In many large houses there is little heat during the daytime, and in a few of them the table is stinted to the last possible degree. Not so in this place. Miss Laura's constant command to the porter, "Uncle Henry, see that the ladies' rooms are warm," resulted in keeping the house like a bake-oven.

I could never accustom my eyes to the sight of such a well-laden table. At times I was afraid I would wake up and find it a dream. The house closed at four in the morning; the rising-bell rang at twelve-thirty; breakfast was at one, but I could not get accustomed to lying in bed until this time of day, and I was always famished in the morning, with the result that I would brave the wrath of the cook, who was old and crabbed, by going down-stairs at the earliest possible moment.

Had I employed half the skill to ingratiate myself with customers that I used to win the good graces of the cook I should have made a barrel of money. I was rewarded, however, not only with an early breakfast, but with many stories of slavery days.

The supposition had been, among those who knew

me best, that I was an exceedingly bright girl. If this had ever been true, it had ceased to be so since I had entered upon the primrose path. I was constantly chagrined by my own stupidity and contrasted myself with women who had not half my intelligence in most matters, but who, as they themselves declared, "could give me cards and spades."

Both my natural reserve and my physical condition made it difficult for me to talk with strangers; but when I had gotten my own consent to do so, I was so deplorably frank that I would insist on expressing my repugnance for the business, and my contempt for the men themselves if they did not happen to please me.

The result was that I made very little money and few men came to see me the second time. The few who did return were very young men to whom it was not difficult to be nice, or who were content to have a girl's body for which they had paid without exacting her soul and her affections as largess.

I was a good-looking girl, but by no means beautiful; consequently few men would have noticed me for my looks alone in a parlor full of good-looking, beautifully gowned girls, each in her own way clamoring for attention and crying her own wares. A less indulgent woman than Miss Laura would not have kept me two weeks; I was not worth my salt, but she was patient. Another of my derelictions was in the matter of drinks. No one expected me to sell them, because few girls who are new in the business are able to sell drinks, but they did expect that I should not "knock" the sale.

The housekeeper had explained to me, with great patience and at great length, that the chief source of income for the house was from the liquor sold, and that all the girls were to help in the sale; she added that this could be done without much drinking if the girls used a little judgment.

It was necessary to remove the glass from the tray and hold it up with an acknowledgment of some sort to the purchaser. It was seldom necessary to drink. After touching the glass to the lips the contents could easily be thrown into one of the tall, vaselike cuspidors which stood beside each chair, or, failing in this, it was very easy to dance around the room, apparently in response to the music, and dance out with the glass untouched.

These lessons were as difficult to me as the instructions upon the art of handling men. I loathed the sight of liquor, and I did not want any one even to think that I liked it. So, despite my resolve to remove the glass when the tray was brought around, I frequently found myself saying, in a voice from which I made no effort to remove my contempt, "No, thanks; I do not drink."

This holier-than-thou attitude of mine, aside from being very bad for business, brought me into conflict with the other girls, who were prone to resent it, and in a less tolerant household life would have been made unbearable for me.

Twice in one week I let men go out without paying

me—great brutes, who had taken advantage of my
ignorance to exact far more than the stipulated entertainment, and had then bluffed me out of my wages.

Discipline required that I pay for the time consumed. I was responsible for collecting the money,
and if I did not have sense enough to get it, it was
my own fault. So I not only did not get paid,
but I had to pay for the torture I had undergone in
entertaining these brutes. These matters of discipline were at the housekeeper's discretion, and she
ruled that the only way to teach me to get my
money was to make me pay if I did not.

She fully believed me when I said that I had been
bilked, but if she had let me off without payment,
unscrupulous girls would take advantage of her
leniency and cheat the house out of its due.

She had remarked sarcastically that if I had got my
money first I would not have been bilked; and the
very next day I offended one of the best customers
of the house by asking him for money in advance.
The housekeeper was exasperated beyond endurance
with me, and told me I would have to learn to dis-
tinguish a gentleman from a blackguard; to which
advice I hotly retorted that I didn't believe that
gentlemen came into a "sporting-house."

Time proved me mistaken in this opinion.

The process of education was painfully slow.
When I had just succeeded in mastering one of the
rules, and had resolved to make a practical application of it, I would stumble over another one that I
had not learned.

The housekeeper gave a sigh of apprehension every time a man "picked me out." If he were an old customer, the chances were that she would have to spend half an hour in applying soothing-salve to his wounded vanity. If he were a stranger, it was almost certain that he would flounce out with the sarcastic taunt, "If that's the way your girls treat a fellow, I'll never come into your d——d old house again."

My difficulties with the patrons arose from two causes. The first was the almost invariable habit of patrons in asking a girl all about her private life; the fact that they had never seen her before, and possibly would never see her again, made not the faintest difference. They considered that her story was one of their privileges and included in the price they had paid for their entertainment.

These questions about my private affairs annoyed me very much. As I had no finesse in evading them, I took refuge either in silence or in impatient outbursts about it's being none of their business. The result was an offended customer.

Secondly, I could not make a demonstration of affection over men nor any pretense at response to their caresses. For the life of me, I could not understand why they should expect it. They had only bought my body. I could not see why they should want more. My love was not for sale, piecemeal, to every man who had the price to pay for my body, and I could make no pretense at a response I did not feel. On the contrary, I made little effort to conceal my repugnance.

MADELEINE

While I suffered greatly from all these conflicts, they were not unique. Every girl who has any sense of decency or refinement goes through much the same experiences as mine. No girl is plunged suddenly from a life of virtue into a life of prostitution. For whatsoever may have been the contributory causes, each girl who enters a house has gone through a period of moral attrition before she takes this seemingly fatal step.

Nor are young girls just entering the business of much value, commercially, either to themselves or to the house. The elements of success in this business do not differ from the elements of success in any other. Competition is keen and bitter. Advertising is as large an element as in any other business, and since the usual avenues of successful exploitation are closed to the profession, the adage that the best advertisement is a pleased customer is doubly true in this business.

Whatever of arts and wiles or even of coercion men may enlist when they seek to betray, all these are laid aside when they go into the open market; they will no more buy from an indifferent, reluctant, or contentious woman than they would buy from a merchant of the same sort.

They expect the same willing, responsive service from the woman whose body they have bought as they do from the waitress who serves their dinner. If the waitress brings in the meal and slams the dishes down in front of the customer, with an air which seems to say, "I am compelled to serve you, but you can see how repugnant the service is to me," the result is a complaint to the proprietor and usually a lost customer.

This is even more true in the case of service from public women. A man soon forgets his irritation in the former instance and merely records his displeasure by remaining away. In the second his vanity has been piqued. The combination of himself and his money having failed to win him a response, he voices his displeasure to every male whom he dares take into his confidence. The result is not only a lost customer, but several lost customers, and often an implacable hostility for the house, an enmity which does not cease even after the cause of it has left the establishment. By some peculiar freak of masculine logic, a man usually holds the keeper responsible for any offense the inmates may give him. She should have trained her girls better.

One evening Miss Laura, who seldom came into the parlors, came to the door and mysteriously beckoned me out into the hall.

"There is a man in my own parlor I want to introduce you to," she said when the door was shut. "You ought to suit him down to the ground. He dislikes having the girls make a fuss over him, and while he always gives a girl more than her price, if she tries to make love to him he flatly tells her she can eliminate that part of it, because she will not get anything extra for it."

I felt that I would be delighted to meet such a man, although I had by this time decided that there was no such animal as a man who did not also want to claim a woman's soul for the price he had paid for her body.

Miss Laura performed the introduction, and I really smiled a spontaneous smile of which I knew not the cause. At a first glance this man struck me as being the ugliest person I had ever seen. But a second glance showed that he had an air of distinction that his plainness of features could not mar. After a little conversation I began picking out his "points" and discovered that he was not ugly at all.

After he had left my room and was on his way to the front door he changed his mind about going out, saying that he was lonesome and wanted to talk to me. We went into the parlor and he ordered a bottle of wine. I went into the hall to look for reinforcements, because I felt that I could not "slough" the wine if I were alone.

The housekeeper looked surprised when I told her what I wanted. "You don't mean to say that that man has ordered wine, do you?" she asked. "He usually rushes out as though he had been sent for. Don't call any of the girls, for he may not like it. I will come in and help you out."

He did not seem to care whether I drank the wine or not. Evidently he had only bought it because he wanted to remain for a while.

He said he would call again in a few days, and when he went out I sat down to ponder about this man who was so different from the usual run of patrons. To my great surprise, he came again the next night.   It was a great joke in the house, a subject for conversation at the breakfast-table, that this man, who was so difficult to please and who had seldom taken the same girl the second time, should have called twice on me when I was never known to have been nice to a man.

"What in the world led you to please him?" they asked.

"Nothing," I answered.

"That was just it," the housekeeper joined in. "He hates to be entertained.   Somebody lied to that boy when he was young, and told him that fast women were a necessary evil.   He believes it, all right. He comes here because he considers it necessary, but he does not consider it incumbent upon him to have social intercourse with us; and it offends him because the girls try to make love to him."

"Don't worry about Madeleine making love to any one," cut in Mamie.   "She is stuck on that man in St. Louis."

"I do not care for any one," I retorted.   "But it *was* a relief to me to meet a man who did not think he had bought me outright.   Some of them even expect you to tell them what you are thinking about.   I enjoyed this man's society, and I hope he will come again."

"Oh, he'll come, never fear," laughed the housekeeper.   "He kept me at the door for fifteen minutes while he sang your praises.   He's been coming here for the past two years, but he never before took any notice of a girl."

He did come again. He came every night for a
week, bringing me candy and books and sending me
flowers betweentimes. He was generous with his
money, but parsimonious with his conversation. It
was evident that he was violating all of his standards
and all of his traditions by showing attention to one
of the lost sisterhood, yet he could not stay away.
I looked forward with pleasure to his coming and
regretted his departure. Suddenly he ceased to call,
and I missed him very much.

When I had not seen him for over three weeks
and had concluded that I should never see him
again, I received a letter headed Winnipeg, Mani-
toba. He explained that he was in that place on
matters connected with his business, that he had
felt it best not to see me before leaving Kansas
City, since nothing good could come from such a
friendship; but he had not been able to forget me
and would see me when he returned in the spring.

This letter came a few days before Christmas,
and as I was still at the age when a month seems
longer than a year, I felt the most sensible thing
to do was to forget all about him.

Besides, I thought that Winnipeg was up somewhere in the vicinity of the North Pole, and it was
not likely that he would ever return.

On Christmas morning I rose at ten o'clock with
the intention of leaving the house for the day. I
had promised my loved ones to spend Christmas at
home with them, and I had perjured my soul in
accounting for my failure to do so. I could not

breathe in the house, yet I was undecided where to go to escape from it. The day was not cold, but clear and bright, and I walked about for a long time. I wanted to go to church, but several reasons prevented me. I did not know where there was a church; then there was an unwritten law among the girls that religion was taboo. Most of them considered it bad luck to mix religion in any way with their profession.

No such superstition hindered me from going to church. I had been taught that Christ came to save sinners, not saints, but since I could not leave my profession, I looked upon it as being in questionable taste to go to church.

I took a Westport car and went out as far as Union Cemetery. I left the car and, wandering about among the graves for a while, I tried to picture myself as lying under the snow, but I did not like the picture.

In the distance I saw a gravestone so much taller than any other that I was moved by curiosity to go and read the inscription.

After the lapse of many years I have forgotten the full verse, but I recall the ending of it:

> LEAVE HOPE AND FAITH ALIKE ADIEU—
> WOULD I COULD ADD REMEMBRANCE, TOO.

Underneath was a notice, reading, "The above inscription was placed here by special request of deceased."

I stood there speculating about the inscription,

and the monument, and the man underneath the stone, until I was nearly frozen. Why should a dead man be bidding adieu to Faith, and Hope, and Remembrance? What had the dead to do with these graces of the living? As I walked back to the car I turned this over in my mind. I did not like him, this man who had bidden adieu to Faith and Hope. But he had reached out of the grave to befriend me; he had raised such a revolt in my soul by his pessimism that I vowed I should never bid adieu to either of these graces.

And deep down in my heart on that Christmas Day, in Union Cemetery, there was born something which can only die when I have ceased to be numbered among the living.

On Main Street I left the car, intending to go into one of the many restaurants which lined that thoroughfare. When I saw two half-frozen newsboys standing on the corner I thought of the little ones at home. I wondered if they were cold; I wondered if they had a turkey for dinner. I could not buy a dinner for them, but I could buy one for these newsboys.

They responded with alacrity to my invitation, and volunteered the information that they knew two more kids on Main Street who had no Christmas dinner. We found the other two, and, accompanied by my four newly found friends, I went into Staley & Dunlop's and asked for a private table.

The head waiter said no doubt they were working me, but I did not care. I was perfectly willing to be worked.   I was used to little boys, and I enjoyed the society of these dirty-faced urchins as much as they enjoyed the dinner which they consumed. Fortunately for me and thanks to the generosity of the man in Winnipeg, I was able to pay the check without going broke.

Christmas Day had not been so dreary as I supposed it would be.

CHAPTER VI

A FEW days after Christmas an unexpected bit of good fortune befell me through a cattleman from Texas who had taken a fancy to me. As a result of his liberality I had ample funds to carry me through my coming ordeal and pay my board until that time should come. I would not be obliged to use the fifty dollars I had hidden in my coat.

Now that I need not worry about money for some time to come, I gave up all attempts to make more. I came down-stairs in the early part of the night, but I did not go into the parlors when men were present. I had grown very nervous and irritable, and cried almost constantly for my mother. I was sure that I would not live through the coming ordeal, and all attempts to induce me to make the usual preparations failed.

The girls vied with one another in preparing for the coming stranger, but I was not interested. They bought many little garments ready-made and they made many others. Bessie, who could do all kinds of beautiful needlework, was busily engaged in embroidering and stitching every spare minute on the little garments that I did not even care to look at.

I was ill and I wanted my mother. I wanted my little brothers and sisters, to whom I had been passionately attached. I wanted to see the children of the neighborhood at home, for I had loved them and they had returned my love; but I did not want this child that the girls talked about.

Yet these women who were not mothers and who would never be mothers, these women who had known me but a few short weeks, were as interested in the coming event as the most normal feminine household would have been. When Mamie, who was the exception, suggested the impossibility of my keeping the child after it came they fell upon her as though she had suggested its murder.

Mamie stood by her guns and declared that I would never be able to take care of it. In her opinion I did not have sense enough to take care of myself, and she would like to ask what I would do with a child? She was sure that the greatest charity both to me and to the child would be to find it a home in some good family.

I wished they would be quiet. I wished they would leave me alone. I did not want a baby. . . . I wanted my mother.

If I lived there would be a chance for me to dis-entangle the web of my life, for I knew that my nature contained more of the elements of decency than of vice. My family loved me and my death would be an irreparable blow to them. I simply had to live—there was no way in which I could depart with good grace.

Miss Laura sent the examining physician to see me, but I did not like him and would not talk to him. His hands made me shudder, for I had grown very sensitive in the matter of hands. Whenever I had been forced to submit myself to customers I looked at the hands that were to touch my bare flesh before I looked at the face of the man who was buying the right to handle me at will.

There was one pair of hands that were firm and kind, beautiful in shape and texture of skin, whose touch had been like a benediction instead of a pollution. These hands had fascinated me by the many things they had expressed, things which the plain, impassive face of their possessor had concealed like a mask.

If I would not have the regular physician of the house, another must be provided, and after a prolonged discussion with the housekeeper Miss Laura sent for an old friend of hers, a famous physician who had retired from active practice, and begged him to take my case. When she brought him up to me and he had taken my hand in his friendly clasp my mind was at rest. I was ready to act upon any suggestion that he might make.

The confidence was a mutual one and he at once consented to take the case if I would go out to the private home of a nurse he knew. We had just settled the matter when Mamie burst unceremoniously into the room with the intention of helping the good work along. "I'll tell you what's the matter with her, Doc," she said, bluntly. "It's not because she's in a family way that she's down in the dumps. It's the result of the 'dose' she had."

The doctor looked grave. "Tell me all about it," he said, and Mamie explained in detail about our meeting in the hospital.

He turned to me. "Why didn't you tell me about this?" he demanded.

"I did not know that it had anything to do with my present illness," I answered. "The other doctor said that I was cured."

"It has a great deal to do with it," he said, slowly. "But you must not be discouraged. We are going to bring you around all right."

After all, the event came much sooner than we had expected—an illness so fraught with suffering and danger that for several days my life was despaired of.

Instinctively I turned to the teachings of my early childhood, and I prayed, not that my life should be spared, nor that the chalice of suffering should be taken from me, but that I should have the courage to bear it.

With every conscious breath I said through my set teeth: "I *will* live! I *will* live!" When my senses were slipping away and a semi-delirium set in I screamed for my mother.

Through a black cloud upon which I floated, and another which surrounded me, I reached forth my hand to grasp a tangibility which was not there. At length a voice from far away penetrated my consciousness. "She cannot last much longer," it said.

I fought with failing breath to speak the words which were struggling for utterance; and finally I achieved my desire. "Don't you believe it," I said, gasping at every word. "I have no intention of dying."

When all danger was over and I was on the highway to recovery the nurse told me of the baby girl whom a merciful Providence had taken to Himself.

During my prolonged convalescence the doctor and I became warm friends. We always had some harmless joke between us, usually founded on the doctor's habit of misquotation. He was an omnivorous reader of poetry, which he quoted in season and out, with little regard for accuracy. If by chance he was correct in his quotation he was sure to attribute it to the wrong author, and I could not refrain from setting him aright.

He was always ready to laugh at his own blunders, and was much impressed by my habit of accuracy, which he always took pains to verify. He could not quite understand how I, an ignorant little girl from Fourth Street, came to know the things which he could never keep straight in his memory.

When I told him of my childhood, and the things of the intellect which had been as daily bread in our home, in those not far remote days, he became greatly interested and wanted to hear more about it. But I could not discuss the events which came later because that might appear to involve a criticism of my father. The struggle of later days and the black, bitter poverty which had darkened my girl-hood were matters that must remain hidden in my own breast.

Besides the reserve which was mine by inheritance and training, there was the tendency to bear the responsibility for my own sins. Knowing the difference between good and evil, I had deliberately chosen evil. The fault was entirely my own. This was the verdict which I had passed upon myself and I did not ask for a more charitable one from others.

It is true that I had not chosen the later steps. They had been thrust upon me, or rather they had followed as a logical result of the first evil-doing.

It is certain that I rebelled against the extor-tionate price I was paying for the curiosity of adolescence, but I did not look outside myself for the reason. I had been a horrible example of total depravity, but I need not remain one. I was young and I had not lost the right to redeem myself.

Something of all this I said to the doctor during the days of my convalescence. He agreed with me and proffered me his assistance. He believed that I had marked artistic talent and that I should not be forced to waste it in uncongenial work. He decided to pay for my education and to help me in the upward struggle. He was a widower without children, and he saw no reason why he should not educate me and give me a chance to develop the talents which he believed that I possessed.

It seemed that I could not do better than to accept the friendship of this great heart, and I had resolved to be guided entirely by his judgment, consequently, when he suggested a visit to my own family as the first requisite step in my rehabilitation I did not demur, although I dreaded the meeting as much as I longed for it.

The doctor's experience with the world had been a wide one, and he declared that he never quite lost hope for the person who had retained that which he termed the "spirit of the clan." He thought when there was a breaking away from all family ties a spirit of bitterness and hardness crept in which made the work of regeneration more difficult.

Miss Laura and the girls had been most devoted during my illness, and the doctor made no attempt to check the intimacy during my convalescence. He realized that social isolation was not good for me at that time, and he had a profound respect for Miss Laura.

When the girls learned that I was going home as soon as I had entirely recovered they were delighted. They were sincerely glad that one of their number was no longer to walk the pathway of shame, even though there was no turning back for them.

They showered me with advice as to my future conduct, and overhauled my clothes to see that no incriminating garment found its way into that which Bessie called my "expurgated" wardrobe. Even Mamie the incorrigible one rejoiced that I had not painted my face, nor smoked cigarettes, nor learned to swear, nor become addicted to drink.

The doctor had written to Mrs. James to tell her of the plans for me and to ask for her co-operation. He would accompany me to St. Louis, and after the arrangements were perfected I would take the train for home, spending a month with my family before returning to St. Louis to begin my studies.

I had remained with the nurse until the last evening, when I went down to Miss Laura's for dinner, intending to take my departure from there.

After dinner Miss Laura called me into her room for a last word of advice. When I tried to express my gratitude for all the kindness that she and the girls had shown me she cut short my thanks by taking me over to the mirror and asking me to take a long look at my own face.

After looking closely at myself for five minutes I turned to ask her what she meant, and she answered me by saying: "You look five years younger than you did before your illness, and sin has left no mark on your face. Neither do you bear the traces in your speech nor manner. You have keen intelligence and the advantage of a good upbringing. Therefore you have no excuse for a return to this kind of a life. While you were still a child in years you made a misstep for which you have paid the price, but you need not let it ruin your life."

"Do you truly think a girl can forget a thing like this?" I asked.

"No, dear. You cannot forget it entirely, but the memory will grow dimmer as the years pass, until you will be able to look back upon it as upon the memory of a bad dream. When I was a girl I was made to believe that the wages of a woman's sin were condemnation in this world and in the world to come, and by the time I had learned different I was too old to change my mode of life. It is a diabolical doctrine this which denies a woman the right of regeneration, which says that a woman who sins must continue to sin and in the end must perish, while it holds forth the hand of fellowship to the partner of her guilt. God never intended that one should perish and one go free."

"But even if a woman redeems herself," I asked, "ought she to marry?"

"There can be no hard and fast rule for those problems. It is a question that each woman must answer for herself."

"One thing is certain," I said. "Whenever I hear any one denounce the women who lead this life I shall think of the kindliness I have received from those I have met in it, and I shall defend them."

"No, no," she said, hastily, "you must do nothing of the kind. The more one knows of our life the more one must denounce it, lest it be suspected that one has a personal motive in defending it. When other women speak of us you must assume an attitude of scorn, not only to protect yourself from suspicion, but that you may also feel it for yourself and have no temptation to return. When you think of us do not remember any small kindness that we may have shown you or that we show to one another. Remember only the things that have shocked you and outraged your traditions and your sense of decency. Remember your sufferings at the hands of beasts who are miscalled men. If you keep these things in view you will never again fall into temptation."

"Miss Laura, there is something else I want to ask you, and I shall do just as you think best about it." I hesitated a moment, then, taking courage from her smile, I proceeded, "You remember the man I met here in your room; the one who came to see me so often and then suddenly ceased to come?"

"Yes, Madeleine. I have known him for a long time. What about him?"

"He is up in Canada, in Winnipeg, and he writes me very often. I think he is fond of me, and I like him very much. Ought I to write him after I go home?"

Miss Laura hesitated a moment. "Madeleine," she answered, "if you can catch that man for a husband you will be a mighty lucky girl. Since he knows of your life here, you would never have to lie to him. Many men marry girls from these houses, and the marriages are often very happy ones. You remember we often speak of Florence who became the wife of a prominent man in St. Paul?"

"Yes," I answered. "And I met her husband when I first came here."

"He always comes to see us when he is in Kansas

City," she said, "because he met his wife in this house. He is madly in love with her, and her life is a very happy one. She does not like to have him come here, but for old time's sake he calls whenever he is in the city."

"Then you think it is all right for me to keep up a correspondence with the man who is in Canada?"

"By all means. He is just the sort of man to be faithful to one woman."

The girls came in after this conversation, and the brief farewells were said. Every one wished me good luck, but no one asked me to write. It was not considered best that I should hold any communication with them.

Mrs. James met us at the station in St. Louis, and her welcome was as cordial as my heart could wish for. She examined the doctor sharply to learn if his designs were honorable, and she frankly told him that she was much given to questioning the motives of fatherly old men.

He laughed at her frankness, but I was embarrassed by it and asked her what she thought he could gain by pretending to help reform me.

She had to admit that the case was different from one which involved an innocent young girl.

It was decided that I should enter a private school in St. Louis, if my mother would consent to it. Mrs. James would tell mother her opinion of the doctor, and leave it to me to invent the necessary lies about my meeting with him.

This was the fly in the ointment, but, having begun

the lies to mother, I could see no end to the deception I must practise. I dreaded my home-going almost as much as I longed for it, and we had come to no definite conclusion about what I should tell mother when I left St. Louis the following day.

I had written to say that I would soon be home, but I had not named the date of my coming and was not met at the train by any member of my family. I looked around the station and was rather surprised to find the same old buildings and the same old loafers who were there when I left.

Every one was unfeignedly glad to see me, and I was as delighted to see them. Wherever mother went about the house or yard there was a small procession, for I followed mother and the children followed me. Already the suffering of the past ten months was fading from my memory.

By all the statutes made and provided by society I should have felt old and sin-battered, but as a matter of fact I felt nothing of the sort. I was a little girl again, tagging after my mother's skirts. My little brothers and sisters were with me, and I entered into their play with the zest of a child.

The black shadow of poverty still hung over our home, and mother's heart was heavy at the sight of her children growing up in ignorance. But even this shadow could not wholly darken the joy we felt at being reunited.

Father had written to mother about three months before from some place in eastern Illinois. Since then she had not heard from him. My brother had had an offer from the firm for which he had worked for several years to go West at an increase of salary, and he was to leave in June.

He did not want to leave mother and the children but mother knew there was no chance for him to better himself where he was, and she urged him to go.

They all looked forward with dread to my return to St. Louis, for with two of the children leaving the home nest, poor though it was, there seemed little chance that we would ever become reunited.

Mrs. James had written about the doctor and his plans for me, but mother did not like the idea. She did not understand how he came to make the offer. I told her what I considered a plausible story, but she was so perturbed that I declared I would not return to St. Louis at all. I would go to Chicago and find work.

Since I had to earn my living away from home, there was no good reason why I should not go to Chicago, and, as I did not know any one there, I would feel safer from discovery than in St. Louis.

At length I won my mother's reluctant consent, and I wrote the doctor and Mrs. James about my change of plan.

One of the first things I did after reaching home was to write to the man in Winnipeg that I had given up the evil life. At the earliest possible moment I received his answer, telling me of his joy at the change and promising to come to see me wherever I should be.

This time when I left home I did not set a date for

my return, because I had failed to keep my former promise to come at Christmas. My greatest grief was at parting from my brother, for I knew it might be years before I should see him again.

The thought of mother alone with the little ones filled me with hot, angry resentment against the bitterness of her lot. So far as I could see, virtue was no better rewarded than vice. My beautiful mother was growing old in a losing fight with poverty. What had she ever done to deserve such a fate? I asked of the Powers that be.

CHAPTER VII

WHEN I arrived in Chicago I was as completely lost as if I had never been away from my home town. I had thought that my experiences in St. Louis and Kansas City had given me quite a metropolitan viewpoint, but in reality I knew very little about St. Louis, and Kansas City was not the largest city on earth, although it had seemed so boundless to me.

I had just passed my eighteenth birthday and was still painfully young and verdant, for all of my experiences. But as I was not now afraid of a policeman, I asked for directions of one whenever I lost my way, which was often enough, goodness knows.

After I had settled myself in a South Side boarding-house, which an acquaintance at home had recommended to me, I went out to look for work. I had decided that I would try for a position in a department store.

During my apprenticeship at Miss Laura's I had been taught the value of a smile, even if I had not learned to exploit it commercially. Nature had not given me great beauty, but she had bestowed upon me a good-looking mouth, my best feature, with an elusive dimple in each corner, and firm white teeth. The girls in Kansas City had tried to impress upon me that this feature was a great asset if I would only learn to use it.

Miss Laura had thought I would be irresistible to men if I would only learn to smile; she cited the instances of the man who had gone to Winnipeg and the cattleman from Texas; in a few days these two men had given me as much money as the girls usually earned in a month, and merely because I had treated them to my rarely given smiles.

Now I was resolved to try the effect of my best feature in my search for work, and I succeeded in getting a position in one of the largest department stores in Chicago. Because I had good manners and spoke good English, I was given a place in the French underwear department, which was patronized by the most exclusive customers.

In the beginning I was asked only to fetch and carry, but gradually I was intrusted to make sales, in which employment I succeeded beyond my greatest hopes. I loved to show the dainty garments, and there was no attraction to divert my attention from my work.

I had quickness of perception and much patience with customers, among whom I made several friends; afterward these women always asked to have me wait on them. At the end of two months I had received an increase of salary and I was as proud of my ability to earn it as I was pleased to receive the additional money. Contrary to the story-books, the floor-walker did not try to make love to me and the head saleswoman of the department did not abuse me.

My two greatest pleasures were my letters from the doctor and my letters from the man in whom I was so deeply interested, and who had now returned to Kansas City.

The doctor sent me a box of books which he felt would be of great value to me, and advised me to spend my spare time in studying them. Occasionally he inclosed a small sum of money in his letters, which he asked me to spend for any girlish frippery I might want.

Instead of using it to procure the little things I so much longed for, I lied to mother about the amount of my salary and sent her two dollars a week out of the money the doctor gave me.

This man's friendship for me was one of those *rarely* pure, disinterested friendships which elderly men *sometimes* have for young girls. I felt no compunction about accepting the money from him, but my mother's code was an inflexible one and she would not have understood; and ninety-nine times out of a hundred her viewpoint would have been the correct one.

There was not much time for study because keeping my clothes in a presentable condition took up most of my leisure moments, but the little spare time I had left was devoted to my books. Education meant more to me than amusement or recreation. No person bearing my family name had been an ignoramus, and I did not choose to be the first to bear the label.

Thanks to the excellent training of my early childhood, I not only had the ideals, but I had the foundation on which to build an education.

My father had held that if a man were to study languages he should begin with his mother-tongue. If he were to study history, he should first know the history of his own country. With these truths firmly held in my mind, I began the study of English literature and the study of American history. Every spare moment was devoted to this object. I had no teacher nor any one with whom I could discuss my plans and efforts. It was uphill work, but I was not to be deterred by obstacles.

I took especial pains with my letter-writing, and when the doctor told me that I possessed the rare art of writing an interesting letter I trod on air for several days.

If it had not been for the sorrows at home I should have been very happy, but I could not forget that patient, calm-faced gentlewoman on whom a cruel fate had laid such heavy burdens. Since the birth of my youngest brother she had been in ill health, but she realized that her failure to keep going meant the breaking up of the family.

One evening when I returned from work I found a letter at my boarding-house which at first glance rather puzzled me. It bore the postmark of my home town, but the writing was unfamiliar. I tore it open and glanced at the signature. Surely I must be mistaken. It looked like "Mother," but this incoherent scrawl could not be from my mother, who had a beautiful chirography and expressed herself in perfect English. I tore up to my room to read it.

Many years have elapsed since I received that letter, but the white-hot indignation which stirred my soul on that long-ago day burns in my veins now as I write.

The substance of the letter was that my father, in a drunken row, had gotten into some kind of trouble. After being in jail for two months without revealing his identity, he had written to a lawyer at home who, in happier days, had been his friend, begging him to come to his aid.

The response of this old-time friend had been unhesitating, for my father was a man of such rare charm of manner that those who had once loved him continued to love him regardless of his derelictions. The lawyer had gone at once to the distant city in which the trouble had occurred; but the letter to him, which had passed through the sheriff's hands and revealed my father's identity, had been published broadcast.

On top of this blow there came another one. A short time after reaching the Western state in which my brother had taken up his new duties he had become ill and for weeks hovered between life and death. He had not been able to send money to my mother, and the family had been on the verge of starvation, having been two days without food

98

when the published story of my father's arrest had caused the town authorities to investigate their condition.

This double catastrophe had prostrated my mother, who was already ill; and at once these cold-hearted philanthropists had settled the matter to their entire satisfaction and after the manner of philanthropists who usually see no farther than their circumscribed viewpoints.

My God! it could not be true! My mother, my beautiful, high-bred mother, who by birth, breeding, instinct, and education was the superior of any woman in our town, was to be sent to the county poorhouse, and my brothers and sisters were to be given out in bondage to whomsoever would take them in!

A blood-red mist swam before my eyes. I wanted to rend and destroy; and to this day when I see "kindly" philanthropists disposing of the bodies and souls of those whom poverty has delivered into their clutches, whenever I hear them suggesting the separation of children from a good mother, I feel the brand of a potential Cain upon my brow, for I must exert all the self-restraint of a lifetime of training if I would withhold my hand.

Until morning I paced the floor of my room. I went down into the depths with my mother; but I suffered no less with that proud man, my father, lying in a prison cell. For I was heart of his heart and bone of his bone. My face, in a much lesser degree of comeliness, was the face of my mother,

but my mind and disposition were those of my
father. I lacked his charm of manner and his
scintillating wit; but I was his; nothing could dis-
sever me from him. My very carriage, my intona-
tion of speech, my weakness and my strength, the
idealism of my nature—they were all his, and I
could not find it in my heart to hate him. I could
only suffer with him.

By morning I had made my decision and was
perfectly calm. During the night I had packed my
trunk and in the morning I went to the mistress
of the boarding-house and told her that I was
leaving, that I would send for my trunk later in
the day.

At the store when I told them I was going away
there was genuine regret in my department. I went
to the office for my pay-envelop, and afterward in
the rest-room I wrote a letter to my mother. I had
previously sent her a telegram telling her to take no
step until she heard from me.

In my letter I inclosed a money-order for ten
dollars, which was all of my pay plus some money
I had received from the doctor. I wrote very
calmly, telling her I had had a raise of salary and
would be able to give her material aid in the future.

I wrote to an old acquaintance at home asking
her to delay the proceedings which were to dispose
of my mother and the children summarily; and then
I sat down and waited for twelve o'clock, when I
went to lunch.

Among my customers had been a woman who lived

in Custom House Place, and at twelve-thirty I rang her door-bell.

In the darkened parlor where I waited, while the maid announced me, I felt a qualm of soul-sick terror, but I girded myself for the interview; and when the maid returned to say that Madame was not up yet, but that she would receive me in her room, I followed her there without a tremor.

The interview was brief and to the point. I was no frightened girl seeking refuge from the terrors of the streets. I was a woman driving the best possible bargain for the sale of my body and my soul.

In reply to the questionings of Madame I said that I had been in a house before, and spoke as if my experiences were much greater than the facts really warranted. I brought my dimples and my beautiful teeth into play, and Madame closed the bargain with me on my terms, which were not onerous. I knew the state of the market too well to make too many conditions.

She was to give me credit up to seventy-five dollars at one of the department stores where she had an account, permitting me to go alone and do my own shopping; and once a week she was to advance me a ten-dollar note, regardless of my other indebtedness to her.

When the interview was over she rang for the maid to show me to my room; after looking around for a moment, I declined the invitation to breakfast and went over to State Street to do my shopping.

Since I was not known in the store to which I went

and had an air of respectability, the prices of goods were not advanced for me. I waited until I was through shopping before saying that the things were to be charged to Madame C—— and sent to Custom House Place, subject to her approval.

Instinctively I had a mind for values, and I did not waste a penny of the allotted sum. I bought toilet articles, towels, underwear, an evening gown, a bathrobe, and a loose gown to wear late at night when custom permitted the removal of the tight-fitting "parlor gown."

When the articles came over to the house and Madame had inspected them she was impressed with my business ability in getting so much for the allotted sum.

In like manner I again became one of the unfortunate sisterhood who "float on man's uncertain tenderness."

A wave tossed up on the shore of his desire
To ebb and flow whene'er it pleaseth him;
Remembered at his leisure, and forgot,
Worshiped and worried, clasped and dropped at mood,
Or soothed or gashed at mercy of his will—
Now Paradise my portion, and now Hell—
And every single, vibrant nerve that beats
In soul or body, like some rare vase, thrust
In fire at first, and then in frost, until
The fine protesting fiber snaps.

CHAPTER VIII

THE life at Miss Laura's was like a Sunday-school convention by contrast with the life at Madame C——'s. I had fully realized my own verdancy before I was twenty-four hours in the house, and in the same length of time I had made myself an object of active dislike to nearly every girl therein.

When I came down-stairs on the first night I was sent into the parlor to help entertain a party of men who had just come in. As they seemed to be well known to several of the girls who claimed them as "friends," I made no attempt to talk with them, but I had been sent into the parlor and, knowing that I was expected to remain, I sat down and tried to look as if I were not wishing myself elsewhere.

A rather good-looking man, who sat across the room from me, with one of the girls perched on the arm of his chair, looked somewhat bored, almost as if he were trying to escape from her. He glanced over at me, and I smiled in sympathy. Instantly he turned to the girl beside him and said: "Pardon me, but I think I know that girl in the pink dress. I am going over to talk with her."

He shook hands as if I were an old friend, but the other girl was not deceived. He had been a cus-

MADELEINE

tomer of hers, and I would surely be made to suffer for his inconstancy. She gave me a malevolent look, and I knew that I had made an enemy.

The others were planning for a bacchanalian dance to take place in the basement parlor, which was reserved for such revels. The girls were delighted because it meant big money, and Madame, who had been called in, was beaming at the prospect of selling much champagne.

The man beside me looked disgustedly at his friends who were urging him to join in the festivity; turning to me, he asked, "Have you ever taken part in one of these exhibitions?"

"No," I answered; "I do not even know what they are."

"I thought not," he said, grimly. "And you're not going to take part in this one unless you want to." Whereupon he explained briefly what would take place.

His explanation made me sick with loathing for the orgy and all who were to be participants in it. At Miss Laura's I had heard such things spoken of as one speaks of some moral leprosy of which one hardly dares to think. I had never dreamed of coming into direct contact with such perversions.

The others surrounded us, coaxing the man to come, for my acquiescence was taken as a matter of course. He wanted to shield me, but he blundered in his well-meant efforts, and finally he brought down upon my head the wrath of the other girls by declaring that the thought of the unspeakable revel had made me sick and that he was going to take me up to my room.

Angry protests at once arose from all the girls, but the one from whom he had transferred his attentions was especially venomous in her objection to his going with me. She goaded me too far, and I stated in plain English what I thought about the matter. I thought she was going to strike me, but Madame hastened to pour oil on the troubled waters by commanding me to go with the man to my room.

He ordered a bottle of wine brought up, and Madame herself served it. She was affability itself, and said in her broken English that she did not require the girls to do these unspeakable things if they did not want to, but she reproved me gently for the manner of my refusal, which made it seem that I felt myself better than the other girls.

That is exactly what I had felt, and I had taken no pains to conceal it. I bluntly repeated my opinion to Madame, but she was all for peace. It was bad business, this airing of household linen in the presence of customers, and Madame intimated that the girls would make life miserable for me if I "got ze beeg head wiz zem."

She went out, bidding me good night as affably as if nothing unpleasant had been said, and I turned my attention to the man who was with me. I was so grateful for his having taken me out of the parlor that I exerted myself to be agreeable to him, and I succeeded so well that he became deeply interested in me.

He asked how I had chanced to come into that "notorious joint," and I explained that when circumstances made it imperative for me to make money I had come to Madame because I had known her as a customer of the store where I had worked; had obtained her address through my sales to her. Every clerk in the store had known the nature of the industry in Custom House Place.

"I inferred from your appearance that you did not know much about this game," he declared. "This house is one of the most notorious joints in the United States. I am not a rescue-worker, but, by Jove! it makes me hot under the collar every time I see a nice girl come into this place, although I am one of the regular customers. If you will take my advice, you will get out of here at once."

"I cannot leave now," I said, "because I owe a bill to Madame, and I must have some money every week for a certain purpose; but if you will tell me about a better place I will move as soon as I am out of debt."

He thought for a minute, and then said: "I'll tell you where there's a good place if you feel that you must remain in this business. I know a woman who keeps a swell house out on Dearborn Street. She is as cold as an icicle, but I think she is fair with the girls. She has the most exclusive trade in Chicago, and her house is so beautiful that the girls must derive great pleasure from living in it."

"Perhaps she would not take me," I replied.

"Don't you worry about that." He looked at me

appraisingly. "Any of them will take you. Besides, if you get out of here very soon she will not know anything about your having been here. I will be down again in a few nights and you can let me know what your plans are. You may count on me as willing to help you."

In the morning I went out before breakfast and, after a hasty meal in a restaurant, I went over to Mandel's and wrote four letters—one to my mother, one to a relative in the East whom I had never seen, one to the doctor in Kansas City, and one to the man who occupied a large share of my thoughts. To mother I said whatever I thought would comfort her. To the relative I had never seen I gave an exact statement of my father's dereliction and the threatened dismemberment of our family, ending with a plea that he should help my mother.

My letter to the doctor was brief. I simply stated that I had betrayed his trust and was again an inmate of a house of ill fame. I made no attempt to justify the step I had taken, leaving him to draw his own conclusion.

When I had achieved the salutation in my letter to the man who loomed so large in my dreams I hesitated. He had been so pleased when I had written him that I had changed my mode of life that I had been hoping for definite results from his contemplated visit to me. It was very hard to accuse myself of the lack of moral stamina which my second transgression would seem to imply. Perhaps it were better not to write at all; but, after all, I thought, defiantly, that was the sort of place in which he had found me.

My letter was a cold statement to the effect that I had found myself unfitted for a life of toil and had returned to the primrose way. I was at Madame C——'s, No. —— Custom House Place, and would be glad to have him call whenever he came to Chicago.

As I did not care to face that hostile crew at the house, I did not return until time to dress for the parlor.

When the maid opened the door she said that Madame had asked to see me as soon as I came in. I went up to her room with a foreboding of evil in my heart; but she was very gracious, and told me that she had made an engagement for me for the night and that I need not dress for the parlor.

Instead, I should go up-stairs and have my bath, dress my hair in a braid down my back, and put on my street clothes. She would send for me when she was ready.

I soon learned that all was grist that came into Madame's mill. If the girls were incapable of making money in one way, she devised another.

Among Madame's patrons was an elderly millionaire who had a penchant for innocent young girls and was willing to pay her a large fee for procuring them. After he had accomplished the ruin of the girl he would compensate her with a sum of money, which sum depended upon her refinement, her education, her good looks, and whatever he estimated her loss to be; his price for a high-school girl was naturally greater than his price for a servant-girl.

Madame, hard and calculating though she was, had no thought of luring innocent young girls into her house, but she had no scruples and found no difficulty in selling him a spurious article, and she thoroughly enjoyed the trickery involved in the transaction. From having spent the greater part of her lifetime in extracting money from men without losing their patronage, she had become so expert that men not only "stood for it," but they appeared to like it, since she again and again worked the same scheme on the same man.

In the case of this old *roué* whom I was to meet Madame had been for years selling him girls who were not virtuous; but he seldom discovered the difference. In a few cases where the girl had not played her part well he had complained to Madame that she had been tricked by the girl, but it never occurred to the creature that she herself would trick him.

When Madame sent for me to come down-stairs she had taken great pains to drill me in my part. I was to say that I lived at home with my parents and was attending school, that on that afternoon I had been sitting in Lincoln Park on my way home, and that Madame, who was driving by, had stopped to talk with me and had invited me to drive with her.

I had thought it very kind of her and had accepted the invitation, although I knew I should be scolded

MADELEINE

for not coming straight home from school. Madame had brought me to her house, and it was now so late that I was afraid to go home.

He would then order champagne, and Madame, after a little byplay, would have herself called out of the room; when he would begin making advances to me. I must repulse him, and he would endeavor to overcome my scruples. The greater his difficulty in overcoming them, and the more modest and refined I appeared to be, the greater his relish for the debauchery; and he would give just that much more money for the supposed injury done me.

If he fancied me he would come to see me several times until he thought the bloom had worn off, then he would drop me without warning. This was the outline of the farce I was to play, and a few minutes later the man himself appeared.

He was such a repulsive old beast that there was no difficulty in playing the part; and, because I looked very innocent and spoke in the manner of a well-educated girl, he was delighted with me.

He presented me with a large sum of money, of which I had to give Madame half. He also gave Madame a big fee for procuring me. Of course I had no share in this.

When I came down to breakfast the following morning I found that the wrath against me had been nursed during my absence and was still warmly alive. I was greeted by sarcastic remarks on every hand.

"What do you think of this one, girls? She don't know she's a whore. She thinks she's a lady!"

"Sure she does. The poor fool don't know that men come here because they've got ladies at home and they like the change."

"She's swallowed the dictionary, girls. She ought to get a job teaching school."

"No, she 'ain't. I was in her room when the maid was cleaning it, and whatcha know? She's got it on her table, and Shakespeare, too, if you please."

"Well, if she thinks she can make more money off Webster and Shakespeare than off that bunch she called down the other night, let her go to it!"

"Oh, Madame has got her playing injured innocence now for old W——. That suits her fine."

These remarks, accompanied by oaths and obscenities, were hurled at me all through breakfast-time; but I held my tongue, although I was so angry that the food choked me.

The rivalry and competition among the girls in this house was keen, bitter, and unscrupulous; but for the moment they were united in their hatred for the girl who not only "possessed the deplorable moral quality of being a stranger," but who had dared to show that she scorned to descend to their level.

I was as completely cut off from social intercourse with them as if they had been early Puritans and I a moral leper. I could not answer them in their own language, and they did not understand mine.

I learned from the servants that all new girls in this house were treated with cold intolerance by the others, but in my case the hostility was an active one. When the man who had declared himself my friend called a few nights later one of the girls who came into the parlor while he waited for me told him that I had left the house, and no one knew where I had gone. She was not at all abashed when I walked into the room.

The parlor rules in this house were the same as in most houses. If a man came in alone all of the girls who were not otherwise engaged were sent into the parlor; and, after urging the man to buy drinks, he was invited to make his choice between the girls and go up-stairs. But, as is often the case with poor, defenseless man, the choice was not always his own.

The ability of a girl to make money does not depend upon beauty, although that may be made an asset. It depends entirely upon her ability to flatter and please men, to be "all things to all men." Many *beautiful* women prefer to please themselves. The result is that in the same house there will often be a beautiful woman who does not make her expenses and a remarkably plain one who is "coining money."

Madame charged the girls fifteen dollars a week and half they made, but despite the heavy percentage many of them had comfortable bank-accounts, together with elaborate wardrobes and costly jewels. On the other hand, there were girls who made very little money, but, since all girls do not have the same commercial value, these others must be kept to fill in.

The contrast between this household and the one I had known in Kansas City was no greater than the dissimilarity between the women who presided over them.

Madame C—— was a French-Canadian who might have been foreordained for the rôle she played, so admirably was she fitted to the part.

One could imagine her as having always been there in her handsome parlor, gorgeous in heavy brocade or velvet, with jewels flashing from her hands and her ears, her throat and her breast, and a benignant smile wreathing her face; and one could easily imagine her as having stood there as the embodiment of the most ancient profession, with one hand outstretched to give a friendly pat alike to the girls and to the customers, while the other itching palm reached eagerly forth to clutch their money and hold it in a grasp of steel.

She could not read or write either the French of her native province or the English of her adopted country. When I expressed surprise that any one should be content to remain illiterate she laughed good-naturedly and told me that she could make the money to pay her many employees who looked after her business affairs. Why should she trouble herself to read or write?

She never lost her affability, but it was purely a business pose. Underneath she was hard and cold, and exacted her pound of flesh from every girl in the house. She well knew how much money her regular customers gave the girls; and when a stranger came in she made it her business to invite him into the parlor as he was leaving the house, and generally she would inveigle him into telling her how much he had given the girl. If Madame discovered one of the girls "holding out" she not only compelled her to give up the money she had endeavored to withhold, but disciplined her by sending her into the parlors to entertain "dead ones" and kept her from seeing good spenders.

Madame was reported to be very rich; but even if this report of her wealth were true, her greed for money was not satiated and she showed no disposition to retire from business for the purpose of enjoying her wealth. It is to be doubted, indeed, if her money could have procured for her one-half the pleasure she derived from her methods of obtaining it. After she had tricked some man out of a sum of money, and he had left the house with every expression of good-will, Madame was in her element. She expanded and glowed with enthusiasm about her victim whom she considered a "good sport" in submitting, with such good grace, to being duped.

She sought constantly to impress her methods upon the girls in the house, but it was difficult to find other women who combined her suavity of manner with her business acumen

In this house most of my waking hours were hours of torture, for I spent most of them in inward combat and protest against the poisonous atmosphere. At Miss Laura's my chief aversion had been the physical contact with men. In this place it was the contact with the women of the house that I loathed.

In Kansas City the inmates were the average American girls from the average American homes, and, barring their occupation, they were no different from other women of the same station in which they were born. But the girls at Madame C——'s were the American-born children of the most ignorant and degraded of foreigners, brought up in the slums of great cities, with nothing wholesome in their natures to neutralize the poison of their environment.

In becoming the inmate of a luxuriously appointed, high-priced house of ill fame they had been promoted in the social scale. They had always known vice, but they had not always known luxury, and they assumed the garb and the air of *grandes dames* without making the least effort to fit themselves for the rôle they played. I do not recall having ever seen a book or magazine in the hands of one of these women. They read the daily papers, or at least such parts of the papers as appealed to them, and they attended the theaters, garbed in costly garments and painted up like circus-riders. Their interest, however, was not in the play, but in the clothes of the women players and in the personality of the men of the stage. The discussions which followed their visits to the theater were always upon these topics; or they would talk of their men acquaintances whom they had seen escorting other women; they might offer a shrewd guess that the men would be down to the house later in the night.

At breakfast the discussion was always about their bedfellows of the night before, given with the most minute detail, particularly of abhorrent perversions, and comparisons of the bed manners of men who had at different times been with the different girls.

These discussions were conducive of much quarreling, especially when a man had been more liberal with one girl than with another. Vile epithets were exchanged, which, in addition to the vile details under discussion, turned me heartsick. When I was not able to conceal my disgust they added more grossness for good measure.

In the parlors I could no more compete with them on equal terms than I could compete with Beelzebub on equal terms; but I could look fresh and wholesome, and I could now smile at men, so that very often a man left one of them after she had fastened herself to him like a leech, and, coming over to me without more ado, took me up-stairs.

The relief of getting out of the presence of these creatures lightened the task of physical labor and contact with men so that I no longer looked upon this part of my life as being the most loathsome.

I simply shut my eyes and repeated to myself some well-known lines of prose or poetry which would keep me from dwelling too much on the repugnance of my task, and when it was over I would smile at the man, and not revile him as I had done in Kansas City.

In this manner, and with the aid of the old *roué* who had bought me, together with the man who had promised to be my friend, I was financially successful beyond my wildest dreams. When I had paid my bill and put one hundred dollars in the bank, which

I did after being three weeks in the house, despite all Madame's urging that I spend it for a new evening gown, I resolved to try for the house on Dearborn Street. But I was at a loss how to get away without a row with Madame, with the prospect of having her hold my trunk for an imaginary debt.

It seemed useless to try to pit my untrained wits against her malignant cleverness, so I consulted with the man who had promised to be my friend. With the aid of a friend of his who was not a frequenter of the house, but who had dined down-town with us on several occasions, we hit upon a plan which we thought a good one.

This other man was to come down to the house and inquire for Madame; when he saw her he would demand to know if she had a girl of my description in the house. He was not supposed to know that I was called Madeleine, since that was not my right name; but he was to describe the clothes I had worn when I arrived; he would go on to say that I was his daughter and under age; he was to threaten all sorts of dire results if I were not forthcoming. It worked like a charm. Madame had never been in trouble with the police, and she was not looking for trouble. She denied that she had a girl of my description in the house, and the man went out, vowing to go to the prosecuting attorney for a search-warrant. After he had gone Madame rushed up to my room and helped me to pack my trunk, for now she was as anxious to get rid of me as previously she had been desirous of keeping me. She urged me to go to a friend of hers in Pittsburg, and offered to advance the fare. I declined her offer and left the house, followed by Madame's best wishes.

I went to a good down-town hotel, and then sent a messenger to my two fellow-conspirators, telling them of the success of our plan and of my where-abouts. In answer to my note I received an invitation to join the two of them at dinner at six o'clock that evening.

We had a hearty laugh over the success of our harmless conspiracy, and our laughter added zest to our appetites. After the excellent dinner had been served the two men invited me to go with them to see Eddie Foy in "The Crystal Slipper," and I was so delighted that I could scarcely refrain from dancing for joy. Here were two staid, well-known business men treating me as if I were the nicest girl in the world, and not hesitating to take me to a place of public amusement.

By their suggestion and at their expense I remained at the hotel for two weeks, during which time I enjoyed to the utmost the many unfamiliar phases of the city. I explored the beautiful parks, and took long walks through the wonderful, flower-lined boulevards; but the Art Institute was, to me, the great objective point from which I departed and to which I always returned. I had rather an unusual talent for drawing, and I cherished secret dreams of being able some day to cultivate this gift.

Although I was rather a silent girl when I was in the presence of strangers, I could, at times, express myself very clearly to those I cared for. Since I felt a deep sense of gratitude toward these two men, I had no trouble in finding words in which to express my joy for the unusual holiday which they were giving me; this was the first real joy my girlhood had ever known.

This period marked the beginning of a long, clean friendship between myself and the man who had played the part of "Father."

He made the discovery that I had a keen faculty of observation and an inquiring mind. He took great pleasure in helping me to develop my latent gifts, and I hung on his every word as if it were a jewel of great price.

When he talked of the Bible from the standpoint of literature he opened up a new and marvelous field for me, for I had hitherto looked upon this book as being one composed only of moral precepts. I now began to feel a growing appreciation of its historical and poetical value; though I assiduously avoided looking at the New Testament, because it recalled too painfully the teachings of my childhood.

Later on, under this man's guidance, I began a comparative study of Job and King Lear. My own preference was for Job, and in after-life I often found myself repeating his despairing cry, "O that thou wouldst hide me in the grave, that thou wouldst keep me secret, until thy wrath be past, that thou wouldst appoint me a set time, and remember me!"

CHAPTER IX

WHEN my brief playtime was over I went out to see the proprietor of the house on Dearborn Street, and the interview was a memorable one, for it brought me into contact with a woman who was as different from Madame C—— or Miss Laura as they were different from each other.

In answer to my ring at the door of a large, unpretentious-looking house in the twenty-one-hundred block, there came a bowing Japanese butler who had a rather disconcerting effect upon me, since I had never before seen either a Japanese or a butler. I entered the hall, which bore no resemblance to the homelike entrance at Miss Laura's or the gaudy, gilt-mirrored hall at Madame C——'s. I think the family story-papers of that period would have described it as "cool, quiet elegance," and that is as nearly as I can describe it now. So beautifully harmonious were the appointments that no one feature stood out conspicuously.

The hall was the key-note of this house, which contained so many rare treasures of art that many men who were not ordinarily visitors to "joy houses" came to view these gems; and when they were accompanied by their women acquaintances of the social, professional, or business world it was not called "slumming," but was referred to as a visit to an "art palace." The statues of Parian marble, the world-famous paintings and bronzes, were no more beautiful nor perfect in their way than were the furniture, carpets, draperies, and other fittings. The famous Japanese room was the model for many similar rooms in the most exclusive homes in Chicago.

Even my untrained eyes saw that the room into which I was shown was perfect in its appointments. After the mirrors and the glittering gilt and glare of the parlors at Madame C——'s this was a room which invited one to rest and dream. My wait was rather a long one, but it was not a tedious one, for my eyes and my mind were drinking in the beauty of this wonderful room.

When the housekeeper entered I was loath to be disturbed, but, since my mission was a business and not an artistic one, I stated my business; inwardly I rather resented being cross-examined by the housekeeper, who was a dignified colored woman entirely dissimilar from the "before the war" servants at Miss Laura's or the "fresh niggers" at Madame C——'s.

In answer to her question as to where I had boarded before, I answered that I had come from Laura B——'s in Kansas City. This house seemed to be well and favorably known to her, although she seemed to consider Kansas City one of the outposts of civilization; she remarked dryly that if Miss

Allen took me she would require me not to mention such a barbarous city in the presence of patrons. Then, after asking my age and inquiring about the state of my wardrobe, she intimated that possibly the landlady might take me, and she went out of the room to call her.

In the other houses in which I had lived the usual daytime garb was a wrapper of some sort, plain or fancy, as suited the taste of the wearer. Having grown accustomed to this style of dress as being the approved daytime garb of the profession, I was not prepared for the appearance of the sandy-haired, austere-looking woman, severely corseted and garbed in a plain, tightly fitting, high-collared dark-gray dress, who looked more like the severe matron of an orphan-asylum than the mistress of the most exclusive "house" in the United States.

Miss Allen spoke with a slight bur which I afterward learned was Scotch-Irish, and I also learned that she had all of the grim traits of the Scot and none of the softening graces of the Irish.

As soon as I opened my mouth I blundered, for I called her "Miss Lizzie," this being the usual mode of address where the landlady did not style herself "Madame." She gazed at me sternly and informed me that that particular mode of address was the one used among "common women," but it did not prevail in *her* house.

She said she would take me, but she evidently considered it necessary to instil some of the refinements of civilization into my mind before pre-

senting me to her patrons. Never, never must I
tell any one that I had boarded in Kansas City.
It was the wild and woolly West; and Western girls
did not take well with her customers. I had better
say that I came from New York.

I protested that I had never been in New York,
and that no one who had could be convinced that I
knew anything about the city. Miss Allen found
me painfully dull, and she continued to insist that
I must have lived somewhere other than Kansas
City; she could not conceive of any one's having the
poor taste to have been born there.

We compromised on St. Louis as a safe place
to hail from; Miss Allen herself had lived there
once, though she seldom spoke of the fact.
Indeed, her enemies—who were legion—said she
did not mention it because she wanted to forget
that she had once been a chambermaid at the
Planter's Hotel.

She impressed upon me that in future I should
be "Miss Blair" and not "Madeleine," though I
could retain that, too, since most people had some
sort of a Christian name.

There was no time during the long interview in
which she showed the slightest indication of a thaw,
and I went out feeling as if I had been taking a bath
in ice-water.

After I had sent my trunk out to the Dearborn
Street house my courage almost failed me, but it
was too late to withdraw. I knew I should never
be able to learn all the rules and live up to the

standards of that misplaced matron of an orphan-
asylum.

I arrived in time for dinner and went down in
my street dress, which was a lucky thing for me,
since otherwise I should have worn a wrapper.
The girls were all dressed for dinner, not in the
regulation evening gown, but in beautiful, costly
"robes" or tea-gowns, wrappers being taboo except
at breakfast.

The girls to whom I was introduced were neither
friendly, as the girls at Miss Laura's, nor intolerant,
as the girls at Madame C——'s. Rather they were
indifferent, in the manner of those who withhold
judgment.

I was assigned a seat at the foot of the table,
where I met the cold, severe eyes of Miss Allen every
time I lifted my eyes from the plate. This presence
had an appreciable effect on my appetite for several
days.

The waiter attracted my attention more than
the girls, for I had never before seen a Chinaman.
I had had a vision of the dignified, bowing Japanese
butler serving, but it seemed that his duties lay
elsewhere—principally in answering the door-bell
and in serving wine; nothing so plebeian as beer
was sold at Lizzie Allen's.

When I went to unpack, Miss Allen came with me
and every article in my trunk was subjected to her
closest scrutiny. She approved of my lingerie,
which was white and sheer, and she scornfully referred to the fashion of wearing colored silk under-

AN AUTOBIOGRAPHY

wear as one which prevailed only among "common women."

My one little evening gown, which had just been cleaned, was too cheap to be worn in *her* house, though she thought it rather nice and acknowledged that it might be becoming. She refused to let me wear it, saying she would see that I had something befitting the dignity of her establishment. I had no robe suitable for the late hours, from two until four, when the girls were permitted to remove tight-fitting gowns and corsets.

I promised to buy a loose-fitting robe, and she proceeded with her examination; she ended by condemning my few little toilet accessories as being utterly unsuitable, though she consented to let me use them until I could make enough money to replace them with silver or ivory.

After everything was put in place she sent me down to take a bath, as unceremoniously as if soap and water were something unknown to me; she told me that I must bathe and change my linen every day, or twice a day if needed. This is a custom which is observed in every first-class house; but, as she considered the matter, there were only two other first-class houses in America—one in New York and one in San Francisco—and women from other places, especially barbarians from Kansas City, were not supposed to know anything about personal cleanliness.

I could see that if Miss Allen ever discovered that I had lived in Custom House Place I should have to move on short notice.

MADELEINE

At length she left me to complete my toilet, after advising me to lie down every evening after dinner, as it helped to preserve one's good looks. This was a rule that Miss Allen herself, who must have been nearly sixty, never observed; but, as she had no looks to preserve, she may not have needed the nap.

At eight-thirty the night-maid came up with a gown of Miss Allen's which I was to wear—a rich brocade of somber hue, trimmed in costly lace. It was quite suitable for a "dowager" of Miss Allen's age and type, but rather oppressive and over-powering for a girl of eighteen, though it fitted my slender figure well enough, Miss Allen being of a spinster-like thinness.

I had finished dressing and was trying to pluck up courage to go down-stairs when there came a rap at the door. In answer to my "Come" there entered a brisk, business-like little gentleman, carrying a brown bag, who announced, with a slight foreign accent, that he had come to dress my hair.

I explained that I did not care to employ a professional hair-dresser and that I had already dressed my hair for the night, but he answered that none of the girls arranged their own coiffures; that even the girls who had their own maids had him to dress their hair. It was Miss Allen's orders, and as there was nothing further to be said, I submitted myself to his hands, and was gratified at the result, for in his profession he was an artist. Indeed, he was more than an artist; he was a sincere friend to every girl in the house, and "Charlie" heard confidences that were seldom given to others, and gave much common-sense advice. Moreover, in his own home on Michigan Avenue he received the mail of girls who were keeping their profession secret from families and friends, and his house served as a place where the girls could meet relatives who came unexpectedly to Chicago.

Charlie's professional prices were high, but these other services were gratuitous and prompted by kindness of heart. From noon until eight Charlie worked among the society women of the South Side; from eight until ten he worked among the girls at Miss Allen's.

Parlor hours were supposed to begin at nine, but there was little business before eleven, so that few of the girls came down-stairs before ten. If they chanced to be wanted before they were dressed, Charlie always shouldered the blame for their dilatoriness; he was the one person Miss Allen never took to task.

When I came down-stairs I found Miss Allen enthroned, in icy stateliness, on the uncomfortable seat of the hall-tree; and as I saw her on that first night, so I saw her every night during the five years that I made her house my headquarters.

During the subsequent years, as might have been expected, I developed into a female "Wandering Jew," who went to and fro on the earth, seeking a peace that was not in her own heart; but during the first five years I always returned to the house on

Dearborn Street; and invariably the first sight that greeted my eyes, when I came down-stairs dressed for the night, was Miss Allen enthroned upon that hard seat of the hall-tree.

Eventually, and in her cold way, she grew rather fond of me, as we girls discovered after I became the second person that she never took to task and the only girl in the house who ever dared to "answer her back." This was also proved by the fact that, no matter how much I rambled among the "common herd," she always took me back, though she never showed her liking by actually "thawing out."

On that first night, as I stood hesitating at the foot of the stairs, Miss Allen called me to her, and I walked down the long hall, feeling as if I were weighted down by the heavy fabric of my borrowed gown.

She examined me as minutely as if I had been a piece of inanimate merchandise sent up on approval. My feet and ankles, being fairly symmetrical and not too large, "passed," and my foot-gear was not condemned. She then lifted my skirt to inspect my stockings and to see if I had obeyed her orders about wearing spotless linen. She turned me around and around to view the effect of her stately gown on my girlish figure. She was not pleased with the effort of eighteen to carry the dignified garments of sixty, but she found solace in the fact that my attire was neither cheap nor common, the two cardinal sins in her decalogue.

She had previously assured herself that my hair was all my own, and now my coiffure was the only part of my toilet that came in for her unqualified approval, for Charlie had made the most of my abundant hair, which was of a beautiful color and texture and inclined to curl.

My discomfort at being examined like a piece of merchandise did not prevent my faculty of observation from working, and I scrutinized Miss Allen as thoroughly as she had inspected me, except that my examination was not accompanied by the laying on of hands.

There was no question about her plainness of feature; "spinster and prude" were stamped all over her; and to picture Lizzie Allen as having ever been clasped in the arms of a man, giving or receiving human kisses, was beyond the power of my imagination.

In her costly evening gown she still had the appearance of an austere matron of an orphan-asylum, dressed in her Sunday best and awaiting a visit from the board of directors. Her gown, which was of the stiff brocade she always affected, was silver-gray in color and plain in outline, with a slight V at the neck, and her only jewels were a bar lace-pin with a single diamond in the center, and old-fashioned, pendent gold ear-rings with diamond drops. I imagined that these ear-rings had descended to her from some ancestor in Scotland, but afterward discovered that they had been made to her order at Peacock's.

MADELEINE

When Miss Allen had completed her inspection she called the butler to show me into the ballroom, where the girls were assembled for the opening of business. He opened the door, with a sweeping bow announced, "New lady," and left me standing motionless inside the door.

Four expensively gowned girls, who were playing whist at a near-by table, glanced up without speaking to me; one remarked to the others, in a perfectly audible tone, "That is Allen's gown she has on," and then proceeded with her game.

I recovered my power of locomotion and went over to one of the alcove seats which lined two sides of the spacious ballroom. In surveying my companions and my surroundings I became so interested that I forgot that I was wearing Miss Allen's gown and that all the girls knew it.

Two other beautifully dressed girls were at the piano practising a new song with the "professor," who was a scholarly-looking, middle-aged man, and the dignified colored housekeeper was wiping non-existent dust from a sporty-looking marble Clytie.

I took a dislike to that Clytie on the spot, and was trying to muster up the courage to get a closer view of her when the butler ushered in four men. The card game was broken up, for the girls arose to greet the men; and the housekeeper whisked cards and table out of sight before leaving the room. The two girls who were at the piano walked over to one of the small alcoves and sat down together, the "professor" struck up a waltz, and in a few moments the four

couples were whirling over the highly polished
floor.

There had been no indecorous scrambling for
possession of the men, as there had been at Madame
C——'s, and I was so relieved that I looked across
the room and smiled at one of the girls who had been
singing. The ice was broken and she came over and
sat down beside me.

She was an ugly little thing, swarthy, and of a
Jewish cast of features; but she had beautiful
shoulders, and when she turned on her ingratiating
smile and displayed her beautiful teeth one forgot
her facial defects. When she spoke in her soft,
Southern drawl she was still more alluring and I
found her to be both intelligent and witty.

She introduced herself as Olga Howard. "*Miss*
Howard, if you please, in Allen's presence, and Olga
or Howard, as you choose, when the old lady is not
around."

Olga offered to show me the ropes because she
thought I was a "titbit"—as young girls who had
not been long in the business were called—and she
did not like to think of another girl being so lonely
and isolated as she had been during her first weeks
at the "Ice Palace," as she called the house. She
had been there eight months, and only recently had
she been admitted to full fellowship with the haughty
dames who possessed a dozen evening gowns and
kept their own maids.

Olga was a Southern girl who had had an affair of
the heart which had driven her from her native city

of New Orleans. She had gone to Duluth, since it was the most remote place she could think of at the time, and it was her bad taste in choosing Duluth as a place to hail from that had aroused the scorn of the haughty ladies at Allen's; it had required a long time and much patience on her part to overcome their prejudice.

The butler came into the ballroom and interrupted our conversation to say that Miss Allen wanted me in the "Copper Parlor."

Miss Allen, with a wintry smile on her face, was trying to make herself agreeable to an elderly man. After introducing me as "Miss Blair" she went out, leaving me alone with him. He asked me where I was from—for Miss Allen had told him I was a new girl —and he did not seem in the least shocked when, to my own consternation, I answered, "Kansas City."

He ordered a bottle of wine, and after about twenty minutes' conversation remarked that he had called on one of the other girls, but had found her engaged. Miss Allen had insisted on his meeting me, but I must excuse him since he was an old friend of Miss Grey's and preferred to see her. If I would kindly find her maid and ask her when Miss Grey could see him he would appreciate it.

I had not the faintest idea who Miss Grey was nor where I should find her maid in that hotel-like mansion, but I was willing to try, and I went out on my errand, only to encounter the icy eyes of Miss Allen, who was again seated on her throne in the hall; she beckoned me to her.

AN AUTOBIOGRAPHY

When I had explained my business she told me,
in a cold, hard voice, that I should never presume
to call one of the other girls when she, Miss Allen,
had introduced me to a man. It did not make any
difference who the man *thought* he wanted; if I were
sent in to him, it was my business to *make* him desire me.

After this lecture she sent the housekeeper to call
Miss Grey, who was in her room, and told me to go
back to the ballroom.

The same men were still there, but they were now
ensconced in couples with the girls, in the alcoves;
the butler was serving wine, and Olga was at the
piano singing a popular song to which the love-
making couples were not listening; the other girl
had left the ballroom.

When Olga had finished her song she sat down
beside me and asked me where I had been. I explained that Miss Allen had sent for me for a man who
wanted to see Miss Grey. Olga smiled. "I do not
in the least blame you," she remarked, "for you
could not know. But that is one of Allen's old
tricks. Miss Grey is not busy at all; she was in
here while you were away. You are a new girl and
Allen wants to boost you, but it's not fair to take
another girl's friends."

I had no doubt about her being right, and I said
so, but I asked her what one was to do about it.

"Oh, there is nothing but to grin and bear it, if
she takes a man away from you, and nothing to do,
if she introduces you, but to get him, if you can.
She sits there in the hall from eight-thirty until the

133

house closes at four; and I will give her credit for trying to give the girls an equal chance to make money. Grey has already made thirty dollars this afternoon and evening and Allen thinks that is enough for her. But when a girl works hard to make her friends and to keep them it is not fair to prevent them from seeing her."

I asked her if all the girls did not go in the parlor so a man could take his choice; she answered that it was not the custom here. Unless a crowd came in, the business was all in private calls. If Allen introduced a girl, she expected her to get the man, whether he wanted her or not. If the girl saw she had no chance, she could tell Allen, who would then send some one else to him.

I remarked that if I were a man with half a dozen girls clamoring at me at once I should leave the house. Olga thought that if she were to go into a room with half a dozen men she would have no hesitation in selecting the one she preferred. But she said she was sure a man often took the girl who was nearest him, or the one who made the most noise, simply because he was embarrassed.

Sometimes a man wanted a girl who sat across the room from him, or one who had nothing to say, but he did not have the "sand" to speak out. In that case it was not an infrequent thing for a man to go out without seeing any one, and then return and ask at the door for the girl he preferred. We were agreed that Allen's plan was the more dignified, though I was certain that I should never learn to force myself on a man who did not want me. And I never did. If I saw a man who did not care to take me I hastened to leave him. And I never ceased to be amazed at girls who could inveigle a man into taking them against his inclination.

CHAPTER X

ON that first night Miss Allen had introduced me to four of her best customers, but none of them had shown any inclination to buy my wares; I had to suffer the chagrin of knowing that the men had taken other girls after I had had the first chance to earn their money.

The ballroom and the great Pompeian room were the places for entertaining men who came in parties, and all the girls had the entrée to these rooms without the formality of being introduced by Miss Allen. All night I had gone back and forth between these two rooms, but no one had paid the slightest attention to me.

The other girls, who looked very alluring in their beautiful costumes, were laughing, talking, singing, and dancing, but none of them had bestowed so much as a glance on me. Early in the evening Olga had become engaged for the night, so that I felt myself utterly abandoned. I lacked the self-assertion to walk boldly up to a man who had not noticed me, and I was acutely conscious of my unbecoming, borrowed gown.

I felt none of the repugnance toward the girls that I had experienced toward the creatures at Madame

C——'s. Miss Allen's boarders were of a distinctly different class, and I earnestly wanted to know them and to become one of them, but they did not even see me. I felt terribly alone and painfully young and unsophisticated. At four o'clock I escaped from Miss Allen's scathing tongue by going up the back stairs to my room. I was in no mood to hear that I was a failure.

As soon as I closed my door I relieved my over-wrought feelings by removing the offending gown and donning my own pretty pink frock. No doubt it *was* cheap and common, as compared with the expensive gowns worn by Allen's girls, but it was also girlish and becoming; so, at least, I decided when I looked into the mirror to discover wherein I was so hideous that no one would look at me.

I saw a face that by no stretch of imagination could have been called beautiful, neither could it have been called unattractive. There were several really beautiful girls in the house, and I could understand any man preferring them to me. But there were also girls in the house who did not possess my good "points," and I could not see why men should choose them in preference to me.

In my pink gown the glass gave back a beautiful pair of shoulders and a perfectly formed chest, which had been covered by Miss Allen's prim, middle-aged brocade. She could cover her bare bones and her wrinkles if she liked, but I had none; whereupon I resolved to brave her wrath by wearing my own gown on the following evening. If I were to make money in a houseful of beautiful women clad in expensive clothes, I did not propose to swathe myself in her horrid old brocade. It did not matter to me that it had cost several hundred dollars, if I looked like a frump in it.

If she did not like it, I would leave. I had not gone to Lizzie Allen's for the purpose of living in a "swell" house, but for the single purpose of making money, and the sooner I made a stake the sooner I could get out of the loathsome business. With this resolution I undressed and went to bed.

Olga was not at table when I came down to breakfast, and, aside from a wintry smile from Miss Allen and an impersonal nod from the two girls who were there when I came in, no one paid any attention to me. That did not affect my appetite, however, for there was an excellent breakfast, nicely served by the immaculately clad Chinaman who presided over the dining-room. Several white-capped maids were arranging trays at a side-table, and I gathered from their conversation that the girls who kept their own maids often breakfasted in their rooms.

After breakfast I went up to my own room and got out my books preparatory to an afternoon of study, having in view a plan for my own future, in which my present occupation had no part. I was deeply engrossed in my book when there came a rap at my door, and upon opening it I found a diminutive colored girl with a harassed expression; she announced that she was Miss Audley's maid and that her mistress would like to see me in her room.

On going with her I found Miss Audley to be the girl who had reminded her companions that I was wearing Miss Allen's gown. She was a beautiful blonde of the purest type, tall, slight, and delicate-looking. Her beauty was now marred by an expression of anger and disgust with which she regarded a behemothian man who was propped up in the middle of her bed.

He had a glass of wine in one hand and a cigarette in the other, and he was imploring his beloved Blanche to come to bed with him. In maudlin accents he continued to call her his darling star-eyed goddess, but the only notice she took of him was to send a glance of loathing in his direction; she now proceeded to explain why she had sent for me.

This man was a friend of hers, who was on a spree, and he had not permitted her to close her eyes all night. He was most liberal with his money, but if she were forced to endure him for another moment she felt that she would kill him. Besides, she had an engagement with her dressmaker, who was a martinet and brooked no broken promises. She could not leave the man alone, because Miss Allen would be angry if he charged around the house, which he was sure to do. Would I please take him off her hands?

My soul revolted at the task, but I was anxious to make money. I went over and sat on the edge of the bed, and instantly became the object of his desire. I asked him if he wanted to come to my room, and he assented with alacrity. Blanche sup-

MADELEINE

ported him on one side and I bolstered him up on the other. As his huge hulk lurched from side to side it seemed that we would all land in a heap in the middle of the floor. Midget, the maid, brought up the rear with his clothes over her arm, and in this fashion we finally got him to my room.

As Blanche, with a sigh of thanksgiving, was leaving the room, she said that he would make no objection to paying another girl, too. If I could not manage him I had better call Olga to help me.

It was not a pleasant situation, as I soon realized. With one breath he was howling for wine and with the next he was yelling for me to come to bed. I had never before been alone in the room with a man in such a state of intoxication and I began to be afraid of him; so I sent Midget for reinforcements.

Olga took charge of the situation that I was unable to cope with by ringing for a bottle of champagne. I looked askance at the quart bottle that the house-maid brought in, but Olga, after filling the man's glass to the brim, only half filled ours; then, while diverting the man's attention, she motioned for me to throw my wine under the bed. I performed a like service for her, but we left half the contents of the bottle untouched.

Olga promised the man a joyful time, but she postponed the fulfilling of the promise until we should have another bottle. He acquiesced and again Olga rang the bell. He handed her twenty dollars and told her to keep the change. She paid the maid at the door, but she did not open the bottle which she took from her; instead she took the half-filled bottle from the dresser and replenished the glasses. The man drank his at a gulp, and again we threw ours under the bed.

With drunken liberality he gave us money as freely as he had bought wine, but he exacted his pound of flesh for his money. From the time he came into the room at one-thirty until he fell asleep at seven he pawed over us constantly, until every inch of my flesh was in a quivering revolt against his huge, hairy hands and I was strangling a sob at every breath I drew. I did not wonder that Blanche wanted to kill him if she had to endure him another moment. I wondered if any girl had ever killed the beast who had violated her protesting body.

When we were assured that he was sound asleep we locked the door and went down for our belated dinner.

The dining-room was deserted except by the Chinamen in charge, so I took a seat beside Olga, and in low tones we discussed our plans of sharing with Miss Allen. The man had paid for one hundred dollars' worth of wine, but only six bottles had come up from down-stairs, and the maid had collected for them. We had simply sold him the same bottle over several times. To me it was a new way of making money, and it did not strike me as being an honest one, but Olga hotly protested that if I were a knocker and a fool she would have no more to do with me.

As she put it, Miss Allen would get fifty dollars

from our afternoon of horror. There would be the thirty dollars for the wine, and ten dollars' "bed-money" from each of us, since Miss Allen never insisted on getting half of what the girls received from their patrons; she was content with taking half the fixed price of the house.

It still seemed crooked to me, but I was not a knocker even if I was a fool, and we compromised by dividing the money.

Olga went to her room to dress, but I had to hold myself at the disposal of the man. I found him still sleeping when I came up from dinner, and without awakening him I got a book and went out in the hall to read. For the next two hours I forgot the man and all my annoyances in my never-failing solace, a good book.

When Olga came out of her room at a quarter of ten she told me that I had better not let the house-keeper find me in the hall, since it was against the rules to leave a man alone, except to go to meals.

I went into my room and, without turning on the light, undressed and lay down as far from the man as I could, every nerve of me tingling with the dreaded anticipation of his awakening. I wanted to creep out of bed and pray to be spared the further pollution of his horrible hands and his loathsome body. Olga had told me who he was, a man whose name was famous in "big business" and whose beautiful wife was a leader of society.

I lay there questioning my Creator. Why had He made beasts like this? Why, since man and woman were created for each other, had He made their desires so dissimilar? Why should one class of women be able to dwell in luxurious seclusion from the trials of life, while another class performed their loathsome tasks? Surely His wisdom had *not* decreed that one set of women should live in degradation and in the end should perish that others might live in security, preserve their frappéed chastity, and in the end be saved.

CHAPTER XI

AT Madame C——'s it was considered bad luck for a man to come in and then leave without spending some money. To remove the curse from the house it was the custom for the girl who let him out of the door to spit on his back.

As I opened the door in the morning to let out the man that Blanche Audley had turned over to me I wondered why it was not the custom to spit on the man that *had* spent money.

When I went up to my room I threw the windows wide open to clear the atmosphere of the odor of stale cigarettes, stale wine, and stale man. It was not yet nine o'clock and I had slept little all night, but as I looked at the soiled and crumpled bed-linen I shuddered at the thought of getting into the bed before it had been aired and changed.

In the bathroom I turned on the water and stepped into a bath so hot that it nearly scalded me. I plied soap and brush so vigorously that I almost removed the skin. I could not wash from my soul the pollution of that beast, but I removed the pollution of his perspiring, wine-soaked body from my skin. An alcohol rub completed my antiseptic bath.

AN AUTOBIOGRAPHY

I felt purer in heart from the very effort to throw off the poison, but I could not breathe the suffocating air of that room. I must get out of the house; I must forget, if only for an hour, that such a place existed.

When I was dressed and out on the street I walked away from Dearborn Street as if I were being pursued by demons; when I reached Michigan Avenue I fell into the long free swing that has always made walking a joy to me, and I walked mile after mile through beautiful streets and tree-lined boulevards, across grassy park places and well-kept lawns, breathing in the fresh air that swept clean and strong from the lake and washed the stale odors of Dearborn Street from my nostrils. But my mind still retained the image of the Beast.

My plan for getting rid of disquieting thoughts has always been to substitute the thoughts of the great minds that have added something to the sum of human knowledge or of spiritual betterment. On this occasion a passage of the essay that had been holding my attention when I was called upon to entertain Miss Audley's friend came into my mind.

The Republic of Venice came next in antiquity. But the Republic of Venice was modern when compared with the Papacy; and the Republic of Venice is gone, and the Papacy remains.

When I began repeating the passage it was not because I loved either the Republic of Venice or the Papacy. It was because I wanted to forget Chicago and the brothel. But my memory took up the essay that I had read but twice, and as I walked I found myself repeating it verbatim.

The marvelous picture called up by that great master of English, Macaulay, swept from my mind the flagitious obscenities of the Beast, as the lake breezes had swept from my nostrils the odors of stale vices.

The brothel became entirely obscured in my mind as my fancy visualized the picture that memories of the essay called up.

The work of human policy that was great and respected before the Saxon set foot in Britain; before the French had passed the Rhine; when Grecian eloquence still flourished in Antioch; when idols were still worshiped in the temples in Mecca.

I saw the smoke of sacrifice arise from the Pantheon, and watched the camelopards and tigers in the Flavian amphitheater. The feeling of shame that lay so heavily on me when I left the house had passed into oblivion when I reached Jackson Park and stood on the shore reaching forth my arms to the turbulent lake.

On the previous night I had wanted to creep from the side of a drunken beast and pray to be delivered from the horror of his touching hands. On this morning I wanted to kneel down on the shore of Lake Michigan and thank God that I was a tiny atom in this great scheme of human progress, even though I was but one of the countless grains of dust that clogged the balance-wheel of society.

When I returned to the house at one o'clock I was happy and hungry, ready to face the world and take up the struggle as best I might, in the path which fate seemed to have chosen for me. I smiled at every one at table, forgetting that most of them were not aware of the existence of one so young and so unsophisticated; and after breakfast I went up to my beautiful room and into my nice clean bed and slept until the dinner-bell rang at six-thirty.

When I came down at nine o'clock, dressed in my own gown, I walked boldly up to Miss Allen and asked her how she liked it. She frowned and said that I might wear it, but that I must order another in the morning. I had made forty dollars the night before from the Beast, and she said she would send Cohen, the credit man, to see me so that I could open an account.

I fled to the ballroom lest I might be tempted to tell her how much we really had made out of Blanche's drunken admirer, and to get Olga's advice about how to use the money without Allen's knowing about it. Olga was not down-stairs, and as the ballroom was deserted except by the "professor," who had just come to work, I proceeded to make his acquaintance, although I knew it was against the rules in any first-class house to talk to the pianist.

This is a rule which is never observed, but landladies make it, because in every society there must be some one who is lower on the social scale. What is the use of having money, if there is no one to look down upon? Not infrequently the landladies are the chief violators of their own unwritten law against the pianists.

MADELEINE

One of the resolutions which I made many years ago was that none of my boys should ever learn to play the piano. Then they would never become "professors."

This particular man was a harassed-looking middle-aged man who had a family of four children to support, and who wanted to be home with them at night instead of thumping out syncopated trash for people who did not give a rap what he played, so long as it was something that did not make them think. The present-day craze for rag-time has floated up from the brothel. So have most of the other crazes, unless it is the one for immodest dressing. No "decent" house of that period would have tolerated some of the styles that are seen on the streets to-day.

If a girl had come into Lizzie Allen's parlors wearing some of the present-day street styles, she would have been told to go up-stairs and put on her clothes.

I had learned all about the pianist's family when Olga came down, and at once we ensconced ourselves in one of the alcoves while she instructed me how I could use my money without Allen's knowing I had it.

It was all very simple, because Cohen was looking out for his own interests, not for Miss Allen's. He made his money from the girls, not from her. He guaranteed the girls' accounts at several of the large shops, and he came every day just after breakfast to collect his money. Miss Allen had nothing whatever to do with the accounts. She made it a point to have

148

the servants watch that none of the girls removed
their clothes from the house without paying him,
but on the rare occasions when they did she was not
held responsible.

It was easily seen that Cohen was not going to tell
Allen if a girl gave him fifty dollars when he had
expected only twenty.

I made his acquaintance on the following morning,
and in the afternoon I went shopping. Olga offered
to chaperon me, but I declined her services for two
reasons. One was that she looked very "sporty"
when she was dressed for the street, and I had never
been on the street with another girl since I had been
in the business, for I had no desire to be pointed out
as "one of them." Then her ideas about clothes
were highly extravagant, and I had no intention
of paying for a gown the hundred and fifty dollars
that my credit order called for.

In the great department store I almost drove the
man-dressmaker mad by what he considered my
parsimony. He expostulated in his broken English
that he could not turn out a gown for one hundred
dollars. He ruffled his bleached pompadour, and
twisted his many rings as he explained that it
could not possibly be done.

The skirts were growing wider, and could I not
see that it required fifteen yards of taffeta to line a
gown? I could not. I would buy five yards to face
the skirt, but an entirely silk-lined gown was a
luxury I did not intend to indulge in. He quoted
girls at Allen's who had paid three hundred for a

gown, but I bluntly said that they were great fools.
I had other uses for my money.

At length we compromised on a gown at one
hundred and fifteen dollars which he declared would
be a disgrace to the house.

When I had been measured I went down to the
silk department and selected an inexpensive silk for
a late-at-night robe. I looked over the laces that
were on sale and found a bargain, and the following
day I became the possessor of a guilty secret, for I
locked my door and began making the robe myself.
Since my early childhood I had been taught to sew,
and I had ideas of my own about the way I wanted
things made.

With my closet door kept wide open, that I might
secrete the sewing, if I had an unexpected visitor,
I cut out and fitted my robe. I made it all by hand,
for I had no sewing-machine, and a few nights later
when I came down-stairs I had to perjure my soul
to account for a piece of work that I would have
proudly acknowledged had I dared. But I was one
of the ladies of leisure and I must not stoop to spoil
my hands with any work so plebeian as sewing.

Olga and I had many things in common, and we
became great friends. She was five years older than
I and looked upon me as being somewhat of a fool
because I lacked self-assertion and was hampered
by scruples; but she grew fond of me, although she
continued to patronize me to an almost insufferable
degree.

Despite her patronage, I had some influence with her, for I succeeded in inducing her to discard her flamboyant hats and leave off her make-up when we went into the street. She reluctantly consented to do this, for she believed in advertising, but I refused to go out with her while she wore the badges of her profession.

From the beginning Olga had taken well with men and she had a host of regular customers. When she was introduced to a man she "got" the man, whether he wanted to be "got" or not. That was what Miss Allen expected of the girls, and Olga's position was secure unless Miss Allen should discover that she had been cheated out of her wine-money.

Miss Allen went on the theory that all her girls were honest, and aside from her strict guard in the down-stairs hall to see that the girls should meet none but the men whom she had picked out for them, she did not spy upon her boarders. In most houses the girls turn in their money as they make it, and the landlady settles daily or weekly, as the rule may be.

Miss Allen did not keep any accounts with the girls. Each morning they turned over to her one-half of the previous night's earnings. She did not handle their money at all. There was no charge for table-board, nor did Miss Allen expect anything but her just share. But she did insist upon getting the last penny of that which was hers; if she found out that a girl had cheated her she did not ask her to leave, but played a game of freeze-out with her. After a girl had sat around for a week without seeing a man except those who came into the ballroom, she knew that it was time for her to go.

But Olga was adroit and Allen was not likely to find her out. Indeed, on one occasion two men compared notes after leaving the house, and the one with whom Olga had gone up-stairs discovered that he had paid twice as much as his friend. He returned to the house to demand a refund, but Olga faced him in Miss Allen's presence and convinced her that the man had lied and was trying to "work" her.

Olga had been madly in love with a man in New Orleans, and he had been most devoted to her, lavishing much money and many gifts upon her. She thought she had won a secure place in his life and in his affections, when she was startled out of her dream by reading in the papers the announcement of his engagement. She had been too loyal to create a scandal, and had quietly left New Orleans. After her adventures in Duluth she came to Chicago, and had been highly successful, winning a long train of admirers. But she still mourned for her lover.

I was not exactly in love, but I had a warm spot in my heart for the man in Kansas City, so I sympathized with her in her broken romance.

We were both actuated by a secret ambition, for the attainment of which we had resolved to lay aside a given sum of money every week, regardless of our other obligations, which were chiefly those owing to Cohen.

Olga believed that she was destined to become a great dancer, and I was equally certain that I could become a great artist if I had the opportunity to study.

I had planned to take up drawing and was ready to begin my lessons when Olga discovered a wonderful dancing-teacher on the West Side, whereupon she induced me to postpone my artistic career and take dancing lessons. She was thoroughly convinced that even a mediocre dancer was always certain of bread and jam, but she was not so sure that the embryonic artist could earn a living.

When the great man-dressmaker made me a gown from my own design her respect for my talent increased, especially as the finished product called forth much favorable comment from those who saw it. But she had far greater admiration for my thrift, for before submitting my design to the great one I had gone through the store and secured a price on all of the materials which went into the gown.

The dressmaker waxed enthusiastic about my design, though he scorned my thrift. However, his scorn did not prevent him from breaking his own rule and turning out for one hundred dollars a gown which would have cost two hundred had I ordered it in the usual way.

The greatest thing that Olga and I had in common was neither our love-affairs nor our ambitions. I was our affection for little children. Like me, Olga had little brothers and sisters to whom she was passionately attached, and her family also was poor But she did not have my soul-destroying secret for her family knew of her occupation, and, though they deplored it, they neither cast her off nor refused her aid. I knew that my family would not only refuse my aid, but that they would discard me if they should find out my mode of living.

It was not the fear of their repudiating me which made my life a burden in the effort to keep my secret. It was the grief it would bring them which blanched my face with fear every time I thought of the possibility of their discovering my manner of life.

It was not possible for me to send them much money, for I had no way of accounting for the possession of it. I could only make vicarious gifts to every attractive little street beggar I met. This was a hobby with both Olga and me. And often when we had been down-town shopping and had spent every cent we had, except car fare, some bright-eyed street urchin would wheedle us out of that, and we would walk to Twenty-second Street, berating ourselves for our folly.

It was easy for Olga to keep to her plan of the weekly deposit because she made a great deal of money, but it was more difficult for me, inasmuch as I was still too shy and lacking in self-assertion to make much money. Besides, I was rather a silent girl who did not take well with men.

But if I did not attract many men, at any rate I held those that I did attract, and I enjoyed the advantage of drawing to myself the men of the highest class who were, for the most part, of a

AN AUTOBIOGRAPHY

rather serious turn of mind. Few of the class known as "bloods" ever looked at me the second time.

When I saw that I should never be able to compete in the open market with other women I made great efforts to be agreeable to those who became my patrons. I was considered lucky by the other girls because I did not have to make my money "at so much per." For my few friends not only treated me with great consideration, but they were more liberal with their money.

My efforts at self-improvement did not meet with the intolerance in this house that they had encountered at Madame C——'s, for most of Allen's girls were of good American stock and possessed some degree of education. If I were foolish enough to waste my time with books when I could have joined a jolly party bound for the races, they considered it my own affair and left me in peace.

As a matter of fact, I longed to go to the races, but, since I could not get over my aversion to publicity, my studies became a convenient excuse for not joining them. It was hard enough to meet the people who came into the house, but I refused to emblazon my shame to the outside world.

Allen always let me see my few friends whenever they came, because she considered me bright, and she conceded that it was necessary to have some one who could entertain the serious-minded men.

The one thing about my intellectual friends that pleased me most was that they never talked "down" to me. Oftentimes their conversation was more or

11 155

less Sanskrit to me, but if I did not understand it was not for lack of interest, and that, after all, was the secret of their liking me.

One especially good customer often talked to me about matters pertaining to natural philosophy, and straightway I went down-town and bought a text-book on that subject, although I could not understand it because I lacked the fundamental training for it. The fact that I did not know the rudiments of a subject never prevented me from trying to acquire some knowledge of it. Since many men of many minds were among my customers, I acquired a most wonderful library in my efforts to live up to their belief in my superior mentality.

My greatest asset was my marvelous memory, and I soon discovered that men were pleased and flattered that I remembered and could repeat with exact nicety the things they had said to me weeks before. One polished political boss was my friend, and though I knew nothing of politics, and cared even less, I would quote his own opinions to him and he would be highly pleased at my interest. He considered that nature had spoiled a most astute politician when she had made me a woman.

He once took me with him on a trip to New York, where we remained for four days before going into Canada for a two weeks' vacation. His admiration grew by leaps and bounds and he lavished generous gifts of money on me while he debated whether or not he should furnish a flat for me upon our return to Chicago.

AN AUTOBIOGRAPHY

His romance was rudely shattered, however, when we reached Quebec, for, of all the cities on the American continent, that was the city of my dreams. As we stood beside the stone bearing the inscription, "Here lies Wolfe, Victorious," I forgot the man's very existence. He talked to me about the alluring dimples in the corners of my mouth, and I talked to him about the conquest of Quebec.

While he attended to business matters I wandered alone about the city. I visited the Citadel and the Lower Town, and returned with a great stock of misinformation gathered from any one who would answer my questions. He talked about his business, about himself, and about the proposed flat. He crushed me to his breast in passionate love-making, and I pushed him away to better describe to him the spot on which Montgomery had fallen. He took down my long hair and wondered if there was another woman in the world whose tresses were so enticing; I disentangled his fingers from it to tell him about the Ursuline Convent where Montcalm's bones lie buried beneath the altar.

At length he flung out of the room with a threat to find some woman who was not crazy about dead men, and I wondered what I had done to offend him. I was glad to get rid of his love-making, and with a fervent wish that he would not hurry back I sat down with a volume of Parkman to further obsess my mind with the stories of the illustrious dead. When he returned at four o'clock in the morning I was still reading. He turned out the

light and left me in the dark, so that I was forced
to go to bed; and then he inflicted upon me the
outrageous insult of turning his back with the
remark "that he had seen all the girls he cared
to for one night."

I never got the flat.

CHAPTER XII

WHEN I had been at Allen's for five months I found out that I was again pregnant, or rather the examining physician discovered it. He had repeatedly assured me that the disease from which I had suffered always caused sterility. For this reason his diagnosis was entirely unexpected and came as a great blow to me.

I implored him to do something for me, but he refused. He did not believe that I could carry a child to full maturity and he would not interfere. According to his orders, he reported the matter to Miss Allen, and she came raging and storming up to my room. One would have supposed that I had deliberately cultivated pregnancy for the express purpose of bringing humiliation on her and upon her house.

Nature had bestowed upon me a great desire for peace and for the line of least resistance. Few women have ever hated conflict and strife as I have hated it. For this reason I have always been long-suffering until the extreme limit of my endurance has been reached. But I have never been a comfortable person to deal with when driven into a corner. In the months that I had lived at Allen's

I had borne the abuse of her scathing tongue in silence, but now I had reached the limit of my endurance.

When I turned upon her I turned with the cumulative bitterness of five months' gathering. It was the impatience of a woman young and fresh for one old and withered; the scorn of the well-born, no matter how lowly their estate, for the ignorant and low-born upstart; the loathing of a woman who was reaching forth to grasp ideals for the woman who had no ideals and who, with a great fortune at her command, knew no other way of using it but to build a palace dedicated to sin and shame.

Within the memory of the oldest boarder or oldest servant such a scene had never occurred; that any member of her household should dare "answer her back" was something incredible. I dared. I answered her fully and completely, and, like the man in the drug-store in St. Louis, she stood aside and in silence let me pass out of my room.

I left her in possession while I went in search of the porter to bring my trunk up from the basement, and, after performing this errand for myself, I went back up-stairs and began packing. The one small trunk that I brought to the house would not hold a third of the belongings I had gathered since. I selected my plainest street clothes, though I possessed nothing obtrusive, and a few changes of underwear; these I packed in my small trunk and went down-town to buy a larger one.

After I had ordered the trunk sent out to the

house I sent a note to the two men who had helped me to get away from Madame C——'s. I told them that I was leaving Chicago, and asked them to meet me at Hogan's at seven o'clock. I told the messenger that there was no answer, for I knew that they would be there at the appointed time.

These two men had been my faithful friends ever since I had known them. They did not fail me now so far as well-meant efforts went, but when I wanted them to suggest a physician who would help me out of my trouble they promptly vetoed that method as being a very dangerous one. Their way of helping was to offer me all the money that I might need.

I had several hundred dollars in the bank, and it was not money that I wanted from them. We debated the matter all through dinner-time without coming to any understanding, and at length one of them suggested that we send out for Olga and get her advice in the matter.

A cabman was called and despatched on the errand, and when Olga came I electrified them all by announcing that I was going home next day. I wanted to see my mother. None of them knew where my home was, for that was a secret I had kept inviolate; but they thought me foolish to go home. I was firm, however, for I retained a most vivid recollection of my illness in Kansas City, and I wanted to see my mother before I had another experience of that kind.

I knew that I could easily remain at home for

two weeks without exciting suspicion. My mother's every letter had urged me to come, for she was in ill health and she sorely missed her two eldest children. My brother was too far away to visit her, but he had recovered his health and was making good in his new position in the Far West.

Olga brought me a message from Miss Allen to the effect that I had been hasty and rude to her, but that she did not want me to leave the house. We all had a good laugh at the idea of Allen's asking me to remain, because that was another one of the things that had never been done. She had never before asked a girl to remain in her house.

When Olga and I were ready to go home my two friends made me promise to let them know where I went after I should leave my own home. I gave the promise, and they then insisted on making me a substantial present of money.

When we were in the cab Olga said she considered me the luckiest girl she knew; she was sure she had never received a dollar from a man unless she had earned it. Some of her friends gave her more money than others, but they all took it out of her in one way or another. I answered that she made twice as much money as I did, and if it were not for the few men who were really fond of me I should starve, because I could not "hustle" fast enough to keep warm.

She laughed in acknowledgment of this well-known disability of mine, and the first small cloud that had ever come between us passed over without doing any harm. It was after parlor hours when we got home, but Miss Allen, who was in her accustomed place in the hall, greeted us with a smile, or what was as near a smile as she could ever muster up.

She asked me to reconsider my decision to leave, but my mind was made up. She then said she would be glad to take me back whenever I wanted to return, and we parted on better terms than we had ever been on during the five months I had been in her house. I went up-stairs to finish my packing, and I did not see her again before I left.

When I came down in the morning with the bag in my hand and stood waiting for the cab to take me down-town, the house-boy handed me a letter in the familiar hand of my friend in Kansas City. I opened it in the cab and then gave the driver a new order; instead of going home I had decided to go to Kansas City.

My sweetheart, for I now called him that, was going to Montana to live, and he had asked me to go out there with him. It was nearly a year since I had seen him, but his image was still fresh in my mind. I had received much attention in the mean time from the few men who were really fond of me, but none had replaced him in my thoughts, although I did not then believe myself to be in love with him. When he met me at the train the following morning, for I had wired him that I was coming, he folded me in his arms and I was all aglow with a rapture which made it hard for me to remember that I had ever known another resting-place.

MADELEINE

When I had been three days in Kansas City he came in one day and asked, abruptly, "Madeleine, when are you going to marry me?"

"Never," I answered, promptly, "because I am going to have a baby."

I had meant to break this news to him in another way, but he had swept me off my feet, and in my surprise I lost all the well-chosen words which I had intended to say.

The next hour was a most uncomfortable one for both of us. For this quiet man had long ago fought the matter out with himself. He did not want to care for me. My mode of life outraged all his sense of decency, all his inherent self-respect, and all his traditions; but he had been unable to put me out of his heart, and he had made his decision after the usual manner of the male of the species, without doubting that I would accept. *He* had made up *his* mind and he then endeavored to make up my mind.

Two persons more incompatible in temperament and in training it would be difficult to find. His was a strong, dominant nature that would have molded the woman of his choice to his own will, and I was as unmoldable as any girl possibly could be. Young though I was, I sensed that indomitable will, and I had no desire to beat out my own individuality against it. With my whole being I wanted this man for my own, though I dimly foresaw the clash of wills which would make our lives anything but peaceful ones.

During the time I had been a saleswoman in

Chicago I had longed and hoped and dreamed of being this man's wife. Despite my harsh experiences before I knew him, I did not feel myself unfit to be the wife of such a man. He saw the scarlet brand as a vivid smear across my girlish brow, and he loathed the stain with all his soul, but his love for me was stronger than his loathing for the life I had led. To him the fact that I had known other men embraced the whole question. It was all a hideous pollution in which there were no gradations; and I could not explain to him the difference between selling my body to a man of his own kind and selling myself to a man like Blanche Audley's "Beast," whose very presence was contamination.

Because he could not get behind the wall of my reserve he thought me cold, almost indifferent to him. He could not understand that I could no more penetrate that wall than could he, nor that I would gladly have torn down the barrier that stood between us had it been in my power.

When I told him of my intention to visit my mother he seized upon this opportunity to press his suit. Why not let him come to my home and meet my mother and my family? He longed to know them and to see my girlhood's home. If I were his wife I should be forever free from the haunting fear of having my family learn of my sins. Surely I needed him at this time. Why not let him stand by me in my hour of trouble? What difference did it make that I was to be the mother of an unwelcome child? Since he condoned the sin, surely he would not condemn the child. He would throw the mantle of his protection and his name around us both. Did I think that I, a young girl not yet nineteen, could stand upright, alone, and unsupported against all the storms of life? It was madness. No woman could do it. I might struggle out of my present mode of life without the handicap of a child, but with that child I could never win. It meant damnation for me and for the child alike.

I looked in awe at this quiet, sober-minded man, ten years my senior, who was so shaken out of his usual calm demeanor. Surely it was not I who was mad; it was he, that he should be pleading for the privilege of marrying a woman of my kind, and be ready to fill the place of a father to a child who might even be the offspring of a man like the "Beast." That this man had lost his mind was quite evident to me. No sane man would do this thing.

Moreover, I was seized by panic at his suggestion to visit my home. Let this fastidious gentleman come into that poverty-stricken hovel! Never! Never should he know the horrors of my childhood. It did not enter my mind to plead the privation of my home life as a defense for my sins. Nothing could have induced me to tell him that I was the town drunkard's daughter, that my father in a drunken brawl had hurt another man and had been sent to prison.

This man who loved me had taken me at my face value, which was that of a girl who had been brought up in a good home. He should not learn differently. I would stand branded and shamed in his eyes, but he should not know the depths to which my father had consigned his family when he had abandoned his obligations to them.

Thus it came about that his desire to visit my home and to know my family only served to build higher the wall of misunderstanding which stood between us. For he looked upon my refusal to let him come as being prompted by sheer perversity on my part. And he came to believe that I did not choose to abandon the primrose way.

When I left Kansas City the next morning we parted in grief and bitter misunderstanding—in silent tears from me and a soft, low whistling from him, which would have seemed highly incongruous had I not known that this was his method of concealing his deep perturbation.

He was to leave in a few days for Butte, Montana, and he had asked me to communicate with him at that place. But I gave no promise, for I could not see why we should prolong the agony when there was little likelihood of our ever meeting again.

On the train speeding homeward I speculated on the futility of love. A week before I had not known that I really cared for this man, but at the first call that had come to me across the miles that lay between us I had gone without hesitation. When I stood once more in his presence I knew that I loved him, and now he had gone out of my life.

When I went into the dining-car for lunch I found it impossible to touch the food which I had ordered.

MADELEINE

I beckoned to the waiter, and in a low, shamed voice asked him to bring me a cocktail. I had scorned the women who brazenly flaunted their vices in public, and now I thought every one on the car must know that I was a fast woman when I ordered a drink. I did not care. I wanted something to help me bear the burden of an undesired motherhood and the bitter grief of separation from the man I loved.

When the waiter brought the drink there came to my mind a little scene of the previous day. My sweetheart had laid his hands on my shoulders and, looking intently into my face, he had inquired, "Madeleine, have you ever been drunk?"

"Never in my life," I answered, truthfully. As I toyed with the glass I felt that it ought to count for righteousness that a girl should have lived where wine flowed freely and yet refrained from more than tasting it. But on further considering the matter I realized that I was laying a flattering unction to my soul. I abstained from liquor because there was nothing in my mental nor my physical composition that called for it. I did not want this drink that I held in my hand. If I took it, I would be deliberately committing a wanton act. I pushed it away untouched.

At home there was great rejoicing over my unexpected arrival, and I spent two weeks with my family in which I forgot so far as possible everything else in the world. I put aside my grief for the man who had gone out of my life and my anxiety about the child who was coming into it. Though I could not foresee it, I was making my last visit to the home of my childhood. The relative to whom I had appealed for aid had been most generous in his response, for he had not only aided my mother, but he had gone to the place where my father had got into trouble and had secured his release.

After this trouble my father never drank again. He went East with this relative and remained for some time in his employ; but he was a doomed man, for he was in an advanced state of Bright's disease, and the physicians had said that his death was a question of only a short time.

Shortly after my visit to the family my father returned home. He was a man who knew the world, and he was not entirely satisfied with the stories I had told my mother. He came to Chicago, made a quiet investigation, and was not long in discovering the truth about my life, which I thought I had so adroitly hidden.

When he faced me in my shame I thought he meant to kill me, but I was no longer afraid of him. I turned on him and all the pent-up bitterness of my childhood poured forth. I hardly knew him—he had changed so greatly—and my heart was torn at the sight of his physical decay and of his mental anguish at knowing that I was lost. But I did not spare him, though I did not raise my voice, as I recounted his dereliction to his family.

It was the first time in my life that I had acknowledged that any one else was in any way responsible for my downfall. I never saw him again, though for years his face haunted me.

The physicians who had pronounced his doom had underestimated the iron vigor of that magnificent constitution, for he lived for three years after his visit to me, fighting back the Grim Reaper and disputing the ground inch by inch. But he never forgave me nor permitted my name to be mentioned at home, though he himself often mentioned it for the purpose of reminding the other members of the family that I was no longer one of them. In the end he had his way, for they cast me out of their lives, and none but my mother remembered that there had been another sister.

BOOK II

CHAPTER I

WHEN Baby was two years old I left him in charge of the nurse who had cared for him since his birth, and went up to Winnipeg for the summer.

My heart was torn not only by anxiety at leaving him, but by maternal jealousy as well, for this woman who had been a mother to him already meant more to him than I. He was always glad to see me when I made my daily visit to him, but when I left his good-by hand-wave held no regret at my going.

This woman and her husband had no children of their own in their comfortable home, and Baby had come to occupy a very large place in their affections and in their lives.

I reproached myself for my jealousy. I reminded myself of the loving care they had given him. Surely I wanted my child to be happy? In the next breath I recalled the goodly sum of money I had always paid for his care, and the fact that this money had been a godsend to them; then I would stand shamed in my own sight, for the voice of Justice whispered to me that money could not have bought the love they gave him.

MADELEINE

When I thought of leaving him for several months my heart misgave me, for I felt sure that he would forget me. But circumstances forced me to make a change. I had returned to Allen's when Baby was eight months, where I lived under a terrific strain, for the expenses of living there were heavy, and the additional expenses of caring for a child made it impossible for me to save money. Several times when I had been almost swamped by my debts I had received a large check from my friend in Montana, and my desperate position precluded the possibility of my refusing it.

Twice in the last two years he had come East to see me. He still cared for me, though he did not again speak of marriage. I felt that his better judgment had reasserted itself; and, for my part, my child occupied so large a share in my life that he had grown to be a secondary consideration. Moreover, I exerted a peculiar fascination over a few men who showered me with attentions, and it was impossible not to make a temporary response to their ardent love-making. I still cared for my old-time friend, but it was rather because of his dependability than through a passionate longing for him. And he was the only person to whom I could open my heart about my beautiful little boy.

The news of Baby's first tooth, and Baby's first steps, and Baby's first word, had been duly transmitted to him through the medium of my letters.

Now I was going to leave my baby, and these intimate matters of a child's development would come to *me* only in letters; but there was no other way. My health was breaking down under the continuous strain, and I did not want to spend all my years in paying for expensive clothes that were of no service outside the brothel. My wardrobe would be considered a strikingly handsome one in a smaller place, and I need buy nothing new for the next six months; but at Allen's it was becoming very *passée*.

One of the girls had spent a summer in Winnipeg and she was filled with the stories of the Northwest— the wonderful ozone-laden air of the prairies; the gentility and liberality of the men one met; the opportunity of out-of-door life; and the advantage of making and saving money. She had returned from there the previous summer with a fat bank-account, and I had resolved to try this, to me, out-of-the-world spot.

With Baby's coming I had been compelled to put aside my cherished dream of studying art, for I could spare neither the time nor the money. I was, however, desperately resolved to acquire enough money to go into some legitimate business before he became old enough to realize that his mother belonged to the "oldest profession."

After I learned of the opportunities offered in the Northwest, Winnipeg became the goal of my immediate ambition, and I wrote to the woman who kept the leading house at that place.

My application for a room met with a prompt response from the landlady, and she wrote that I could meet her in St. Paul ten days later, for she was going down there to procure new girls.

Baby's nurse and her husband came to the train with me, and then for the first time Baby cried after me. He clung to me with all his might, and we had to loosen the clinging little hands when the train pulled out.

Madame von Levin met me in St. Paul; she was a stately woman who, both by birth and through her marriage, belonged to the German nobility. After a dinner together at McGee's, she took me to her heart in a manner unusual to her; for she was the *grande dame* to her finger-tips. She explained that she was sending up four girls from St. Paul, for business was good and girls were scarce. We were to leave that night over the Great Northern, but I flatly refused to be shipped with a carload of prostitutes; I had lost none of my old-time repugnance to being publicly known as "one of them."

I felt, as I made my declaration, that Madame would consider me a snobbish creature, but I could not help it. This was a firm principle with me and I would not break it.

On the contrary, she liked my standpoint, for it was one she herself would have taken. So we settled the matter by my going alone over the Northern Pacific.

At this period the bawdy-houses in Winnipeg occupied one short street, which stood alone in the midst of the prairie. It was more than two miles from town, but it was within the city limits; for the public men of that day had a vision of the great city which was to be built on those prairies, and the city limits extended out into the wheat-growing district.

In front of the houses, for there were no other buildings on this street, was a long stretch of unbroken prairie extending into the town, and behind them were the waving wheat-fields.

The unwritten law of the public and the police was that the houses must be far away from residences or other buildings; the girls could have the prairies to themselves, and they would not be molested so long as they did not make themselves conspicuous in the town. But no girl should be allowed to remain in Winnipeg who "made a show of herself" on the streets.

So far as I ever heard, there was no graft, nor were there any fines unless a complaint was made against the landlady for selling liquor without a license.

This restricted district was often facetiously referred to as the American Colony; because all of the girls "on the prairie," with the exception of two or three, were American by birth. Our Canadian cousins seemed to think that the United States supplied the Canadian market with prostitutes; they expressed great surprise if they chanced to find a girl who had not come from the States.

Business was good for girls and for the houses and the profits to the house were enormous, for "short" drinks were sold and everything from lemon-soda to Scotch whisky cost twenty-five cents a glass. Indeed, every tray that came into the parlors contained several whisky-glasses of water, which the girls ordered under the name of gin. Champagne also was bought freely, and the men of this small city spent money with a grace and ease that I had never seen equaled. I heard many stories of champagne baths, but I never saw one; although I remember seeing one girl pour glass after glass of champagne over her head with the declaration that she intended to go back to St. Paul and say that she had had a champagne bath.

Winnipeg kept early hours, and most of our business was over by one o'clock in the morning, except in the case of men who remained all night. The house closed at two, and our early breakfast at eleven o'clock gave those who cared for it the opportunity for a long day in the open air. Adhering to my rule, I usually went out alone. I soon learned to row, and I spent long hours on the river

At other times, when I had spent the night alone, I arose early and took long walks over the prairies, which soon came to exert a wonderful fascination over me. Often, if I were up late at night, I took a long walk before going to bed; for the dawn begins to break at two o'clock in midsummer, and every daybreak was a new revelation to me. I wanted to paint that first pink streak of dawn. I wanted to burst into poetry, and I did break into tuneless song as I tried to express to myself just what I felt was behind the rim of the prairies. Life became fuller and more beautiful than I had ever thought it could be.

AN AUTOBIOGRAPHY

The men of this country exerted as great a fascination over me as the whispering prairies, and I met them with a glad response I had never before known. I awakened to find myself the most sought-after girl in town, and I rejoiced in my popularity. Time after time men came in from the outlying provinces of the Northwest who had heard about Madeleine from some friend in Medicine Hat, or Calgary, or Regina, or some other distant point.

I examined my own heart, day after day, to discover if the fascination of the prairies was the cause of this spiritual and physical awakening; or was it an awakening? Was it not, rather, an evidence of moral decay that I could meet each new day as if it was a great adventure?

Despite the ache in my heart for my little boy, I was happy.

I began to dream again of art—to seek a medium for expressing the joy of life which thrilled me all through the day and made my nightly tasks so much less irksome than they had ever been; yes, and often made them a pleasure. Was it an awakening or a moral decay? I did not know. I only knew that I was changed in every way. I had broken through the wall of my own reserve, that reserve which had been the cause of so much suffering, which had kept from me so much of the joy of life. My thwarted girlhood was behind me, and in my dawning womanhood I felt that somewhere and somehow I should demand from life the things that had been denied me.

MADELEINE

Was it the prairies, or was it the men of Winnipeg, or was it both? For surely these men were as different from the men in Chicago as the prairies were different from State Street. Here were no *blasé habitués* of wine-rooms and bawdy-houses, seeking a new sensation by learning a new perversion. Here were men, fine and strong, courtly gentlemen such as I have never met anywhere else in the world. Their visits to the houses were a part of their playtime; they were not seeking a new sensation, these red-blooded men of the Northwest; they brought their sensations with them, and they showed a tenderness and courtesy toward women which often brought a choking into my throat

The only exceptions were the English remittance-men; and they were often so charming when they were sober that one forgot they were fools; or remembered that, if they were fools, at any rate they were not "cheap skates," for when they had spent the "money from home" they betook themselves out of sight and were seen no more until the next remittance came.

Late in October I returned to Chicago. Just before leaving Winnipeg a friend who had been very generous with me asked me to stop over in Fargo for a few days with him. I was glad to earn the money which I knew would be forthcoming, and acceded to his request. While in Fargo I wrote to my child's nurse, announcing the date of my return, and I counted the hours until I should see my little boy. On the last lap of my journey, between St. Paul and Chicago, I could not sleep, for I was exulting in the thought that I should see him in the morning. Had he forgotten me? Would he call me mother? I got up and dressed before daylight, and sat looking from the car-window. At the Union Station I took a cab and made the driver break the speed laws in my haste to reach the South Side home of Baby's nurse. I arrived to find the house deserted. A neighbor living next door told me that the people had left the city a week before, and they had told her that they were going to keep Baby, for his mother had deserted him. They had not heard from her all summer.

CHAPTER II

IN a breath's space my whole, happy, prosperous summer had become a source of bitter regret to me. I had returned to Chicago restored to vigorous health and with a comfortable sum of money in my possession which would permit me to have my little boy with me for a few months. But of what avail was my money if I had lost my son while I was making it?

I tried to be very indignant with the woman whom I will call "Nurse," but I succeeded only in feeling very sorry for her. She could not help resenting my claim to the child to whom she had been a real mother. No doubt when she received my letter telling her of my intention of taking care of Baby myself she had yielded to the temptation of running away with him; and I knew that her husband would abet her in anything that she did, for I had had several clashes with him on account of the air of proprietorship which he had assumed toward my little boy.

Knowing their attitude and their hope of finally gaining possession of my child, I had been a fool to leave him in their undisputed charge for more than four months. Yet what was I to do? I could never get ahead in Chicago, after Baby came, for the cost of living took every dollar that I could make. In Winnipeg I had saved the greater part of my earnings; I had recovered my health; and my hopes for the future ran high, only to be shattered by this blow which my better judgment told me was not entirely unexpected.

There was little time now for regret. If I could not find my baby the joy of life was over for me; I must reclaim my child. Now was the time for action. There was no use going to the police. If any one could find him, it was I.

The logical place to begin my search was at the home of the woman's parents, who were prosperous farmers living near LaCrosse, in Wisconsin. I was certain that her mother would know where they had gone.

When I arrived in LaCrosse I enlisted the aid of the local police in finding out where Nurse's parents lived. My respectable appearance stood me in good stead, and the chief was all sympathy, leaving no stone unturned in his search for the people I sought to find.

Their name was a very common one, and my ignorance of the father's first name made it difficult to locate one farmer in a large community of farmers. We received little aid from the post-office authorities; but our inquiries among the liverymen brought better results.

The people we were looking for should be one of four families of that name—so they told us. I

MADELEINE

visited each of these families in turn, and each place was a long drive from the town, over the worst roads I had ever traveled. But my search was rewarded at the last place, for when I walked into the kitchen of the large farm-house I found Nurse, her husband, and Baby seated at the dinner-table, together with Nurse's family.

The scene which followed was a painful one for all concerned. Nurse was determined that she would never give up my son to me. Her husband attempted to bluster, calling the attention of the assembled family to the terrible sin of a woman of my kind bearing a child, which was rather beside the question, seeing that I had *borne* one. Baby refused to have anything to do with me. When I attempted to pick him up he drew away from me and kept repeating: "I don't like you, lady. Go 'way!"

Two stalwart sons of the house kept casting hostile glances at me, until the liveryman who had brought me to the place was obviously uneasy. He kept urging me to return to town and invoke the aid of the law; but I refused to leave without my baby.

When I reproached Nurse for her treachery and for the lies she had told about my desertion of Baby I found an unexpected ally in her mother, to whom she had told the same mendacious story. When I showed her the weekly letters which her daughter had written me, and the photographs of Baby which she had sent, and the Dominion Express Company's receipts for large sums of money which I had sent from Winnipeg, she denounced her daughter and her daughter's husband in scathing terms. She herself was a mother, and she thought that the claim of a mother, who had done what she could, came before all others. She peremptorily ordered Nurse to pack up Baby's clothes and prepare him for the long drive to LaCrosse, otherwise she herself would go with me to the proper authorities.

Nevertheless, the parting scene was a heartrending one, for Nurse clung to Baby and he clung to her. I would not tear him away by force, and I was at my wit's end what to do, when he became interested in the waiting horses which he could see through the window, and he allowed the driver to carry him out to the carriage. He would not let me touch him.

On the train returning to Chicago he cried so lustily that he attracted the attention of every one in the Pullman. He would not make friends with me, and he refused to touch the food that I ordered brought in from the dining-car.

A man in ministerial garb, who sat in the section opposite to me, came across the aisle and, sitting down beside me, undertook to quiet Baby.

"Your little brother, I suppose, madame?" he inquired.

"No," I answered, shortly. "He is my son."

The man looked his incredulity, for Baby at two and a half years was as large and spoke as plainly as most children of four, while I looked younger than my twenty-one years. Furthermore, it must have struck an observer as strange that the child should not know one who claimed to be his mother; for he still kept reiterating: "Go 'way, lady. I don't like you!"

The ministerial-looking man had little difficulty in attracting the child's attention, and they were soon romping away in the seat in great glee. I thought it time to make another effort to induce him to eat something, and when the porter came in with the bread and milk which I ordered, Baby ate without protest from the black hand of the porter, though he had refused to let me feed him.

My cup of sorrow was overflowing to know that my little son would make friends with every one but his mother.

It was several days before he learned to trust me, and it added greatly to my embarrassment that he would not call me anything but "Lady."

I rented a small flat and employed a steady-going colored girl, who had formerly been Olga's maid, to keep house for me, while I devoted all my time to cultivating the friendship of my son. He was a strong, healthy child, remarkably bright, but with a quietness and poise not usually found in highly intelligent children. As soon as he had ceased to grieve for "Auntie" he began to care for me, and we became very happy together.

With a flat of my own I could have made an easy living by receiving a few of my best friends, but I had resolved that no man other than the one in Montana should ever come into the home in which my son lived. I wanted him to see my little boy and become interested in him. He was coming East to spend Christmas with me, for he still held a large place in my life. I wanted him to love my baby, and I knew that no normal man could keep from loving a child so beautiful.

The plan for a legitimate business of my own still loomed large in my consciousness, but I did not have all the capital I required to carry out my plans, so I planned to "assignate" until spring, for I had found out the expenses of private women were not half so large as those of women in public houses.

I consulted Charlie, the hair-dresser, who knew all the best assignation-houses in town, and he advised me to leave my name and address at two or three places on the South Side, for that was more satisfactory than sitting for company at one place.

The woman who kept the most exclusive place on the South Side would not take me when I informed her that I had formerly lived at Allen's, for she must have women who were not known in the underworld. But another woman, who kept a good place on Indiana Avenue, was very glad to have me come, for I was just the type of girl to take well in a private house. We agreed that if I should meet men whom I had known at Allen's I was to relieve her of all responsibility by saying I had deceived her in the matter.

This woman wanted some one who would live in the house, and she gave the resident girls the first chance. I could go home to my flat when the house

closed, at one o'clock, and return in time for dinner
at seven.

As this would give me all day at home with my
baby, I agreed to the plan.

During my stay in this house I learned a great
deal about two phases of prostitution which hitherto
had been unfamiliar to me.

These two phases, occasional and clandestine
prostitution, have always struck me as being far
more pernicious from a social standpoint than public
prostitution; although they do not make such havoc
in the lives of the individual, since most of the
women who follow these lines still retain their accustomed place in the social order.

My fellow-worker in this house was a student at
the Conservatory of Music, whose family had made
many sacrifices that she might study in Chicago.
She was engaged to a rising young lawyer in the
Western state from which she came, and she had deliberately chosen this means of earning money for
her trousseau.

Since we were thrown so much together, we came
to know each other very well, though we had little
in common. She thought that a girl who had been
in a public house was beyond the pale, and I thought
that a girl who would deliberately deceive the man
who was to marry her and whom she professed to
love was beneath contempt.

This man, to whom she was afterward married, rose
to a high position in the affairs of the nation, and
she, his wife, became famous for her political acumen

and her social graces. Society placed no scarlet brand upon her nor upon her kind, and it is to be supposed that her four children rise up and call her blessed.

We each had a small hall bedroom in which we kept our clothes and personal belongings. We were always dressed in our street clothes, and when we were wanted down-stairs we donned our hats and outer garments and stole out through the basement. We would walk around the block a couple of times in order to acquire an outdoor glow, and then come up and ring the front-door bell.

To the men we met we were anything that the occasion might require. We were married women, widows, girls from good homes, working-girls, business girls, professional women, or whatever else the men in question had ordered.

Since we were both intelligent girls of modest demeanor, who let the men do most of the talking, we encountered no difficulty in playing the different rôles we assumed.

There were several other women who came to the house and "sat for company," and others who were "on call." Most of these were the real articles of which we were the spurious representatives. These women came two or three times a week to meet friends, some of the married women keeping their engagements in the daytime because they could not leave their husbands at night. Some of the girls on call were students at the Conservatory of Music and at the Art Institute. One woman who came was a famous church organist, while still others had no other means of support. But all wore a distinctive garment which differentiated them from the public prostitutes whom they openly scorned. This convenient garment was the Mantle of Respectability.

Although I scorned the cowardly, hypocritical wearers of this cloak, there was something in my own conventional pharisaic soul which grasped at this garment as though it had been made of cloth of gold. I longed to become a respectable member of society, but, failing in this desire, I was glad to have the outside world consider me one. Because of this attitude of mine, I was eminently fitted to fill the various rôles assigned to me. I not only played the parts well; I lived them.

One elderly visitor, whose name was famous throughout the United States, wanted to meet some sweet young girl who earned her own living and who would accept the attentions and the money of a gentleman of sterling character. He required that she must have known just one man before meeting him, for he was no seducer of young girls; he only aspired to be a protector. I played this rôle so well that he fell madly, though discreetly, in love with me. He extolled the purity of my character, my sweetness of disposition, my grace of form and feature, until I really believed that I was as sweet and innocent as he thought me.

I had an engagement with him one night, but he came before I was dressed and the landlady sat down to entertain him. He told her he was afraid that

I might become corrupted by coming into an assignation-house to meet him, therefore he was going to rent a flat and keep me all for himself. He would procure the best art-teachers for me, and I should have every opportunity to develop my one gift. He had drawn from the bank that day six new one-hundred-dollar bills, and he showed her the present that he intended giving me when I came.

The landlady was delighted to know that I had found such a splendid friend and protector, and she joined with him in singing my virtues.

When I rang the door-bell after my run around the block he was impatiently waiting for me, and after a couple of hours spent together in one of the beautiful guest-rooms he told me of his plans for me and gave me the six hundred dollars. We went down-stairs to say good night to the landlady, as he insisted on taking me to my car, now that I was to be his own dear little girl forever. This meant that I would take a car for Nowhere and get off at the next corner.

The landlady was so pleased at my good fortune that she invited us into the parlor to talk about it, and he ordered a bottle of wine. As an after-thought he gave her fifty dollars to show his appreciation of having met me through her.

As we waited for the car he instructed me to send him a message next day, telling him where I was going to live; if I did not have sufficient funds, he would supply me with whatever was needed.

When I returned to the house a transformed landlady met me in the hall and sternly commanded me to follow me to her room. There she turned on me in fury.

"So this is your trick, is it? You are planning to take one of my best customers away from the house. You don't seem to appreciate the fact that you met this man through me."

"Nor do you seem to appreciate the fact that I am here for that purpose," I retorted. "Also that it is I, and not your house, that the man is in love with."

"You may as well understand that you can't take him away from here. I can queer you in five minutes by telling him that you came from a public house, and if you want to see him again you will have to give me half of that six hundred dollars."

High words followed her demand, and I lost my head. For this had seemed my golden opportunity, and the thought of losing this man drove me wild. He was a dear old gentleman, and I really liked to be with him. His money would enable me to realize my dreams of a different kind of life. The thought of losing this chance when it was within my grasp was too much to be borne with equanimity.

At first I refused her demand that I share my money with her. I knew that she was hard and unscrupulous, and that even if I gave her the three hundred dollars I might never see the man again. But assuredly if I did not give it to her, I should lose him. At last I decided to take a chance with her and I handed over three of the hundred-dollar bills.

AN AUTOBIOGRAPHY

The next day she went to him, almost with tears in her eyes, to tell him how I had deceived her. She had discovered that I had been a public prostitute, and she begged him to investigate for himself. He could easily learn the truth. Not only had I lived in a public house, but I had a child that I had told him nothing about. She was sure my designs on him were evil—perhaps blackmail or open scandal and divorce would follow from his affair with me.

In answer to the message I sent him next day he returned a verbal answer to the effect that the lady must be mistaken in addressing him; that he did not have the honor of her acquaintance. In the next morning's mail there came a typewritten unsigned letter from him, setting forth in detail my various iniquities and my great sin in breaking the heart of a man who had trusted me. He did not see that he himself had set a premium on lies and deceit and that I was merely trying to supply the market with "something just as good" as the article which he had ordered. And the poor man lived for twenty years longer and died full of years and honors, despite his broken heart.

CHAPTER III

ALTHOUGH I regretted the lost opportunity and the wasted three hundred dollars, I did not grieve long over them, for it was not in my nature to mourn long over anything that did not touch the well-springs of my affections; moreover, any release from the House of Bondage, however temporary, always filled me with gladness.

In this instance I had great cause for rejoicing in my freedom, for I could spend all my time with my little boy, who was daily growing in beauty of character and intelligence. When I told him stories and watched the marvelous unfolding of his mind, or cuddled him to sleep in my arms, singing to him the songs my mother had sung to me, I thanked God from the bottom of my heart that the joy of motherhood had not been denied me. He was mine, this child who possessed such beauty of body and mind. What did it matter that somewhere in the world, unknown to me and to him, there was a prodigal sower of the seed of life?

When I took up my pencil it was to make numerous drawings of the beautiful head of my baby. My dream of art, this dream, this ideal that was always being frustrated, again filled my mind to the exclusion of my plans for a business career.

AN AUTOBIOGRAPHY

A malignant Fate awaited my moment of supreme happiness before delivering her cruelest blow.

One morning as Baby and I romped around the little flat my maid stood intently looking at me. I was wearing a clinging negligée which outlined my figure quite distinctly, bringing into prominence my matronly stoutness, which was increasing in spite of my best efforts to reduce it.

I became annoyed at the persistent stare and told the maid to go about her work; but instead of doing so she fired a bombshell of her own conjecture at me.

"Look here, Miss Madeleine, you know I don't bother my haid very much about the white folks' business, but I am botherin' my haid a whole lot about you. You certainly air gettin' fat and losin' your shape. First thing you know there's goin' to be another baby around this house."

I laughed at her as I took my little boy up in my arms. "Don't worry, Sadie," I said, easily, "there will be no more babies. I don't know what put such an idea into your head."

"Because you air gettin' too fat, and it ain't natural for you; I'm tellin' you that there is something the matter. If you was one of them beer-drinkin' gals, I'd lay it to that, but you don't drink beer. You know very well it's natural for you to be slim. You bettah go see the doctah."

I laughed at her fears. I had borne two children and I ought to know the symptoms of pregnancy by this time. There had been absolutely nothing to indicate it. I was in such buoyant health it was not to be wondered at that I was growing stout. I took long walks every day, regardless of the biting March wind, and I had an appetite like a school-boy. Sadie was full of negro whims; this was one of them.

Still, the idea had been implanted in my mind, and because I was jealous of anything that threatened the security of my life with Baby, I went to see the doctor. He confirmed Sadie's diagnosis; in about five months' time I would have another child.

As I walked homeward with all the lightness crushed from my heart I debated the old question that I had faced twice before. Should I refuse to bear another child, risking my life by an abortion, which I mortally feared, or should I add to my burden the care of another child?

The baby that I already knew and loved was one thing, but a second child by an unknown father was quite another proposition. I questioned God as to what He meant when He had made the male parent such an unimportant factor in the scheme of life. A mere sower of seed, who neither toiled nor reaped. Or why, since He had given me a limitless capacity for motherhood, had He denied me the usual emoluments of motherhood, a husband and a home?

Sadie met me at the door with a worried expression on her face. "Oh, Miss Madeleine," she exclaimed, "I am shore glad that you've come. Baby is so cross I cain't do anything with him."

I went in to him and found him fretful and feverish and demanding to be put to bed at an unusual hour.

I sent for the physician that I had so recently

visited, and while I awaited his coming I gave Baby a bath and put him to bed. When the doctor arrived Baby was sleeping soundly, and the doctor made light of my fears. He said the child had a slight cold, but that he would be all right in the morning.

By midnight Baby's labored breathing resounded through the room, and I again sent for the doctor, urging him to hurry and to bring a trained nurse.

When he had made a brief examination he called the nurse into the hall for a conference, and in five minutes I followed them, demanding to know what was wrong with my little boy.

The doctor was reluctant to commit himself, but when I insisted he said he thought it was pneumonia.

When he came the next morning my darling was worse. I asked the doctor in charge of the case to call in another physician for consultation, and I sat beside the bed with every nerve braced to bear the shock that I felt was coming.

The child was suffering intensely, but he was fully conscious and would take no medicine from the nurse. With labored breath he announced, "I will take the medic' from my mother."

Whenever I left his side for a few moments when he appeared to be sleeping he would open his eyes and with gasping breath exclaim, "I want my mother." It was not a plaintive wail; it was a demand for something to which he was entitled.

On the sixth day, when the two physicians had suspended their labors, and as I looked up into the face of the strange doctor I read the answer to my unspoken question, but I would not accept his verdict. I turned to the man that I had known for several years. "Doctor, is there no hope?" I asked.

This man had brought Baby into the world and had attended to his physical welfare throughout his brief life; he knew what his answer meant to me, but there was no hope and he must tell me the truth.

The frightful struggle for breath filled the room, but the brave little soul who had battled for his own life and supplemented our efforts for him in a manner almost uncanny in a child so young, looked into my face and asked me to hold him in my arms.

As he struggled with failing breath the words he was striving to say found utterance, "Mother, I am your good boy."

And then, as the beautiful eyes were fast glazing, "Mother . . . I . . . love . . . you . . . tongue . . . can . . . tell."

CHAPTER IV

I HAVE never had a clear recollection of the first week which followed my little boy's death. My faithful maid sent over to Allen's for Olga, who came bearing messages of condolence from the girls, and flowers and offers of financial assistance if it should be needed. But these women of the underworld showed a rare delicacy by forbearing to obtrude their presence into the house of grief.

Olga made the necessary arrangements for the funeral, and in response to the telegram which she sent him my friend from Montana hastened to Chicago, but I remained semi-oblivious to all that went on around me. I was indifferent also to the presence of this man until he attempted to take me into his arms to express his sympathy.

When he touched me I drew back from him and struck him in the face with all my force. While I poured forth my protest against life he stood motionless, with the red mark of the blow on his fair skin, but he gave no sign that he was hurt.

"How dare you touch me? Don't you know that my baby is dead? Do you suppose I want a man offering me caresses when my child is not yet cold in the ground? Do you know that I am to have

another fatherless child? That God has chosen me
to be the mother of all the fatherless children that
want to be born? Go away from me, before I yield
to the temptation to kill you; for you, too, are one
of those who go thoughtlessly along the way, casting
the seed of life wherever it may fall, not knowing
and not caring that in some hapless woman's body
it may bear fruit."

He left me alone, but he remained in the city to
be within call if I should send for him. Olga
remonstrated with me, but I was adamant; I would
not see him; I hated him; I hated every man that
I had ever known, from my father down to the
physicians who could not save my baby for me.

When he saw that I was beyond reason he returned
to his home in Montana. There was no use trying
to do anything until time should have softened my
grief and cured my madness.

A month after my little boy's death I made my
decision. I would not bear another child, and I
would not call on a physician to help me until it
was too late for him to protest; then I would call
in my own.

I made careful arrangements, and after the birth
pangs had begun I sent for him, for I knew that he
would not refuse to aid me. When peritonitis set
in he sent me to the hospital, and for the second
time in a few weeks I heard from his lips the words,
"There is no hope." He was talking to the nurse,
and I did not know that it was I of whom he was
speaking.

When my vigorous constitution conquered and I came slowly back to health without having the operation that had at first been thought unavoidable, he told me that I should have borne twin children if I had not interfered with the design of nature.

I laughed bitterly. "I fooled God that time, didn't I, Doctor? I refused to furnish the soil for the free nurture of the seed of life."

"Hush, Madeleine, you are talking sacrilege."

Within two months I was sound and well physically, but the dark veil of sorrow which had settled down upon me shut out all the joys of life. I was twenty-two years old, and life seemed over for me. The roots of my affections had been deep ones, but they had been torn violently up, and I was spiritually dead.

My little boy's death and my own illness had brought such heavy expenses that my bank-account was almost gone. I must earn my living, and so I went back to Allen's. But I had no ambition to make money.

When I tried to smile at men the smile froze on my lips. A few old friends came to see me, but the strangers, who looked at me curiously and asked countless questions about me, never sought my company, for I was that terrible incongruity, a living picture of Sorrow in a house dedicated to Joy.

My arms ached for the form of my beautiful son, and with strange perversity and inconsistency I mourned for the twin children that I had deliberately destroyed. I yearned for the infant who had died at birth and who was laid to rest in Kansas City. Baby faces stared at me from the corners of my room. Baby hands upon my face awakened me from my troubled sleep.

When I went out into the streets I passed familiar places that I had visited with my lover, and I began to yearn for the man whom I had driven from me. In his arms there were healing and comfort, yet I had struck him because in trying to comfort me he had taken me into his arms.

One night when Olga was singing in the ballroom the words of the song kept beating themselves into my brain until I began to repeat them under my breath:

> "Phantom footsteps just behind her
> Lightly patter on the green;
> Back she glances, while tears blind her,
> But no little one is seen."

I tried to get up from my seat in the alcove, but I could not move, though that terrible song was putting into words the thing that was crushing out my life. Those phantom footsteps that followed me wherever I went, those phantom voices that called to me, sleeping or waking.

Olga's clear, high voice took up the next stanza:

> "Phantom footsteps, hear them falling,
> Now wherever she may be.
> And a baby voice is calling,
> 'Mother, mother, wait for me.'"

Something galvanized me into life, and, walking over to the piano, I snatched the music from the rack and tore it into shreds.

Leaving the ballroom, I went up to my own room, with my heart burning with indignation against the unfaithful friend who had publicly mocked my grief.

A few minutes later Olga came bursting into my room. "Oh, Madeleine," she exclaimed, "can you forgive me? I did not know that you were in the ballroom. A fool man asked me to sing that song."

"A man asked you to sing it!" My anger almost choked me as I spoke. "What does any man know about phantom footsteps or phantom voices? What does any man know of anything but sexual gratification?"

"For Heaven's sake, Madeleine, do have some sense! Men are human beings. Don't let any one else hear the remarks you are always making about men being an unnecessary sex or they will think you are like French Lottie's women."

"You know how I hate men. What is the good of discussing it? Go away and leave me alone."

Olga sat down on the bed instead of obeying my order to leave the room. She did not care how angry I got, she had something to say and she would say it. "Madeleine," she began, "I am going to talk business with you before I go. You know what this life is. You are a woman of strong desires, who must come into daily contact with men, and your present attitude toward them is abnormal.

If there is anything out of place under the sun, it's a prostitute who hates men. I know how you feel about Baby's death and about your condition at that time, but that is no reason why you should go on hating all the men in the world. You will lose your mind if you don't brace up."

I did not want to discuss the matter; I only wanted to be left in peace, and I told her so. She lost patience with me altogether. "For goodness' sake, Madeleine," she snapped out, "come out of it. You've got to live, haven't you? You are not making your salt, and you give everybody in the house the willies. It's a wonder that Allen does not ask you for your room. She would not stand for any one else sitting around looking like an early-Christian martyr and not making their expenses. You had better take a drink once in a while and cheer up. Get a lover, play the races, or do something human. Why don't you go up to Winnipeg again this summer and let the wind blow the cobwebs out of your brain?"

"I was too happy last year when I was in Winnipeg. I could not stand the place now. I would be always thinking of my lost happiness."

"You talk as if you were forty instead of twenty-two. Tell me the truth. Don't you ever want to see Paul again?"

"Oh, Olga, I want him so badly, but he has never written to me since Baby died. He must hate me, for he cannot understand that I struck him because I was insane from grief and trouble."

"Don't you worry about Paul not understanding. I had a long talk with him before he left, and I found him the most 'understanding' man I have ever met. He is waiting for you to tell him that you want him. If you have any gumption you will pack up and go out there. You are not broke, are you?"

"Not quite," I answered. "I have about five hundred dollars left."

My bell rang and we had to go down-stairs, but I kept thinking of what Olga had said. Why not go? If Paul would forgive me, he would be my salvation. For with his help I could take hold on life again. I could not do it alone.

I turned the matter over in my mind for several days, and after I had decided to go I was filled with all my old-time impetuosity for doing things at once.

Twenty-four hours after I had made up my mind I was on my way to Butte, Montana.

CHAPTER V

SOMEWHERE west of Minneapolis I began to feel a lightening of the burden of grief that I had carried for so many months. Some part of my great love of the out-of-doors came into play as the train rushed through western Minnesota and eastern Dakota; for the young wheat had just begun to thrust its head above the earth, making the prairies one vast, tender, soft cloth of green.

Hour after hour I sat looking out of the car-window; but when the fields of growing wheat were left behind us and we had entered into the desolate Bad Lands I pulled down the blind. Their barren desolation brought too vividly to mind the waste desolation of my own heart.

The plains were behind us, and as the train labored upward into the mountains I lay in my berth watching the stars, which did not seem very far away. Somewhere in that vast starlit silence were the children that my heart cried aloud for, and as we ascended the mountain I felt very near to them, but it was a kindly, loving nearness that brought consolation and peace—altogether unlike the haunting presence which was always near me in Chicago.

206

AN AUTOBIOGRAPHY

The beliefs of my childhood were very close to me in those quiet hours. The mountains held a message for me that was as unlike the message of the prairies as they were dissimilar in outline. To me the prairies spoke of the awakening, and the joy of life, the will to dare to do, to live to the utmost. But the mountains were the ramparts of God.

From the sacred Mount of Sinai He had given unto Moses the law for His people. When He would deliver to mankind the sermon which was to ring down through all the ages until man should walk no more on earth, the Great Preacher had gone up into the mountain, thereby placing forever His seal upon the temple of His Father.

A great peace filled my turbulent heart, dispelling the sorrow and bitter pain which for months had darkened my life. To-morrow the aching pain in my arms would be easier to endure, because a train which was bearing me to a city where God was not had passed through the silent places where He dwelt with His little ones.

CHAPTER VI

IN the cab which took me to the hotel where Paul lived I speculated about his probable reception of me. Would he understand, and forgive that blow from a grief-crazed mother?

When I registered at the Butte Hotel I tried to ask for him, but my voice failed me. I had been guilty of presumption; he had not asked me to come. Suppose he should refuse to see me? Perhaps he no longer cared for me. No word had come from him since I had driven him from me.

In my room I walked back and forth until I could summon the courage to ring the bell and inquire for him. When the boy came up I asked him to find out when Mr. Martin would be in.

He returned in a few minutes to say that Mr. Martin was out of town and would not return for several weeks.

"Will not return for several weeks." I kept repeating the words after the boy had gone. Here was I, alone in this hole in the top of the world, and Paul would not return for several weeks. The shock of the disappointment was so great that I could not breathe. I walked over to the window and threw it up, but the sulphur-laden air which blew into the room caused me to close it again.

AN AUTOBIOGRAPHY

As I stood looking through the window at the hurrying throng in the street I wondered if I had not lost a day somewhere. I had thought it as Sunday, but surely I was mistaken, for men who wore the garb of labor hurried through the streets, carrying dinner-pails in their hands, and Chinamen with laundry baskets on their heads mingled with the crowd of alert-looking business men, debonair gamblers, pasty-faced pimps, overdressed shop-girls, and painted, gaudily garbed harlots.

From a near-by saloon there came the familiar sound of rag-time being pounded out on a wheezy piano, and high above the noise of the street arose the voice of the prompter in the corner dance-hall, "Take your pardner and promenade to the bar."

"The greatest mining-camp on earth," I remembered hearing a well-dressed man in the Pullman asserting about Butte to a party of women from the East. I was not sure what constituted a mining-camp, aside from taking ore out of the ground, but I half expected to see a band of savage Indians ride into that motley throng. I was thoroughly awakened from my self-absorption. I put on my hat and went down into the street to get a nearer view of "the greatest mining-camp on earth."

Although the day *was* Sunday, the big dry-goods stores were the only business houses which were closed. Clothing-stores, groceries, saloons, small dry-goods shops, cigar-stands, dance-halls, and variety shows, elbowing one another and wide open for business, gave a shock to mv sense of the fitness of things. I myself did not keep holy the Sabbath day, but my puritanical instincts revolted at the idea of outraging the feelings of those who did.

The strident chords of piano and violin which came from the saloons and dance-halls rivaled the din from the streets. Again rose the stentorian voices of the prompters with their incessant cries of, "Two more couples for the next quadrille," together with the cacophony which came through the swinging-doors of the pool-room: "They're off at Hawthorne! Wildfire in the lead!" "Rubicon against the field!" "It's a hundred-to-one shot you can't win. You're crazy with the heat!" "They're off at Oakland!" "Come on, you Rubicon!" And over all the discordant clamor there hung that awful, thick cloud of sulphur-laden smoke from the smelters, which made one gasp for breath and feel that the city itself with its rampant vice was an outpouring from the slag-pots of hell.

I turned into a side-street to get away from the noise, thankful to find a quiet spot in this horrible place where the sounds of vice did not penetrate, when from a window over my head I heard a loud, clear voice announcing, "She is seventeen, gentlemen, and a black one." I rushed back into the main street, with the belief firm in my mind that they were selling colored women at public auction in that up-stairs room.

When I returned to the hotel I almost walked over a man in the lobby, for my eyes and ears were filled with the sights and sounds of the street. I turned to apologize, and found myself confronting a man I had met some weeks before in Chicago. He had made very little impression on me at the time, but now a stray tomcat from Chicago would have been welcome, and I greeted him as effusively as if he were a long-lost friend.

"What in the world are you doing in Butte?" he inquired. "But pardon me, are you here with some one?"

"I came out to see the wild and woolly West, and I am alone."

"Good!" he answered. "I have to go to Missoula to-morrow, but I can show you the elephant to-night."

"I think I have seen him this afternoon," I said. And we sat down while I told him of my sight-seeing tour, personally conducted by myself.

He laughed as I told him of the auction of negro women, and explained that "seventeen and a black one" was a number on a roulette-wheel which had won. I had thought my experiences very thrilling, but the man assured me that I had not seen anything at all; and then, after a dinner in the Butte café, he took me out to see the night life of the town.

We did not tarry long in either of the two first-class houses. They were interesting only because I had not expected to see girls so well dressed nor houses so elaborately furnished in this out-of-the-way place. But the variety shows and the dance-halls were a source of wonder, and the "cribs" a source of horror to me.

MADELEINE

I had never seen the seamy side of the underworld in all the five years that I had belonged to it. I had never had any desire to see it, but in Butte it was underfoot at every step and there was no avoiding it even if we had not gone out for the express purpose of sizing it up.

Despite my shuddering horror, the sight fascinated even while it repelled me. It gripped me by the throat and forced me to examine it, even though I was sickened and faint at the horror of it. It filled me with many sad forebodings. I drew my skirts back from contact with the poor creatures who represented this seamy side of prostitution; I could not help it. I wanted to take them by the hand and tell them that I was one of them, but I could not touch them. I could barely touch my lips to the glasses of beer which they served.

In one place where the woman was at least forty my heart was so filled with pity that I urged the man to buy and buy, and when he would no longer order drinks I bought them myself, though I was not in the habit of spending money for booze. But this poor old creature, offering her body for sale, wrung my very heart-strings, and I was determined she should have at least one profitable night. But if my life had depended on it, I could not have fraternized with her, and when we left her place she came to the door and poured forth a stream of filth because I was a "stuck-up parlor-house tart." I did not blame her.

CHAPTER VII

A FEW doors farther down the street I heard some one calling my name; I turned, and was surprised to see a woman beckoning me from the doorway of a crib which we had just passed. As we came closer to her I recognized her as a girl who had formerly lived at Allen's.

She caught her breath with a sobbing intake as she shook hands with me, and I was so embarrassed I did not know what to say to her; for girls of the higher class, who have fallen into reduced circumstances, feel their position as keenly as do women in other walks of life; the social gulf between the first-class courtezan and those who have become the dregs of prostitution is as great as the gulf between the sheltered woman in her home and the street-walker.

When I had last seen this girl, two years before, she had been a star boarder at Allen's and one of the most beautiful women in Chicago. Her face was now so lined with the marks of dissipation and care that she looked ten years older than she had then.

When we had exchanged greetings I introduced my escort, who ordered drinks, and we girls sat down to compare notes, for this sad girl was hungry to talk with some one who had known her in her prosperous days. She begged me not to speak of her when I wrote to old acquaintances in Chicago, and I gave the desired promise.

I was curious to know how she, who had always been so successful, had come to this pass, and she answered my unspoken question by saying:

"It's the same old story, Madeleine. I got stuck on a gambler, who kept me for a while. I am keeping him now. In fact, that is the story of every crib woman. Those who never knew anything different are here because their first lover assigned them the task of supporting him, and the first-class women are here because they have fallen in love with some man whom they have to support if they want to hold him. No girl can meet the expenses in a big parlor-house and keep a man at the same time, even if the landladies would stand for a *macque* in the house, which they won't."

She then explained that she had gone out to Denver after leaving Allen's, and that there she had fallen in with a gambler with a "big roll" who had taken her out of the business and lavished money on her for several months. The previous year they had come out to Butte for the big race meeting, where he had lost all his money. She had pawned her furs and her jewels and given him the money in the hopes of making the "big killing" which every race-track follower looks forward to.

When she had nothing left to pawn she had gone into one of the two first-class houses in Butte.

At this point she had interrupted her story to ask me if I intended to "board" in Butte.

"No," I answered, "I came out West to get away from myself; I do not expect to go into a house here."

"Don't try it, Madeleine. It's a tough game in this town. The girls in the big houses are all hundreds of dollars in debt, with no chance to get out. Board is not high, because they pay twenty-five dollars a week straight. All the rest they make is theirs, which would be fine if they cleared anything over their board. But they don't, and the cost of clothes, and laundry, and cleaners' bills, and toilet articles— in fact, everything we use—is double the price it would be in Chicago. The girls are required to dress very elaborately, and when they get in debt they either have to stay or lose everything they have, because the landladies in the East will not send a railway ticket or pay a bill for a girl who has been out here any length of time. They seem to think that the girls in the West, especially in Montana, become tough after they have been here for a short time."

"I do not see why business is not good, if there are only two big houses. I never saw so many people on the streets and in the places of amusement; and at the hotel I saw so many well-dressed, prosperous-looking men that I concluded that any girl who was in business in Butte would have a gold-mine of her own."

"Forget it," said Norma, with an air of disgust.

"If you stay in Butte awhile you will discover that Montana liberality runs to buying booze and playing the races and 'stacking them up' on the high card; never to giving women a good price for their services."

"I don't understand that. In Chicago the men who spend the most money for drinks are those who pay a girl more than the price of the house."

"Well, you will find the contrary in Butte. I have known men to spend a hundred dollars for wine, and then want to stay all night with a girl for nothing. In Butte a girl can be wined and dined and entertained to her heart's content, if that kind of thing appeals to her, but she can't earn a living to save her life, nor call her soul her own, for the landladies own them. That's the reason why the first-class women go to the devil so fast when they get stuck in Butte. Take my advice and keep a little cozy corner in your pocketbook for the price of a ticket back to Chicago."

"I don't want to hurt your feelings, Norma, but I do not see how you can stand it. Think of going to bed with one of these unwashed beasts who are tramping up and down these alleys; think of sitting with your face in a window and having them pass along leering and peering, as if you were a part of a live-stock exhibition; and then think of receiving a dollar for entertaining the beasts."

"It isn't the dollar for our personal services that counts; it is the drink-money. We charge a dollar a bottle for beer, just as the big houses do. The

216

saloon that serves us takes twenty-five cents and we keep the remainder. We sometimes make a touch when a man is drunk and we think we can get away with it."

My escort, who had been listening with an expression of disgust on his face, now arose and cut short the conversation. We bade the girl good night, but after we had walked half a block I asked him to turn back with me; I wanted to ask Norma to have breakfast with me the following morning.

When we reached her window she was eagerly talking to a dirty, big laborer who was so drunk that he rolled from side to side, although he tried to steady himself against the window-casement.

Norma appeared embarrassed at having us see her companion, and the creature reached forth his dirty hands to grasp at me, but my escort prevented him. I gave the invitation, which was accepted, and I asked Norma to name the place, since I did not know the town. She made the appointment for two o'clock at the Chaquamegon and we hastened away, leaving her to "rope in" the drunk if she could.

We walked on in silence, for I was too heartsick for words, and my companion did not interrupt my thoughts until we turned into the main street and passed a decent-looking restaurant.

"Let's go in here and have something to eat before we go to bed," he proposed.

At the table he looked so long and earnestly at me that I grew nervous under his gaze. "Why do you stare at me so?" I asked.

MADELEINE

"Because I am trying to understand you, but you are too much for me. You remember the night I took you 'hopping' in Chicago a few weeks ago?"

"Yes," I answered, "but what of it, and why do you say I am too much for you?"

"It struck me that night that you were a haughty dame and a darn poor mixer. Or, as one of the other girls in the party said, you were not a good fellow. Yet here you pick up a low crib woman who by her own voluntary confession is a thief, and you invite her to break bread with you. I am wondering why you did it."

"I am sure I don't know," I answered, "but it all seemed so horrible and so hopeless to me, to think of a girl like Norma living in this way. She is only twenty-six and this is the beginning of the end for her. I can't express what I feel about it; my emotions and my thoughts are too chaotic; but this horrible town, and these awful streets of vice, with the women displayed like so much merchandise in the windows, while the endless procession of leering men of all races—whites, negroes, half-breed Indians, and Chinese—pass them in review, fills me with terror. Think of Norma having physical contact with that great, unwashed brute she was talking with when we came back to her. There are no depths of poverty nor stress of circumstances which could make me a thief, but I am not so sure that I would not become a murderess if I were forced to consort with such creatures. I thought I knew all the horrors of prostitution, but I have learned

218

to-night that I know very little about them. I have learned that there is a sheltered class, and that I belong to it, yet I would have laughed yesterday had any one spoken of 'sheltered prostitutes.'"

"But you can't do anything for this girl. Why do you harrow your own soul by association with her? The best thing for you to do is to break your engagement and forget her."

"Never! I know I can't help her, but I must stretch forth my hand; if not to draw her back, at any rate to let her know that somebody cares. It may be a premonition of what is coming to me that makes me want to be kind. I cannot say. It is something I have never felt before."

"Madeleine, it is a premonitory birth-pang of the social consciousness."

"What is the social consciousness?" I asked. "I never heard of it."

"It is summed up in the question you are now asking yourself. 'Am I my sister's keeper?'"

15

CHAPTER VIII

THE iniquities of Butte lay as heavily on my heart as if I alone had been responsible for them. Here was no kid-gloved vice with a silken veil across its face; but vice naked, raw, and rampant. The noxious fumes from the smelter became as pure ozone when compared with the vitiated moral atmosphere.

Day after day I lingered, fascinated yet frightened, in this upper chamber of hell, my soul racked and agonized by conflicting and contending emotions.

From the hotel clerk I learned that Paul Martin had gone to a remote part of the state on business connected with placer-mines in which he was interested, and that he would not return for several weeks. I wrote to him announcing my presence in Butte and telling him that I had come to Montana for the purpose of begging his forgiveness.

In great trepidation I awaited his answer, which came in the form of a telegram. "There is nothing to forgive," it read. "Come to me at once. Am anxiously waiting for you."

I made inquiries about the place, and learned that it was to be reached by a stage journey of seventy miles from the nearest railroad point, from which station the telegram had been sent.

I was wild with delight at the prospect of seeing Paul again. The thought of being alone with him filled my heart with a glow of joy. The mental picture which I drew of the tiny hamlet in the mountains appealed to my imagination as an ideal setting for our reconciliation. I was still at the age of romance and looked eagerly forward to the proposed journey by stage, not daunted by the stories of its discomforts.

The malodorous, ugly town held me in its grip. I wandered through its hideous streets, and in and out of the dance-halls and variety shows, buying drinks which I did not consume, but because it was the thing to do. Since there was nothing in my manner nor appearance which proclaimed me a member of the profession, I was an object of much curiosity to the *habitués* and of audible speculation on the part of the inmates.

I spoke only in answer to those who addressed me, but these were few, for my manner did not invite approach.

Returning to the hotel, I made futile efforts to reproduce in drawing some of the scenes which had held me spellbound, and equally futile attempts to put my impressions into words. My impotency to grasp and my inability to portray this living melodrama which was being enacted before my eyes caused me many bitter tears.

Why had nature given me the power to feel these things in every fiber of my being and then denied me the ability to express myself? I paced the floor in an agony which wrung great drops of sweat from my body, my hands clenching and literally tearing at whatever came within their grasp, as if in this senseless manner I could rend the invisible and intangible bonds which held my mind enthralled.

And because I, an untrained girl of twenty-two, could not produce a masterpiece I destroyed my work which mocked my puny efforts at self-expression and thereafter gave up the attempt. "A mustard seed which refused to grow because it could not become a stately oak."

In the early morning of a gloomy day I drove through the dirty streets on my way to the train which was to bear me out of the city which had gone mad of its own lust. Two days later I was in the heart of God's great out-of-doors with the man I loved, and Butte with its raw and rampant vice had become to me as the memory of a bad dream.

CHAPTER IX

THE little mining-town in which I was to spend several weeks was one of the first settlements in Montana, and in the early 'nineties it still preserved its primitive appearance. Except for the dredges on the creek, which had replaced the old-time rockers and gold-pans, everything about the camp still spoke eloquently of the early days when gold had first been discovered.

The straggling main street of the village which stretched out along the creek was lined on either side with great log buildings. Stores, residences, saloons, and the two rival hotels were all of logs. Many of these buildings were whitewashed, and one enterprising hotelkeeper had erected a brick addition to his log structure. This building presented a most incongruous appearance and formed a blot upon the landscape.

The one other street—which was in reality a road—led up through a cañon which bore the euphonious name of Hangman's Gulch.

When questioned about the name, the old-timers told me many thrilling stories of the events which led up to giving this beautiful cañon such a gruesome name. While their stories were widely at variance as to detail, they were agreed upon the fact that a former sheriff of that section had played the dual rôle of guardian of the place and leader of the road-agents who preyed upon the gold-seekers.

When the Vigilantes had secured undeniable proof of this double-dealing they relentlessly hunted down the man and his gang. Those members of it who were not killed in fights with the Vigilantes were captured and hanged in this gulch, the gibbet being a log beam which projected from the cabin occupied by one of the band.

Cattle-stealing had also been one of the early industries, and neither cattle-stealing nor highway robbery had entirely fallen into desuetude. As Butte was Montana's chief hotbed of vice, so this section was still the most lawless part of the state.

One desperado, who belonged to a family of "bad men," and women hardly less desperate, had been tried for nearly every crime on the calendar, including arson, murder, and incest. But, because of the fear of reprisals by his lawless family, few could be found to give evidence against him, and no jury could or would convict him. A few years later, when he tried his hand at counterfeiting, the United States performed the duty which the state dared not, and he was sent to prison for a long term of years.

As the name of Hangman's Gulch commemorated a phase of the history of the village and the state, so the name of Road-agents' Rock bore evidence of the early activities of this class of criminals. And the private conveyances which now carried out the gold-dust still went through to the railroad under the guard of armed men who gave Road-agents' Rock a wide berth.

The romance of the West held me in its grip, and to me this isolated hamlet in the mountains presented the most fascinating phase of Western life.

I stayed in the same hotel where Paul was living, but I seldom saw him before supper-time, for his days were busy days, and he was up and gone long before I responded to the call of the last bell for breakfast. Every night I resolved to join him at breakfast, but I was not accustomed to undisturbed slumbers nor to early rising. Now, when I went to bed, I wanted to kneel down and thank God that there was no lecherous man present to awaken me at his will, and the health-giving air of the mountains made me sleep like a little child.

I was an object of much curiosity to the natives, both as to my social status and my occupation. They were not long in discovering that I was Paul Martin's girl, and they soon concluded that I must be an Eastern school-teacher, for no one else could possibly be so eager for information nor ask so many questions. I rode horseback over all the trails in the country, dismounting to explore every abandoned mining-shaft or prospect-hole into which I could descend, risking life and limb upon the rotting timbers, and coming back with the inevitable questions upon my lips.

On a bleak, bare hill back of Hangman's Gulch I discovered an old burying-ground, which had long

since fallen into disuse. I tore away the weeds
which had overgrown the head-boards and found on
every one which was as yet decipherable the statement that the deceased had been massacred by the
Indians in the early 'sixties. Again I came back to
the village with my everlasting "Why?"

Why had they buried those persons on the top
of that bleak hill? Why had they not buried them
in the valley? But even the old-timers who had sur-
vived the massacre could not answer my question.

But the place of all places that I had the most
curiosity about was the creek from which the
dredges brought up the treasure, and that was forbidden ground.

I spent two months in this place in the mountains,
and they were among the happiest months of my
life, although my heart and my arms still longed
for the child who was gone. Olga had been right
when she had referred to Paul as an "understanding"
man. When I tried to explain my actions in
Chicago and to beg his forgiveness, he only smiled
at the idea that there was anything to forgive, and
we never discussed the matter again, though we
often talked of my little boy. Paul had much of the
paternal instinct, and he understood many things
of which we never spoke. It was this instinct that
made him shield me and shelter me in the bitter
years that afterward came to me. There were many
times when he ceased to be my lover, but never did
he cease to be a father when a father was what I
most needed. We hear much of the maternal

instinct which causes a woman to look upon the man she loves as her child as well as her lover, but I have known men in whom this instinct of parenthood was equally strong, and Paul was one of them.

We spent the long summer evenings together, talking over every conceivable subject but the one uppermost in my mind, that of our future together.

I spoke to Paul of my long-cherished dream of studying art, but he was filled with the idea of sending me to college. This idea did not appeal to me for several reasons. My hand was never at ease except when I was striving to portray the life that I saw around me. I had never received any training and my drawings were crude, but this was the one thing within myself that gave me the greatest pleasure.

Then, again, nothing could ever induce me to confess to Paul that I had not even been through grammar-school, for this deficiency in my education seemed to me a shameful thing. Through self-study I had acquired a wide knowledge of good literature and general history, but I could not have given the definition of many of the subjects required to enter high-school, to say nothing of trying to break into college.

On one thing I was determined: Paul should never know of my wretched childhood. And because of this determination eventually I built for myself a wall which kept me apart from him through many years; for when once he had conceived the idea of educating me he reverted to it again and again, until he thought that nothing but sheer perversity on my part prevented my going to college.

It was not strange that Paul failed to understand, for he had no way of knowing that to my mind poverty and ignorance were the cardinal sins, and that these accompaniments of my unhappy childhood were to be concealed at the cost of my future happiness, if indeed that were the price of secrecy.

However, I was now so happy with him that I was ready to dismiss the future. I snatched every moment of happiness until I could have cried aloud for joy. But in my supreme moment there came to me a haunting thought that would not be dismissed, try as I would to banish it. When I tried to formulate my thoughts and express to Paul the thing that troubled me I could not make him understand, because I myself did not understand the meaning of many things that are now clear to me.

The wonderful out-of-door life that I was living brought to me such a sense of the Infinite that there were moments when I felt that I stood in the presence of God. Oftentimes after a dash across the uplands I would dismount from my horse and stand looking at the panorama spread out "where the hand of God had hung it"; and then I would kneel down and press my face to the grass, the rocks, and the sage-brush.

But when these brief moments of bliss had passed they were followed by a reaction of sadness, for I stood in that Presence convicted not only of my own sins, but of the sins of all the sinners that I had ever known. And several times I found myself asking aloud, "Am I my brother's keeper?"

In some way the awful conditions which prevailed in Butte had awakened in me a sense of personal responsibility. I had always been deeply conscious of my own transgressions, but only as they tended to destroy me. I was not a "good mixer" and I had always held aloof from most of the women of my class, conscious of the sense of superiority. But since I had seen the dance-hall girls and the crib women of Butte I was filled with a great desire to take them all in my arms, to soothe them and comfort them and heal them.

Poor little fool that I was, I could not even heal myself.

About this time I received a letter telling me the story of one of the girls that I had known in Chicago. She had been, apparently, so corrupt that no thought of her redemption had ever entered the minds of those who knew her. Two years before she had startled us all by announcing that she was going to quit the business. We gave her a month as the longest possible time in which she could remain decent, but now at the end of two years she was still making good.

Of all the girls that I had ever known, she was the last one whom I should have expected to reform. But there was no doubt about it. When I read the story of her redintegration I began to realize something of the wonderful recuperative powers of the human soul.

Then I began to see, as through a glass darkly, that every fallen woman who is restored to decency means more than an individual redeemed. It means the healing of a contagious ulcer on the social body.

I expressed this thought to Paul, but he had the lie of the ages at his tongue's end, "Prostitution is a necessary evil." To be sure, he did not want me to be one of the burnt-offerings, but another man's sweetheart could serve without in the least disturbing his peace of mind.

CHAPTER X

AT the end of two months, when Paul went back to Butte, he took me with him. I had talked of returning to Chicago, but he wanted me to remain with him for another month. He still purposed to send me to college; and I still purposed to circumvent him, without giving the true reason.

I hoped and prayed that he would renew the proposal that he had made to me in Kansas City, but he said nothing which could lead me to believe that he still thought of it. I came to the conclusion that however much he cared for me he had no intention of again asking me to marry him.

I was to remain in a hotel in Butte, though not the one in which Paul was living, for we wanted to avoid scandal. I did not see him every day, as I had in the mountains, for in the city he had his own circle into which he could not take me. There was no longer the wonderful out-of-doors, for the sulphurous atmosphere of Butte precluded the enjoyment of open-air exercises. Time hung heavily on my hands, so that when I met an old acquaintance from Chicago I made the excuse to myself that Paul had neglected me for his society friends and that I was free to accept this man's invitation to dinner.

As we sat at dinner in the café of the leading hotel

my companion began a long-drawn-out story of a poker game in which he had sat the night before in this hotel.

This big game was in progress nightly and "the ceiling was the limit." The man asked me if I would like to witness the game. Women are barred from the card-room, but, as he remarked, "Everything goes in Butte, if you know the ropes." He could take me in if I cared to go.

I had no interest whatever in a poker game, but one thing was much like another in Butte. I had let myself "in for it" by going out with this man, and I thought it would be easier to shake him if he became interested in the game; accordingly, I accompanied him to the card-room.

After a brief parley at the door we were admitted to the room, and my escort began to explain the intricacies of "stud" poker.

Fifteen minutes after we had entered the room he had removed his coat, bought a stack of chips, and become oblivious to my presence. Since I was accustomed to being made much of by the men who were my friends, I was not flattered at being ignored for a poker game.

I was wondering if I could not slip out unobserved, when one of the players who was the greatest winner handed me a stack of chips, saying as he did so, "Try your luck, kid."

Instantly an onlooker offered to coach me, and I took the seat of a player who had "gone broke" a few minutes before.

AN AUTOBIOGRAPHY

The players had been drinking whisky, but some one ordered a bottle of champagne in my honor and the game went on. I did not know one card from another, so far as their value in the game went. When I got a five-spot in the hole, and on the next turn of the card drew a trey, the man who had constituted himself my tutor in the game told me to throw them in the discard, and I obeyed.

My stack of chips were worth twenty dollars, but they meant nothing to me, since they had cost me nothing. A few minutes later, when I had a nine-spot in the hole, my tutor told me to "stay," and I pushed in a bunch of chips, unconsciously raising the ante. This struck the other players as good sportsmanship on my part, and they all "stayed" with me.

On the next turn of the cards I drew a king. The dealer said, "You are high with the king; it's your bet first," and I bet the remainder of my chips. The other players called me, and the game went on.

On the next turn I drew another nine, but could not bet again, since I was "all in." One man had two jacks in sight, and was making side bets with another player. On the fourth turn this man drew an ace and "bet his head off." His opponent dropped out, and when the dealer turned over the last card I drew the third nine. I had almost forgotten my escort's existence, when he recalled himself to my attention by telling me that I had won a "fat pot" and it was up to me to buy a bottle of wine.

I bought the wine, and then because I was winner
the game assumed great interest for me. When I
arose from the table at four o'clock in the morning I
was two hundred and twenty-five dollars ahead of the
game. This was partly due to "fool's luck" and
partly to the generosity of the other players, who
could have broken me if they liked.

When I returned to my room I found Paul, white
with jealousy and rage, pacing up and down the
room. When I came in he walked up to me and,
placing his hands on my shoulders, said in an even
voice, though his eyes snapped like steel, "Madeleine,
where in the world have you been, and is there anything you want to tell me?"

I knew what he meant, but that was not the thing
that I had to tell. I related the experiences of the
night, and instantly his face softened as he realized
the truth of my story. However, he at once began
to lecture me on the evils of gambling. "This vice
is worse than whisky, Madeleine; promise me that
you will never play again."

I was ready to give the promise, for I did not
think that I had been caught in the toils, and Paul
kissed me and went out.

Since "everything went" in Butte, he could visit
my room whenever he liked, or stay as long as he
liked, and I was sorry that he had not chosen to
remain. But I did not waste much time in thinking
about it, for daylight was breaking as I tumbled
into bed.

A few days later, disregarding my promise to Paul,

I went "down the line" and won a hundred dollars at roulette, and with this winning I placed upon myself shackles which held my soul in bondage for many years. I played poker, roulette, faro, the races, or anything else on which money could be staked. There were times when I would have sold Paul for a stack of red chips.

I had escaped the usual vices of my class, liquor and drugs, only to fall a victim to as great an evil.

CHAPTER XI

WHEN Paul discovered that I had broken my word to him he was furious and he gave me a curtain-lecture that left my ears tingling. I had violated my word to him and he found it very hard to overlook. A little later he relented of his harshness, though I richly deserved all that he had said.

I renewed my promise never to gamble again, and once more matters ran smoothly between us. But a week later I heard of a system to "beat the wheel," and I went into one of the open gambling-houses and lost every dollar I had. Paul had kept me abundantly supplied with money, and on that day he had given me fifty dollars. When I left the gambling-house I did not have the price of my dinner.

It was the first time that I had ever been completely broke since I had been in the "business," and I could hardly realize that I did not have a penny in the world. I dared not confess to Paul that I had again broken my word to him.

I could easily have made more money if I had chosen to take the easiest way, but with the picture of Paul in the background the thought of doing so was abhorrent to me. At any rate, I would not deceive him in that way. I pawned a valuable ring, and tried to keep my peccadillo a secret from him.

I attempted to appear unconcerned, but I did not succeed in deceiving Paul. He knew that something was troubling me, and then he missed my solitaire, for he had a great admiration for my hands and a fashion of caressing them.

This time he sat very silent after I had confessed the truth. Then he kissed me very gently and went out without saying anything. In an hour he called me up to say that he was sending me some money by messenger and that I had better redeem my ring.

He stayed away for three days, and I was in an agony fearing that I had lost him. Then I received a note from him saying that he would not again ask me not to gamble, since he did not believe in putting a premium on lying. But he hoped that I would feel free to tell him the truth and to come to him when I needed money instead of going to a pawnshop.

I soon returned to the roulette-wheel, though why I played was as great a mystery to me as it was to the onlookers.

It must have been for the sake of the game, for, in the words of one of the interested bystanders who watched me break the bank and then lose hundreds of dollars against a twenty-dollar bill that the dealer took from his pocket: "You were not playing to win. You were only trying to see if you would keep your own money or give it to the dealer."

Then, because I would not ask Paul to keep on

paying my gambling debts, and because I would not remain with him and make money in the easiest way, I left him and went East again.

For the next three or four years I wandered over the face of the earth, always finding that the place I was in was the one place where I did not want to be.

I saw them all, the "lost sisterhood" of the nations. I met them in Europe and in the Orient; in Canada and in Mexico. And I met more American women than those of any other nation, for they were in every city and every land that I visited.

I met the public prostitute, the clandestine prostitute, and the occasional prostitute. I met the trusting girl who had been betrayed, and the unfaithful wife. I met the college woman, and the illiterate child of the slums. I met the deserted wife and the wife of the profligate; the girl from the sheltered home and the girl who had been allowed to run wild; the girl who had sold her honor for bread, and the girl who had sold it for luxury and fine clothes. I met the girl who should have been a nun, and those others who were "predestined by ancient conditions" for the life of a harlot.

But the one girl I never met in all these years and in all the cities and the countries that I visited was the pure girl who had been trapped and violated and sold into slavery, and held a prisoner unable to effect her escape—the so-called "white slave."

Because I had more intelligence than the average harlot I was enabled to go into many places that they could not enter, and to make money in many ways not open to them. But whenever I found myself up against a blank wall I came back to Paul or he came to my rescue.

At length I went to live with him, and after this I gambled no more. For one year I had much happiness, mingled with much sorrow and bitterness; for we belonged to different spheres of life, and we had but the one point of contact, our love for each other. And that was not great enough to cover the multitude of disparities between us.

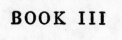

BOOK III

CHAPTER I

WHEN I went up into the Canadian Northwest, after a prolonged and bitter quarrel
with Paul, I had planned to remain for six weeks
and then go on to New York, but the six weeks
lengthened into six years before I again took up my
residence in the United States.

Two years before, Nona Blake, one of my few
intimate friends, had gone up into that country and
opened a house of ill fame. With a small place
and but three girls, she was doing a phenomenal
business and piling up a bank-account which gave
her gratified astonishment every time she contemplated it.

It was not, however, the stories of her commercial
success which induced me to make Nona a visit;
it was the lure of the "Just Beyond" which caused
my vagrant feet to turn in a northerly direction.
To my mind, the Canadian Northwest represented
a land of great adventure, an unexplored country
in which there was something hidden from me;
when once I had heard the call of it my restless heart
could know no peace until I had gone "to search
behind the ranges."

I left Helena, where I was living at the time,

and went up to Great Falls in Montana on the first lap of the journey into Canada.

After a night spent in a comfortable hotel in Great Falls, I departed in the early morning, over the narrow-gage railway which ran up into Canada and was familiarly known as the "Turkey trail."

The mixed train, consisting of freight, empty coal-cars, and one passenger-coach, dragged itself wearily along, making long stops at the isolated stations, apparently from sheer exhaustion.

The agent in Great Falls had told me that there was a station on the line where the train stopped for lunch, but when one-thirty came without our having reached the place, I consulted the conductor about the prospect of getting something to eat. He offered me a part of his own lunch, saying, as he did so, that we were already two hours behind time and there was no telling when we might reach the lunch-station. He gravely assured me that this road which led across the arid, desolate plains of Montana and the equally barren plains of southern Alberta was the worst railroad in the whole world, barring none. And I agreed with him.

There was no way in which one could mitigate the discomfort of the trip unless one partook of the booze which circulated freely among passengers and train-crew. These community bottles were replenished at every stopping-place, for the country through which we traveled was as long on whisky as it was short of water.

Since I was the only woman passenger, many

apologies were offered me for this free indulgence; but, as one expansive commercial traveler declared, it was the only way to forget the "Turkey trail."

It was eight o'clock that night when we reached the Canadian boundary, where we made a long stop for the customs examination of freight, and where we sat down to something that was miscalled a meal. It was midnight when we reached Lethbridge in southern Alberta, where I was to change to the Crow's Nest Pass Railway.

As I dragged my exhausted body from the train I was nearly swept from my feet by the terrific force of a wind which seemed to blow from all points of the compass at once. And as I went into the ill-smelling, crowded waiting-room I execrated my folly in coming to explore these wilds. A three hours' wait in the dirty, uncomfortable waiting-room at Lethbridge did not improve my disposition. Another change of cars and a prolonged wait at Macleod still further ruffled my temper, until I envied those passengers who had found relief in whisky.

After I had eaten a fairly good breakfast the world seemed brighter, although the wind had increased in violence, until it seemed that the cars must be blown from the track.

I was told that Macleod was the windiest place on the Pass.

We did not, however, leave the wind behind us in Macleod, for it was still blowing a gale when we arrived in Calgary. But the Calgarians indignantly repudiated the wind. It did not belong; it was unusual. Of course, the wind always blew in the Crow's Nest Pass, and in Macleod, which was at the foot of the Pass, but *not* in Calgary.

When at length I reached my destination, and was met at the train by Nona Blake, there was still no diminution to the fury of the wind. As we drove out to Nona's place, which was three miles from the town, the carriage rocked and swayed in the wind until it was in imminent danger of being blown over. But Nona, who was thoroughly imbued with the spirit of the country, denied that there was much of a wind.

"Had I noticed the wind in Macleod? If I wanted to talk about wind, I might speak about that place, for it was well known that Macleod was the windiest place in Canada."

Before I had been six months in the Northwest I, too, had adopted this attitude, and was ready to do battle with any tenderfoot who complained about the wind, and to make the inevitable comparison.

And, anyway, the wind did blow harder in Macleod.

Nona's home was a ramshackle old ranch-house, furnished with a view to producing the greatest possible offense to the eyes and the last degree of discomfort to the body.

The wall-paper was torn and discolored, and the plaster had fallen from the ceiling in many places. The carpets, from which the pattern had long since been worn away, were ragged in spots, with only a few upstanding tufts of nap to bear witness that in a better day they had been Wiltons. Apparently the mattresses were stuffed with brickbats, and the springs on the beds sagged down until they swayed like hammocks; again, there was not a comfortable chair in the house.

On account of the difficulty of getting laundry done the dining-table was covered with a white oil-cloth, on which was placed a miscellaneous assortment of cracked china, and tableware splotched with occasional flecks of silver. proving that it had once been plated.

Nona had always been a "first-class" woman, living in the most luxurious houses, and I could not understand how she could endure such squalid surroundings, when for a thousand dollars she could at least have made the house habitable.

When I spoke to her about this she explained that no woman could bank on being allowed to remain in that country, and since a thousand dollars was a great deal of money, she preferred to have it within reach in the bank rather than tied up in a house that she might have to leave at a moment's notice.

Nona's three girls—all old-timers with the marks of age and vice and alcohol ineradicably stamped upon them—were a living refutation of the "statistics" which prove that the life of the scarlet woman is ended in seven years.

Not one of these women could have competed in the open market with the younger members of her profession, but here in this new country where hundreds of single men were hungering for feminine society they were making a great deal of money.

Notwithstanding that the actual cost of living was exceedingly high, the cost of running the place was not great, for Nona herself served the drinks, one of the girls played the old piano, which had four soundless keys, and a Chinese servant did the general housework. Each girl took care of her own room.

The time was late in September, but the icy wind which swept in from the mountains found every crack in the old house, and it was impossible to keep warm. Loosened boards on the outbuildings flapped in the wind; and this sound, mingling with the fearful shrieking of the wind, wore nerves and tempers into fiddle-strings.

The girls cordially invited me to join them in trying to "beat the climate with booze," but their invitations did not find me responsive.

The trade of the house, while highly profitable, was sporadic, and there were days and nights when no one came near the place. Then a wild horde of savages would sweep in from the cattle-ranches or the town, and tear things open, figuratively and actually. Or perhaps some one man with a big roll of money would stroll in and "buy up the house."

But the in between times left the women to sicken of one another's society; to quarrel constantly, drink heavily, and count the days until they should be able to return to the States with a fat bank-account.

At the end of ten days I told Nona that I could not stand the discomfort and the monotony, to say nothing of the drunken women, the savages, and the climate. I was going on to New York, but first I intended spending a few days in Banff.

Nona tried to induce me to remain for the six weeks that I had contemplated when I came to Canada; for she, too, was tired of the drunken women and the savages, and I helped to bring her relief from the monotony. As to the climate, she assured me that if I would wait until after the equinoctial storms were over I would find it one of the most glorious climates in the world.

But I had been spoiled by soft living, and I could not long endure discomfort. Furthermore, no one could convince me that the wind would ever stop blowing. Still, since I was in that God-forgotten country, and wanted to visit Banff before returning to civilization, I would endure it another week while I made the proposed trip to the mountains.

Nona protested against my going to Banff, for she believed that I should get into trouble if I went there. Sporting women were not permitted to stop in the hotels in that country, and if I attempted it I would get a six months' job scrubbing floors for Queen Victoria.

I threw up my head and asked her if she knew of any reason why I should publicly proclaim my profession. I had never done so in my life; there was nothing in my manner or appearance that proclaimed it; and I had always gone where I liked and stopped at the best hotels or wherever else I chose. I intended to do the same in Canada or any other country on earth.

Nona insisted that I had no knowledge of the implacability of the Northwest Mounted Police. Other American women had gone up into that country, believing that they could do anything they liked, and several of them were confined in different police barracks at that very moment. I had better take warning.

"That is because they are fools and cannot behave themselves," I answered. "I don't belong to that class. I am quite ready to take my chance with the Mounted Police. No doubt they are a terror to criminals, but I am neither a criminal nor a fool, and I have long ago discovered that men are very much alike under their uniforms. If a woman bears the outward marks of respectability, plus brains and a knowledge of men, she has nothing to fear from the sternest of them."

Nona was not satisfied, but she waived further responsibility. "Go if you like, Madeleine," she added, warningly. "You may get away with it, since nobody ever takes you for a sport, but I am telling you that you are taking a big chance."

"Don't worry about me; there is no danger of my getting into trouble; I don't look the part," I retorted.

It was not an idle boast. I never either then or at any other time had my profession suspected by those who met me outside the market-place.

I was at this time twenty-eight years old, but I looked much younger, and nothin either in my manner or appearance branded me as a fallen woman. The most acute observer had never detected it. The previous year I had been with Paul in Minneapolis, and on meeting in the street one of the girls whom I had known in Chicago I promised to call on her. A few days later I went across the river to the address given, and as I stood on the corner wondering in which direction I should go a policeman came along. I stopped him and asked him where I should find No. 25. He looked at me sharply for a moment, then asked, sternly, "Young woman, do you know what kind of a place that is?"

I hesitated for a moment, shamed as usual at not being able to live up to my appearance of purity, and then answered him: "Oh yes, I know. It is a young women's boarding-house, isn't it?"

The policeman smiled indulgently. "I knew from your appearance," he said, "that you did not know the character of the place. Girl, that house is one of the most notorious bawdy-houses in Minneapolis."

In the face of this it was impossible for me to go into the house. Because that man believed in my decency, and because I believed him to be a real guardian of the peace, I could not disillusion him. I went back across the river.

At times I tried to live up to this appearance of respectability; at other times I tried to live it down. I never quite succeeded in either effort. But some inner sanctity which remained undefiled by my mode of life kept from my face the brand of infamy. My own conscious will kept my speech and manner free from contamination; and because of these things I knew that I could go wherever I liked and not be subjected to questioning.

Therefore, I went up to Banff and crept a little nearer to God for a little while. The mountains were still to me a temple, where I went not to pray, but to feel the touch of the Infinite.

Then, because I was in a softened mood, I wrote a long letter to Paul, pleading for a better understanding between us. There was no doubt about his love for me, and, since this was true, why could he not take me as I was? Why could he not recognize me as an individual with a mind and a soul of my own and cease from his efforts to remold me?

At the end of my month in Banff I had decided to remain in the Northwest Territory, for here was the land of opportunity. With a small capital I could open a house in some one of the busy towns, and in two years have a working capital of twenty thousand dollars. I would then be independent.

In the nature of things I should lose Paul some day. Notwithstanding our love, our lives had been led apart except for a few brief weeks of nearness, which only made our apartness seem wider. We had lived in the same house with a world of misunderstanding between us. And we had lived on different continents when the understanding between us was so great that we seemed to be holding hands, for both of us had the disposition and the power to forget all unpleasantness, once it was over.

During the past ten years I had traveled thousands of miles to be with him, and he had crossed the continent and the Atlantic once when I greatly needed him; but in the end the wall always rose between us.

Paul had other ties and other interests into which I could never enter; and on my part, no man could ever fill my life, no matter how much I might care for him.

It was part of Paul's paternal nature which made him want to guide and direct the woman he loved. It was my nature to find a trail for myself, no matter what the cost might be. If I went out into the mountains, and two trails lay before me, one of which was cleared and blazed and the other narrow, dim, overgrown with underbrush and almost impassable and leading no one knew where, I invariably took the unmarked trail.

Paul was conventional to the core, and he would follow no path which had not been marked out and trodden by the members of his own class.

We could never hope to be any nearer than we were at present. Some day Paul would marry, and I must then depend upon myself. I was getting into the old-timer's class, notwithstanding my youthful appearance. If I ever intended to have any money of my own, I must grasp my chance in this land of opportunity.

Having settled the matter to my own satisfaction,

MADELEINE

I left Banff and went up to Edmonton, seeking a location.

I did not find what I wanted, but I heard of a place in which the Mounted Police had closed the houses two years before because the women had made themselves so conspicuous that the citizens objected to their presence in the town; and because the Mounted Police would not tolerate the *macques* who had begun to infest the place. After two years the business men had raised an objection to the "closed town" because of the decrease in business. They attributed this to the fact that the town had no attraction for the hundreds of single men employed in various capacities in that section. They maintained that as soon as the men drew their money they went to one of the neighboring towns to spend it.

Partly because of this pressure from the business men, but mostly on account of matters that had come under his own observation, the commandant of the Mounted Police had decided to let one house open in the place, if the right woman applied for the privilege.

There were many dissolute squaws and half-breed women in this section, and the O. C. had discovered among his own men an alarming increase in venereal diseases, undoubtedly from these sources. He believed that a house which could be put under medical supervision was the lesser of two evils.

My informant was one of the leading professional men in this town, thoroughly familiar with the situation, and he gave me the full details. I took the first train to the place, which I shall call Malta, because it is not the name.

I saw the commandant of the Mounted Police and the chief of the Municipal Police, and I found that I could open a place; so long as I ran it in an orderly manner I would not be disturbed. The O. C. warned me against investing too much money, because of the severe penalty for selling liquor without a license. For the first two offenses there was an increasingly heavy fine; for the third offense a long term of imprisonment. The police would not take official cognizance of any violation of the law unless a complaint was made by some citizen or hotel-man. The hotel-men were the sole licensed purveyors of liquor and they were the persons most likely to complain.

I must expect sooner or later to pay a fine, but after the second offense I must leave Malta, for the third meant prison, and I must not stay to take the chance. If I got along without any trouble, it might be a year before any complaint was made.

This head of the Mounted Police was a stern man, thoroughly dreaded by all classes of offenders, and held in awe by his own men; but he was clean, and unbribable. I knew that if I played fair with him I could expect his protection so far as he was able to extend it.

There was a bitter rivalry between the Mounted Police and the municipal authorities, and each suspected the other of unspeakable corruptions. As I turned to leave the barracks the O. C. called me back to say, impressively, that if any officer, of either the municipal or Mounted Police, tried to exact graft money, I was to report the matter to him at once.

I gave the required promise, which I knew would be impossible to keep, and went out with a full knowledge that I should pay graft, not to him nor to his men, but to the municipal officials. I had already settled that matter.

I negotiated a loan on my jewels, and then made a big payment on an eight-room house, which stood alone on the prairie half a mile from any other habitation, but within the corporate limits of the town. Before I could take possession of this house I would have to complete the payment.

I telegraphed to Paul for a thousand dollars, saying that I was sending particulars by mail. I received a message in return saying, "What do you think I am, a bank?" But he sent the money.

When he got my letter he began bombarding me with telegrams of protest. At length a message came saying that he was on his way to see me and asking me to meet him in Lethbridge.

I reached Lethbridge an hour in advance of the train on which he was to arrive, and I came prepared to do battle for the right to do as I liked. But when Paul stepped from the train I saw by the expression on his face that he had come, not to command, but to plead.

I knew that he was hurt to the core, for, in common with many other persons, he looked upon the keeper of a house of ill fame as a modern Moloch who could be appeased only by the souls of the women victims who fell into her insatiable maw.

As soon as he had greeted me he said, tenderly: "You are coming home with me, Madeleine. I will never stand for your doing this thing you are contemplating."

I could combat his sternness, but the most difficult thing in the world for me to withstand was his tenderness. I had always been as wax in his hands when he chose that method of managing me.

But now my mind was fully made up. I would never sit quietly down, waiting for him to grow tired of me and discard me. I had seen it too often when some woman of the underworld loved a man in a different station of life. Sometimes it was many years in coming, but the final rupture was inevitable.

I endeavored to make the matter clear to him, but, like all other men, he believed that he would never change. He had cared for me for ten years; he had gone to Europe to find me and bring me home when I was sick and friendless; he had paid my gambling debts times without number; and he had never refused me anything within reason that money could buy. What was it that I wanted?

All this he said to me as we walked up and down the station platform at Lethbridge, waiting for a train on the Crow's Nest Pass line. I had told him that we were going up to a little resort in the Crow's Nest Mountains to spend Sunday.

As I looked at him, tall and strong, with his plain

face drawn by the pain which I was bringing him, my heart wavered, for he represented the best that had ever come into my life. Without him I might have been—but I drew a veil across the depths to which I might have sunk without his constant friendship and understanding.

The separation was as painful to me as it was to him, but I saw no other way. I wanted to be free to follow my own path, let it lead where it might. And generous as he had always been about money, dependence carried a sting which I could not forget. I wanted to be financially independent.

We talked of all this on the train, but we were no nearer to an understanding than at first. After I told Paul that I had already bought the place, pawning my jewels to raise a part of the money, he said no more for a time.

I had been told that this resort in the Crow's Nest Mountains was a beautiful place to spend a few days; this was true if one wanted only scenery. But the hotel accommodations were vile—poor food, poor beds, and no heat except in the dining-room. As there was no train on Sunday, we had to remain, and it did not make us any less unhappy because we were acutely uncomfortable.

We went up to Calgary on Monday, and then Paul renewed his importunities. I should have no trouble in disposing of the place I had bought. But I was not to be persuaded. At last, in desperation, he turned to me. "For God's sake, Madeleine," he exclaimed, "don't go into this nefarious business!

Come home to Montana with me, and we will be married."

I could hardly keep from smiling at Paul's idea that marriage would prove a cure for our incompatibility, but I refrained because I knew he was deeply in earnest.

We parted the next night in Calgary, and as his train was pulling out from the station he held out his hands to me. "Come home with me, Madeleine," he pleaded. "Life is pretty blank without you."

As I walked beside the train, which was moving slowly, I shook my head. "I can't do it, Paul," I protested; "it's too late."

CHAPTER II

THE first acquisition to my new household was Fawn Kee; after his name I write the words: Christian, gentleman, and friend.

I had been seeking for a Chinese house-boy to help me get the place in order, but for one reason or another I had rejected all applicants. This one was too "fresh," that one was too dirty or in some other respect undesirable. I was ready to abandon the search when I dropped into a Chinese restaurant for lunch.

The waiter who took my order was so clean that he presented the appearance of having recently been scrubbed with Sapolio, and he served me with such deftness that he drew from my purse a generous tip. He bowed almost to the floor as he held out my coat for me, and hope returned again. Perhaps somewhere else in these wilds there was another such as he. I asked him if he knew where I could get a good cook who was clean and honest.

All his white teeth glistened as he turned his beguiling smile upon me.

"All China boy honest," he answered, "but not all China boy good cook. I likee good job. You likee habee me?"

I assured him that I should be delighted to have

him, asking him where he had worked and if he could cook.

He poured forth a flood of broken English in which he extolled his own virtues. "I come from Vlictory. I good cook, work for before lady slix years. I no talk lie, no sass, no cheatee, no glit flesh, keep house clean. What you pay?"

In the face of so much virtue I offered good wages and engaged him on the spot. He came to me that afternoon.

I had furnished the house well, but not expensively, though everything had been bought with a view to comfort as I knew it. I had not much idea what to get for the kitchen, never having been in one since I left home.

After Fawn Kee had explored the house he came to me with a saddened look upon his face and then proceeded to explain the cause of his dejection.

"Nice dining-loom. Belly nice parlors, pletty nice bedloom. Not muchee good kitchen. Come, I show you."

I meekly followed him while he pointed out the deficiencies of my kitchen, and as meekly I placed the matter in his hands, telling him to have the kitchen fixed up to suit himself and order whatever he liked.

My weak yielding to Fawn Kee's wiles cost me one hundred and fifty good American dollars, but it won me a friend who was unwavering in his devotion.

I had told him that my household would consist of four women, three others and myself. I was wondering if he understood the situation, when he came to me, his work being finished, and with the utmost confidence asked me to help him with his reading lesson. His "before lady in Vlictory" had been teaching him to read English, and he took it as a matter of course that I should do the same.

I hardly knew what to say, and in order to gain time I asked to see his book, which I found contained simple lessons from the Bible.

There was nothing for it but to make him understand the incompatibility of my profession with Bible-teaching. I tried to envisage an American harlot as a missionary to the heathen, but I did not enjoy my mental picture.

Turning away from the trustful eyes which had regarded me as a Christian and a lady, I told Fawn Kee as well as I could what the business of the house was to be. When I had finished he nodded his head, saying, "Oh yes, I sabee, you keepee ladies' house," and in no other terms did he ever refer to the business. A little later he came back to say: "I tellee you about Jesus. You no sabee him?"

Fawn Kee's idea of Jesus was not that of a Divine Being, but of an upright man—"allee same Confucius"; a man kind and tender, a good friend; in short, a gentleman who could "no talk lie, no glit flesh, no cheatee"—and Fawn Kee lived up to the spirit and the letter of his belief, so far as we of the household were concerned. But he would deny all knowledge of English or lie until he was black in the face to protect one of us.

Throughout the Canadian Northwest, from Winnipeg to Vancouver and from the American boundary to the farthermost outpost of transportation, every town and hamlet was a port of missing women, or the wrecks of women, time-battered derelicts who had drifted up from the States seeking an undiscovered harbor. But these derelicts, far from being water-logged, were usually sodden with whisky.

When it became known that there was a new house about to be opened in Malta, which was the center of a rich wheat-growing and cattle country, these women began pouring in to see me. I could have opened a full-fledged dance-hall had I been able to accommodate all who came. But I would not have tried to live in the house with these poor creatures for all of the gold that ever came out of the Caribou.

Victoria was Queen of the "Dominion Beyond the Seas" and her picture held the place of honor in every hotel parlor and public building, but Alcohol was the uncrowned King, and few women remained long in the country without coming under his dominance.

I sent down into the States after three girls that I knew, young, attractive girls, not overly given to the use of liquor; and late in November I opened my place of business. The afternoon was like a mid-September day in the Middle West, for, as Nona Blake had predicted, a glorious Indian summer had followed the equinoctial storms. But by nightfall the wind was blowing a gale and the air held a promise of the coming snowstorm. I was keenly disappointed at the change in the weather, for I felt it was inauspicious for the opening of business, but I was mistaken.

As soon as it was dark the men began to arrive in buggies and in hacks, in hotel buses, on horseback, and afoot—men of all sorts and conditions, gentlemen, hoodlums, and all the gradations between. There were railroad men and bank officials, cowpunchers and professional men, wheat-growers and business men, Mounted Police in mufti, bartenders, clerks, and most of the male choir members of the English church. Inside of an hour after my house was opened I had discovered that I could make no social distinctions. If I did not want the house torn from its foundations, I would have to admit any white man who came to the door.

I had no thought of running a "hurdy-gurdy" nor of mixing patrons who had not come to the house together; therefore, when both parlors, the dining-room, and even the kitchen were occupied I began trying to turn men away. But it was no use, they simply brushed past me and came in.

Each party was overflowing with good-fellowship for their own members and for us women, but decidedly inimical to the others. All were united in their hostility to the Mounted Police—until one big policeman captured the piano and began to sing in a voice to "charm the birds from the trees"; then the hatchet was buried, for the evening at least.

I had done my best to keep the different parties separated, but I could as easily have stopped the blizzard which was gathering outside. When the

264

more exclusive visitors discovered that there could be no privacy they departed, after telling me that I should have to manage better if I intended to make a success of my business. The "wild bunch" had previously given me the same advice when I had tried to exclude them. If I was going to put on airs and cater only "to dudes and big bugs," I could count them out; that is, unless they decided to take possession of the house.

By midnight the three girls were drunk, and, as the only sober person in the house, I was going about trying to keep peace between the different men who were contending for them. Many of the customers thought me more desirable than the girls and were trying to buy me outright. I managed to evade the issue by showing them how impossible it was at that time and by making promises for future delivery, which promises I had no intention of keeping.

I had laid in a stock of liquors sufficient, as I had supposed, for a week, but by three o'clock in the morning there was not a drop of liquor in the house, outside of the skins of the imbibers. All the men had departed except those who were to remain for the night; but before they left one drunken and disgruntled customer, whose money had failed to get him a girl, hurled a lamp through one of the parlor windows, and the storm which had now become a blizzard came sweeping through the "banquet-hall deserted," with the snow piling up in heaps over carpet and furniture.

I was nearly swept from my feet as I closed the

MADELEINE

hall door behind the last departing guest. All the others had gone to bed. Fawn Kee had left the house after the midnight lunch, for I had no place for him to sleep, and, to all practical purposes, I was alone in the house, to prepare for what proved to be the worst blizzard the country had ever known.

I made no attempt to go to bed, but, having removed my evening gown and donning a warm bathrobe, I went from basement to kitchen, then to the big base-burner in the hall, and back over the same route, shaking down the grates and piling in the coal.

At eight o'clock I could no longer stand the loneliness, and I awakened one of the girls and her bedfellow. They sat up in bed, holding their swollen heads and clamoring for a drink. But I had neither drink nor sympathy to give them, for I myself never drank to excess and I could not understand the horrible craving for it on the "morning after."

I insisted upon their getting up and helping me to keep the house warm. After the man had fully awakened he began to swear loud and long. When I inquired into the cause of this outbreak he announced that it was Sunday morning and that he was the leader of a church choir.

I told him if he would harken to the noise of the elements he need have no uneasiness about the congregation's missing him on that day, for they would not be at church.

A little later, when the others had been awakened by the fury of the storm, we girls went out into the

266

kitchen to prepare breakfast. The men had tried to leave the house, but they came back in a few minutes, declaring that it meant their lives if they got ten feet from the door.

It was the first time in my life that I had been faced with the necessity of cooking a meal, and I did not know how to go about it. I was ashamed to confess this, but one of the girls, seeing my awkwardness, came to my rescue, and we had a bountiful and well-cooked meal.

For three days we were marooned. I turned my house into a life-saving station and kept the lights burning all night. Four wayfarers lost on the prairie saw the light and came to us. It is certain they would have perished had they not seen it. One at a time they straggled in, and we nursed their frost-bitten feet and hands and shared our food with them.

Fortunately for us, Fawn Kee was a good provider and had laid in a sufficient supply of food. But the furnace and the stoves ate up the coal so rapidly that I was beginning to have visions of freezing, when the storm began to subside.

I seemed to have gone through ten years in those three days, and it was many months before the terror of them faded from my memory.

CHAPTER III

THE first person to reach us after the storm had abated was faithful Fawn Kee, who came floundering through the huge drifts bearing a basket almost as big as himself.

When we had disentangled him from his manifold wrappings we found that his hands and ears were frozen. We dragged him, struggling, to the hall door and began vigorously rubbing him with snow. As soon as he could catch his breath he broke away from us and began a malediction on the climate of Alberta, in the next breath extolling that of Victoria, which was his standard of comparison for everything in Canada. Then, uncovering his basket, he bade us examine its contents, while he explained with much gesticulation:

"Maybe so more blizzard come. I catchum lotsee glub. Bimeby man come blingum coal. I not go home. I stay here keepee house warm so ladies not fleezee. I sleep on couch."

We never knew what arts of persuasion he had brought to bear on the coal-man, but we received the first load of coal which left the yards after the storm, notwithstanding that the "best families" were all clamoring for fuel. The town was always on the verge of a coal famine, but we were well supplied throughout the winter, thanks to the untiring vigilance of Fawn Kee.

The storm was followed by such intense cold that we gave up all hopes of having any business until the weather moderated. But we were gratified to find ourselves mistaken and to learn that the horde of single men in the Northwest were not to be deterred from their pleasures by a mere matter of temperature. Rather, the long cold evenings sent them forth to find companionship, and there were very few nights when we did not have highly profitable visitors.

The house was not half big enough to accommodate the growing trade, and I needed twice as many girls as I had room for. By Christmas-time I had given up my own room to a fourth girl and was sleeping on a folding-bed in one of the parlors.

I imported a pianist from Spokane—which made my unwieldy business easier to handle, for the men of this country were all music-mad, and would entertain themselves for a reasonable length of time by singing with the "professor" while the girls were otherwise engaged.

These men were not *blasé roués;* they were great, boisterous boys in their hours of recreation; and if the piano and the furniture suffered from their exuberance, they spent enough to pay for the damage.

Although they poured out their money like water and were easily entertained, they were not so easily managed, for the jealousies of caste, creed, race, and occupation were many and virulent. When the men of one class conceived that they were being slighted for those of another it took all of my diplomacy and patience to soothe their ruffled feelings.

When I was not with the largest party, which always occupied the parlor containing the piano, I was flitting from room to room, "jollying" men who were waiting for some particular girl to become disengaged.

Sometimes these waiting men were tucked away in the dining-room or in the kitchen. Quite by inadvertency I found a new source of income and one which added greatly to the growing fame of the house. Again I owed something to the vigilance of Fawn Kee, for he, ever on the alert to be helpful, became a great favorite with the men who came into his domain; I often came in to find him serving an appetizing lunch to some man who had grown tired of waiting. No man who had the opportunity of eating Fawn Kee's cooking was ever in a hurry to go, and, as I did not accept payment for the meals served, it came to pass that many drinks were served with them.

After a while the fame of my table spread to such an extent that we seldom sat down to a meal without having visitors, and I had to provide an assistant for Fawn Kee.

Late in February a Chinook wind swept the ground clear of the great drifts of snow and the weather became like spring.

I rounded up all the available carpenters in town

and had two rooms added to the house before the next storm broke. I had not meant to spend any more money on the house, but I was worn threadbare from the discomfort of having no room of my own. And the proceeds of two weeks' business would pay for the improvements.

Just as I was congratulating myself upon my increased facilities for handling the trade there came an unexpected slump in business. For three or four days at a time the only men who came near the place were the tradesmen or an occasional Mounted Police trooper. We were no longer new girls and there was not the rush to seek our society that there had been earlier in the season.

Then, too, most of our customers had spent so lavishly at first that they were now compelled to retrench.

The winter rush was over, the spring trade had not begun, and we felt that we must look forward to lean days. There were not, however, as many of these as we had anticipated; for though the volume of business decreased to an alarming extent, from time to time some lone man with a big bank-roll would drop in upon us and make things lively, especially for "the house."

During the dullest month I cleared six hundred dollars, but business was not correspondingly good for the girls. To offset this and keep down a growing discontent, I did not charge the girls anything for board during that month.

As they did not pay me any percentage of their

earnings, they did not go behind in their expenses, but their complaints about dull times were long and bitter. By some process of reasoning which I have never been able to fathom, the girls always blame "the house" when business is quiet. And a houseful of idle women can find more cause for complaint against the scheme of things entire than fifty I. W. W.'s can discover.

One of the most prolific sources of discontent at this time was the weather. The wild March winds which swept down from the mountain passes, growing in volume and fury as they traveled, broke over the prairies with all the force of a tornado. The different sounds produced by these winds were maddening to the nerves, especially since it was difficult to disabuse the mind of the idea that there were those outside who were calling for succor.

At first there would come a wild howling, as if all the souls in bondage were shrieking for release; then, gradually, this sound would die down into a piteous wailing, as if many little children were lost on the prairie and crying in the dark.

I was now asked to abrogate a rule which I had made when I established my business, namely, that I would not sell liquor to the girls.

Two of the four girls came to me declaring that no one could endure the isolation and the abominable climate without the aid of liquor, and they intimated that I was a tyrant who sought to coerce them into temperance because I myself did not care to drink.

I indignantly denied this allegation, for it was only half the truth. My chief reason for not selling to them was entirely a matter of conscience. I had no wish to make money *from* the girls; I was keenly aware of my obligation in making money *through* them.

I now saw that, unless I expected to live in constant discord, I must assert my authority. I put my foot down firmly and asked these two girls for their rooms. Two days later I had replaced them by two girls from Medicine Hat. The next morning after their arrival I announced to my household, assembled at breakfast, that I was tired of hearing complaints about things over which I had no control. I was not responsible for the business depression nor the climate. I, too, had to endure both. I could relieve them from most of their expenses by making no charge for board during the dull season, while my own overhead and current expenses went on alike in good and in bad times.

As to the rules of my house and my business policy, I intended to adhere to both. The road was open in either direction for those who cared to leave. As I had the most comfortable house in the country and lived in the center of the richest district, the girls were not anxious to go and I heard no further complaints.

CHAPTER IV

THE first summer of my business career was one of extraordinary prosperity and good-will. The volume of business was so great that it taxed every member of the household to handle it. By the first of August my bank-account had swollen to a size that was far beyond my wildest expectations. My head caught the contagion, and, disregarding the advice of the O. C. of the Mounted Police, who sent for me when he heard of my plans, I began the erection of another addition to the house. This one was to contain a large ballroom.

I told the O. C. that my business justified the expenditure. I needed more girls to handle my large trade, and I wanted room for a housekeeper who could relieve me of my arduous duties, for I was worn out from overwork.

The O. C. shook his head, for he felt that I was investing too much money and standing to make a big loss if anything happened to shake my present popularity. There were too many warring factions in the community. I could not hope to please them all for any great length of time. The O. C. hoped that I would reconsider my plans for building.

This man hated the profession which I followed,

but he liked me personally and he wanted to see me win out. The idea of my settling down into being an ordinary "madame" did not please him. I was sorry to disappoint him in his good opinion of me, but I had grown money-mad and nothing short of a positive command from him would have caused me to forgo the proposed plans.

He did not feel justified in giving the command, and the building went on. In the midst of the work Paul arrived unexpectedly on the scene.

When he saw the half-finished building he took it as an indication that I was irrevocably wedded to my evil profession. He bitterly denounced me and all my kind in terms that I found hard to bear with equanimity.

Still, it was easier for me to withstand his rage than to harden my heart against his tenderness, and I was glad that he had chosen the former method. When he left me as suddenly as he had arrived I was greatly relieved. He had annoyed me very much, and I preferred to go to the devil in peace.

I felt that I no longer cared for him. The one best thing in the world was money. The woods were full of men who would gladly play the rôle of lover for me if I were not too deeply engrossed in my business to think of men in anything but their spending capacity. If it were simply admiration that I craved, I was surfeited with that, and I had no time for love.

I ought to make a small fortune by the time I was thirty, and then I could choose my own career. My hand had lost its cunning, and my soul was losing the ideals cherished through many years. I no longer dreamed of art. But there were many avenues open to a woman of means, and they were mine to choose from.

The addition to my house cost far more money than I had anticipated, and in furnishing it I went still deeper into my bank-account. But heavily as I drew on my financial resources to pay for this monument to gross ambition, I drew still more heavily on both my physical and my spiritual resources.

I had succeeded, to a flattering degree, in pleasing both of the warring police factions. I was heralded by each as the "whitest" woman that had ever come into the country. I was such a general favorite with my customers that it required all my ingenuity to evade the attentions of many of these men and to keep from arousing the ever-ready jealousy of the girls; for I labored under the disadvantage of being as desirable as any of them and of being younger than two.

I was more than liked by my girls, though I had the reputation of being a strict disciplinarian; and the general public, who believed that prostitution was a necessary evil, conceded that it was far better to have an unobtrusive, straightforward woman running an establishment than to endure some unscrupulous creature who would be an open offense to the public decency.

All this general good standing had cost me dearly

in every way, physically, financially, and spiritually; and the more money I had invested in my business the less could I afford to offend any one.

The "white-slave" myth had not been begotten at that time, but if there were such a creature in my house, I was that slave, and I was chained to a smile.

As a "boarding girl" I had only my own particular customers to please, but as a "madame" I had to placate every one in a country where the standing of my class was most precarious, where any private citizen might put me out of business, if he chose.

In common justice, I will say that I never paid a dollar of graft money to the Mounted Police, although they levied other forms of tribute; and the amount of money which I gave to the town authorities was small and always a voluntary offering. But the amount of graft exacted by citizens of the highest standing would have put a Tammany alderman to shame.

Day or night I was on call to any one who chose to invade my privacy or to disturb my sleep. I remember one good citizen who, mistaking me for one of the girls, offered to share his spoils with me if I would help him "pull the old lady's leg."

Yet the entire sum of money which I paid out in this way was but a tithe of that which was demanded; but I was able to stand off some of the grafters. And, since I was still young and desirable, many of these persons demanded the use of my body as well as money. This was a form of tribute that I refused to pay, though to evade it often required more skill than to evade giving money.

It was at the beginning of my second year in business that Mildred came to me as housekeeper. She was an acquaintance of many years' standing and I knew her to be true as steel. I could intrust my business to her with the knowledge that she would do nothing to jeopardize my good standing.

Mildred was a "good fellow" and the girls and the customers took to her at once. The one person whom she could not win was Fawn Kee. He could not see any reason for there being a new "bossee lady."

I turned my house over to her charge and went South for the winter. As soon as I got away from my business I lost my money-madness, and the one thing needed for my happiness was to see Paul. I wrote him from Chicago saying I was going to spend the winter in Hot Springs and asking him to write me there. I spent ten days shopping in Chicago, and when I reached Hot Springs I found Paul awaiting me there.

Save for his brief visit to me the previous summer, I had not seen Paul for over a year, and I now looked forward with anticipations of the keenest pleasure to being with him for a few weeks. I knew he would not have come had his mood not been one of tenderness.

We avoided any discussion of my business affairs, dwelling only on the present and our joy in being together. Since my profession always fell from me like a discarded garment the moment I got away from it, this was not difficult.

We had been four weeks at the Springs when I received a telegram from Mildred demanding my immediate return. And on the heels of Mildred's message came one from Fawn Kee giving particulars. Mildred was under arrest, though allowed to go on her own recognizance, for procuring women from the States.

I started homeward, torn with anxiety for Mildred's safety and for the security of my business. I was sure that it was a "plant," but that did not make the situation less precarious.

Paul accompanied me as far as St. Paul; he was fearful that I was walking into the lion's jaws.

When I arrived in Malta I found a much-perturbed household, and then learned the cause of all the trouble.

A few days after I left two girls in Spokane had written me for railway tickets to bring them to Malta. Mildred had sent the transportation and the girls arrived a few days later.

A few days after their arrival they had asked to borrow clothes so that they could make a presentable appearance; they explained that they were going down-town to meet an acquaintance from Spokane.

Mildred had dressed one of them in her own clothes, and had drawn on my wardrobe to clothe the other; thus attired they had gone to the Mounted Police and represented themselves as innocent girls who had been inveigled into Canada for immoral purposes.

A man confederate appeared at the proper juncture and declared himself a near relative who had followed them into Canada, to save them from a life of shame.

Evidently they had reckoned on making the complaint and then demanding a big sum of money for their silence. It was a case of "shake-down" pure and simple, and I was the intended victim, since they did not know of my absence when they sent for the railway tickets.

But as I was not in Malta, the conspirators made a scapegoat out of poor Mildred.

The only flaw in their plan was that they had gone to the Mounted Police instead of the town police. The word "compromise" not being in the Mounted Police lexicon, Mildred was promptly arrested. Then something occurred which had not entered into the calculations of the conspirators. They were locked up at the barracks, to be held as witnesses.

When everybody else in the house had talked themselves hoarse, telling me about the affair, Fawn Kee beckoned me out to "talk sleclet" to me. Then I discovered that the "heathen Chinee" had two cards up his sleeve.

One was a half-finished letter which one of the girls had left in her room. The salutation was "Dear Papa and Mamma," and from the contents of the letter it was easy to infer that "Papa and Mamma" were entirely cognizant of their daughter's plans, which she set forth at some length.

Fawn Kee's second card was a visit which the man in the case had made to his kitchen in an attempt to bribe him. The Chinaman's ethics did not forbid him to take the man's money, and he gleefully exhibited it to me. But as for bearing witness against "the house," no power on earth could have made him do it.

The lawyer whom I employed to defend Mildred advised me to go over the line until the case was tried; for though she was sure to be acquitted, yet, now that our existence had been brought to the public notice, there would be a charge of some sort filed against her.

I went down into the States and remained until after the trial, but I heard the full details when I got home. Fawn Kee had made a most impressive witness, and his story had carried conviction. Mildred was acquitted of the charge. The man in the case was given a six months' sentence for vagrancy, and the girls were ordered to leave the Dominion of Canada.

Since it had been brought out at the trial that liquor was being sold in the house, Mildred was "summonsed" and paid a fine for selling liquor without a license.

As Mildred had been "summonsed" as a principal and not as an employee, this left me still clear of ever having been convicted on this charge.

To be sure, it was I who had to pay the expenses in both cases. But Mildred shouldered the responsibility because she had no property at stake.

CHAPTER V

IN the Canadian Northwest the sale of liquor and the profits therefrom were greater than I had ever seen elsewhere. The country had just entered on an era of remarkable prosperity and was rapidly being settled, not only by the European peasant immigration, but by the flower of British and American immigration.

Men came into this country bringing money for investment purposes. A large proportion of them were single men, and the time not devoted to business or labor hung heavily on their hands. There were no amusements and in the winter few recreations, so that drinking was the great indoor pastime.

The bars closed at ten o'clock at night, and at six on Saturday nights. The sporting-houses remained open as long as they liked, usually until four o'clock in the morning. And Saturday nights and Sunday afternoons were the times when we did the big business.

In the parlor-houses in the States bottled beer and champagne were about the only drinks served. But all through the Northwest the houses sold "short drinks," and served about everything that could be bought over a bar except mixed drinks.

Each drink served was twenty-five cents, and we managed to get six glasses of beer from one bottle. From the first I had refused to serve whisky to the girls, so that they usually took beer or light wine. But when I thought they had had enough of these drinks I gave them lemon-soda or "gin," which was simply plain water.

Sometimes there would be four glasses of "gin" on one tray of drinks, which meant that I got twenty-five cents each for four glasses of water.

I did not by any means always succeed in keeping the girls sober by serving them with whatever I considered good for them, for it is a part of the creed of nearly every patron of a sporting-house to help the girls circumvent the landlady. And the men frequently ordered whisky for themselves and then gave it to the girls.

Again, as in the previous spring, the murmurs of discontent and dissatisfaction began to arise as soon as business grew slack, for our prosperous winter was followed by the usual depression, coupled with abominable weather during March and April. And as I now had a larger house and more girls, the dissatisfaction was not so easily quelled.

Both the city police and the Mounted Police held me to strict accountability for the actions of my girls, not only in the house, but in the streets as well.

If the girls went down-town shopping and attracted attention in the streets, either by their actions or their attire, I was sure to receive a visit from the chief or be called up on the carpet by the commandant of the Mounted Police. I protested that it was unfair to hold me responsible for whatever some irresponsible girl might do when she was out of my sight. But my protest was unavailing. It was my business to manage the girls, and I must do so or shut up shop.

I could not put the lid on their going out whenever they claimed to have business, but I forbade more than two going out on the same day. This order was attributed to tyranny on my part, and in self-defense I was forced to urge the chief to give his orders in person to the girls.

As in the previous spring, there were complaints because I would not sell them drinks. If I would not let them go out whenever they liked, would not permit them to buy drinks, and refused to let them have lovers, how did I suppose they were going to pass the time during the dull season?

I will acknowledge my lack of sympathy in the manner of whisky and pimps. I had never been addicted to either, and I could not get the viewpoint of those who were. I sold liquor because it was my business, and I was perfectly certain that I would always remain on the "sober side of the bar."

In the matter of lovers I had been fortunate, for the men whom I cared about and who cared for me had always been men of education, standing, and means. And I had a loathing for the professional lovers, which was only equaled by my loathing for liquor.

For this reason it afforded me great pleasure to obey the injunction of both the Mounted Police and town police that I should not permit undesirables of the male persuasion to frequent my house.

The conditions were also unfavorable, for there were few men of this class in the country, though there was some available timber for producing them. But I had seen *macques* in the making too often to enjoy the process.

I was fully aware that the pimp was a ripe product of prostitution, instead of prostitution being the offspring of the pimp, as a recent public delusion would lead us to believe. Therefore I set my face, in so far as I was able, against fostering the growth of this excrescence of society.

It was not difficult for me to find occupation for my own hands and brains, when business was dull, for I had never acquired the habit of absolute idleness.

Through generations of thrifty, industrious men and women, the habits of thrift and industry had come down to me, and they were too deeply ingrained in my nature ever to become lost. It is true that at times my habit of thrift was in abeyance, but the habit of industry was not. I had always been a source of scandal to those who held that a scarlet woman should not use her hands. And I had never given up the habit of study nor the effort to educate myself.

I now had the opportunity to learn the art of cooking under a master of his craft, and, to the disgust of Mildred and my boarders, I invaded the kitchen. I succeeded so well in learning my lessons that I am to-day as complete a master of the art as Fawn Kee himself.

I assumed a motherly attitude toward the girls, though I was a year younger than the oldest of them, and I endeavored to teach them to sew. I bought a sewing-machine and induced them to buy the materials for some simple gowns. I cut and fitted and basted garments that were easily finished, but I never succeeded in getting the girls to sew except while I worked with them. They would not even mend the clothes they had, to say nothing of making new ones.

The average prostitute is more scrupulously clean about her person and her lingerie than any other class of woman, but she is hopelessly untidy when she depends upon herself to take care of her clothing. A button gone is a button gone forever, for it is never replaced. A pair of five-dollar stockings which have a stitch dropped are worn until they are past repair, and then discarded. And so with every garment these women possess, yet, in my zeal, I tried to teach the art of mending and darning. One of my pet aversions was a petticoat tucked up around the waist to keep it from hanging below the skirt. When my own petticoats were too long I put a tuck in them, and I did not see why the girls could not do the same. But I wasted my breath when I tried to induce them to perform this simple task, and it was a joke among the girls in that part of the country that "if you board with Madeleine Blair she will want you to tuck your petticoat."

One well-meaning sob-sister has written as an axiom, "Prostitution always destroys manual dexterity." The lady in question is mistaken. These women lack manual dexterity because they have never been taught to use their hands. Perhaps that is the reason why many of them became prostitutes. It may also be one of the reasons for the respectable parasite.

Failing to interest the girls in sewing, I tried to foster in them a taste for books and reading. I had a well-selected, small library, and I subscribed for several of the best magazines. But my books and my magazines did not appeal to the girls, and my efforts in this direction only tended to estrange them, for they looked upon me as a "highbrow" who did not understand their viewpoint.

At that period of my life I thought that my own class of women were the only empty-handed, idle-minded women in the world, but I can see them now on every hand, women who have never learned to use either hands or minds and whose sole object in life is to murder time.

CHAPTER VI

THE woman I am now about to write of is to me almost a stranger. As I look back across the years that have elapsed since I knew her she seems to me to be "the delusion of a dreadful dream" rather than some real person that I have known. Yet I dwelt in the house with her for two years. She bore no resemblance to any one that I had ever known before, and she bore no resemblance to any one that I now know; this woman who descended into the blackest depths of hell, and then demonstrated the marvelous recuperative power of the human soul by emerging triumphant from the depths. And yet this woman bore my name.

When I had been keeping house for about four years I began to drink, and I began to drink secretly.

I was harassed with business cares to the extent that insomnia was my nightly companion. One night when I was unable to sleep, and it seemed that I had been awake for years, I arose, went down to my liquor-closet, and took a drink of whisky. Almost immediately I fell asleep, and slept for several hours without awakening.

At length this became a nightly habit, and after

I had slept off the effects of the first drink I would get up and take another one; in this way I was enabled to get a night's slumber.

I drew the whisky from a demijohn instead of from the bottle, because I feared that Mildred would miss it if I took it from the bottle. I had said so much to Mildred and the girls about the evils of intemperance that I did not want them to know that I was not practising what I preached.

Since I went to this length to conceal my delinquency I was in effect stealing my own whisky. A little later I began taking a drink in the morning before breakfast, and it required some ingenuity on my part to get this drink without Mildred's knowledge.

Liquor had at first a most soothing effect upon me, and on this plea I excused myself for taking it. I needed something to soothe my tortured nerves, for under the stress of my many business cares I had begun to grow irritable; it was only by the greatest effort that I now preserved my equanimity and my smile in the presence of the customers, the girls, and the servants.

Another house had been built alongside of mine, and while the competition did not cut into my trade to any great extent, it added greatly to my anxiety, for the woman who kept it was a feather-brained creature who had little at stake; she had only a cheap shack of a house and would not suffer a great loss if her establishment should be closed.

Her girls ran wild over the town, and her house

was infested with male parasites. Two months
after she opened her place we were all arrested,
charged with vagrancy, since the Canadian law does
not recognize prostitution as existing.

Her house had been raided first and she and her
girls were given a heavy fine. Then a cry went up
that I was receiving protection, that the police dared
not arrest me. The chief came to me in great distress
to discuss the matter, and I told him that for the
sake of peace he had better notify me to appear
before a municipal magistrate. My household was
let off with a very small fine. And again the cry
of "protection" went up.

The O. C. of the Mounted Police sent for me in an
endeavor to find out if I were paying graft to the
municipal authorities. He vowed to "break" them all
if he discovered that graft was being exacted, and the
fight between the two conflicting authorities was on.

I could not afford to offend either of these contending factions, though each suspected me of aiding
and abetting the other. I could only smile and try
ingratiation and conciliation with both.

A party of the male parasites connected with
the house next door came into my place one
night and started a "rough-house." I sent Fawn
for the police, and impressed upon him that I
wanted him to get the town police. He came
back with a detachment of the Mounted Police,
and when I upbraided him for disobeying my
orders he stoutly maintained that "lotsee bad
men needee lotsee police to catchum."

The men received a heavy fine and had to pay for the damage to my furniture, but they testified to having bought drinks in my house, and I got my first summons before the Mounted Police for selling liquor.

The chief of the city police came to me in a rage. Was I giving him the double cross? Why had I not sent for him instead of for the Mounted Police? And the hundred dollars that I slipped into his hand did little toward mollifying his wrath. He announced that he had been my friend through thick and thin, and that I had thrown him down. I would get all of the Mounted Police I wanted before I was through with them.

Then the magistrate, before whom the municipal cases were tried, sent for me to inquire if I were trying to make a grand-stand play by recognizing the authority of the Mounted Police over that of the town authorities.

When, a few days later, the chief made me another call, and a heated discussion arose between us, I recommended him to try a hotter climate. Mildred, who was present during this controversy, tried to quiet me, but there was no stopping me now. As always, I had been slow to anger, but when once I had loosened the curb on my temper and my tongue there was not much left unsaid.

The chief left me vowing vengeance, and following in his wake came one of the officers of the Mounted Police. The matter between this man and myself was a personal one. For three years he had hounded me with his attentions, and I had evaded him by various subterfuges. I did not want his enmity. Time after time I had paid one or another of the girls to take him off my hands. Now my blood was up, and I was ready to begin on him where I had left off with the chief.

The house was full of people, but I did not take the trouble to lower my voice, although we were talking in the hall. The man fled before the fury of my unexpected attack, but I knew that there would be a "come-back."

I went out into the ballroom, which a slow crowd had been holding down for several hours, and I told Mildred that I intended to put a little ginger into them by treating them to a bottle of wine. Mildred looked her astonishment, but I repeated my order; then, seeing that one bottle would not go around, I ordered two.

Inside of half an hour I was drunk and still buying. After the men had gone one of the girls came to me and asked if she could buy a bottle of wine, and I replied by telling Mildred to sell her the house if she had the price to buy it.

CHAPTER VII

I KEPT up my spree for weeks, and since alcohol continued to have a soothing effect on my disposition, I patched up a truce with the chief the next time he called. Before he had conceived the idea that I had flouted his authority he had in reality been a great admirer of mine, though his attentions had never been obtrusive, as was the case with the Mounted Police officer of whom I have spoken.

The girls took advantage of my relaxed discipline to go on a tear for themselves, and Mildred and poor harassed Fawn Kee had their hands full with my demoralized household; finally Mildred, in exasperation, declared that the best thing I could do would be to go away from home until I had come to my senses.

I very promptly acceded to her proposal; I packed up and went to Spokane, where I took an expensive suite at a leading hotel, and then proceeded to make ducks and drakes of my money.

I learned that one of the big gambling-houses had a private room containing a roulette-wheel, and that women were admitted to this room. Night after night I went down to this place and played the limit on the wheel. When my losses amounted to such a large sum that I was afraid to think of them, and when alcohol had wrought such havoc with my nerves that I was afraid to try to get sober, I thought of Paul.

I had seen him only at rare intervals during the past two years, but we still kept up a correspondence. I now felt that he was the one person in the world who could help me, and I began telegraphing him to come to me, and kept it up until he answered in person.

He did not reproach me for my conduct, for which I was truly thankful, for I was too sick to bear reproaches. He put me to bed and then sent for a physician.

I was in bed for a week as a result of my dissipation, and then Paul was compelled to return to Montana. But before leaving he prevailed upon me to go out to the coast for a while until I could get a hold on myself. I went to Seattle, where I remained for a week, and then took a steamer for San Francisco. I did not make any acquaintances in either place, but I was not lonely, for I had always possessed the faculty of entertaining myself. After three weeks in San Francisco I went to New Orleans, stopping for a few days in El Paso.

The change of thought and scene wrought a great healing in my physical and spiritual being. I had no trouble in breaking away from alcohol, and I was no longer playing the rôle of mistress of a bawdy-house, used as a pawn by contending police factions. I was a woman of means, traveling for pleasure, and

I thoroughly enjoyed the part. I wrote to Paul every week, describing the places I had visited and the people I had met, for, after leaving San Francisco, I began to form pleasant acquaintances with my fellow-travelers.

I spent four months traveling about in this way, and then Mildred began writing me letters of protest for the great sums of money I was spending, though it was not the money I had spent in traveling that had made such a crimp in my bank-account. It was the money I had lost gambling in Spokane.

I went reluctantly back to Canada and found that business was flourishing, and that Mildred and Fawn Kee had never failed to work for my interests, each in their separate way, for Fawn Kee would take no orders from any one but me. And as he had always done the buying for the house and paid the bills for his department, he took great pride in making a good showing during my absence.

I was touched to the core by the faithful friendship of these two, who, while thoroughly disliking each other, were yet united in their loyalty to me. Fawn Kee was intensely jealous of Mildred, and she, on her part, resented his attitude toward her. Yet both were my faithful friends and remained so to the end.

But I was thoroughly disgruntled with my business and with the Northwest Territory. I found that I could no longer smile and smile, no matter what happened.

I had only been home two months when I began

drinking again, and this time alcohol had no soothing effect upon my disposition. Two of my best girls disregarded a rule of the house that had never before been violated, and I asked them for their rooms. The pianist, who had been with me for two years, "got fresh," and I discharged him on the spot. One of my best customers complained about something that one of the girls had done, and I told him that I did not remember ever having sent him an invitation to visit my house. If he did not like the place he could stay out of it.

The chief came out to see me, filled with goodwill. Remembering my advances to him before I had gone away, he glowed and bowed and tried to kiss me, and I told him to go to hell. He went away vowing that he would break me, and I laughed in his face.

I drank and drank; I went to bed drunk and I got up drunk, and every time I thought of the many scurvy tricks that life had played me I took another drink.

I insulted every customer who gave me the opportunity to do so, and my business decreased until I was not making expenses. But I went on drinking and antagonizing both my customers and the authorities. Fawn Kee protested and Mildred implored, but I paid no heed to either.

One of my most faithful friends was the young doctor who was medical examiner for the house. He had come to the town with his young bride when he was just out of medical college, and through the solicitation of the chief I had given him the practice in the house. The medical examinations were made weekly, and the fee in each case was three dollars. It was a comfortable little addition to the income of a young doctor, and he had been grateful for the practice. But, further than that, he had a certain liking and respect for me, and he now exerted himself to stop me in my downward course.

He knew all about my affair with Paul, and when he found that all other efforts to stop me from drinking were unavailing he wrote to Paul.

Paul came at once and took me away. I went without protest, and for a short time I stopped drinking. I had so crippled my business and my bank-account that Mildred wrote me imploring me to remain away until she could get the business again on a paying basis.

I stayed sober as long as Paul remained with me, encouraging and helping me. But I could see clearly that his love was dead and that he was helping me only for old time's sake.

I fought with all my strength to regain a hold on myself, but my sobriety was short-lived, for I learned that Paul was paying attention to another woman, and rumor had it that they were engaged. Then I knew that he had broken his shackles, and the only hold I had on him was for the sake of the woman that I might have been.

We went through a scene that was filled with anguish for both of us—I, crushed and broken, with no other hand to cling to, and he, filled with sorrow, because he believed that no human power could save me from the pit that I had dug for myself. He said, sorrowfully, again and again, "Madeleine, you are beyond redemption, you are beyond redemption."

At length I went back to my own house, and I kept out of sight as much as possible, for I had come to be the most hated woman in the Northwest Territory. Nothing was too bad to be attributed to me by my enemies, who were legion. I drank now "more in sorrow than in anger," for I no longer railed at those who did not meet with my approval. I drank until I was in a state of sodden sullenness, and yet all decency had not departed from me, as the following incident, which occurred during two of my rare sober intervals, will testify.

I discovered that the young doctor had been carrying on affairs with two of the girls, each of whom had considered herself the sole recipient of his attentions, until they began comparing notes.

It made me heartsick to feel that everything that I had ever touched had been corrupted by my touch. I had meant to help this young man, but I had only succeeded in bringing him into contact with this horrible vice of prostitution, which corrupts everything that comes within reach of it.

I took the young doctor to task, but he did not understand the personal responsibility I felt in the

matter, and he simply looked upon what I said as
an unwarranted interference with his affairs.

Then, a little later, there came the meeting with
the preacher, which seemed to point out that some
latent spark of womanhood still lay hidden in my
whisky-sodden brain.

20

CHAPTER VIII

"YOU are going to catch it, Madeleine," said the young doctor, one day, as he made his weekly report to me. "There is a Presbyterian minister from Toronto in our midst, and he tells us that unless we suppress the red-light district he will do it single-handed. Evidently there are no sinners in Toronto, so he has come West to clean up the country."

"I wish some one would suppress me," I answered, "for unless they do I will be doing business in the same old way for the next forty years. I would enjoy being put out of business by a preacher. At any rate, it would be a change from being harassed by the police. Can't you bring him out to see me?"

"He has boasted that he is going to call on you, and that when he is through telling you of your iniquities you will be on your knees. You've been misrepresented to him as several different kinds of monster, and he is girding himself to beard you in your den. I hope you won't be drunk when he calls. There is no good in antagonizing him."

"My dear Doctor, do you suppose that I am going to sit quietly down and permit some would-be reformer to annoy me? I will have the servants throw him out if he comes here bothering me."

A few days later as I returned from town I saw a tall man in ministerial garb coming from the house next door. His face was flushed and he was wiping the dust from his hat, which had been thrown into the street. Several drunken women stood in the doorway jeering him, and one called to me, "Has the preacher been to see you yet, Madeleine?"

I had stopped to witness the disturbance, but I shook my head and went on, with a sense of shame and disgust almost choking me. Of course the preacher was a fool and would better mind his own business, but, singularly enough, my sympathies were with him and not with the harpies who jeered him.

Turning into my own house, I went into my room and, after removing my hat, I pinned a large white apron over my severely plain street dress and set about dusting my rooms, a task I usually did over after the house-boy. A ring at the outside door of my private sitting-room disturbed me, but I did not answer it, because few visitors were ever admitted by that door.

Whoever was ringing the bell, however, was persistent, and, still holding the dust-cloth in my hand, I went to the door, intending to send the person to the front of the house. As I opened the door with a rebuke on my lips I found myself confronted by the minister who had recently been ejected from the other house. When he saw me his glance

traveled from my face to my gown and then
down to my white apron. He was evidently
nonplussed.

The rebuke which had been on my lips died without utterance, and I found myself saying, courteously: "Good afternoon. sir. Won't you come
in?"

He entered and I invited him to sit down, apolo-
gizing for the long time I had kept him waiting at
the door, explaining that I had been busy when he
rang. He sank into the armchair beside my reading-
table; then, finding his voice, he said, "I want to
see the madame." And again his puzzled glance
traveled over me and then to the books on my
table.

"I am the mistress here, sir. What can I do for
you?"

He gasped, wiped his forehead, and irrelevantly
exclaimed: "Bless my soul! but you live in a bad
neighborhood, madame. Is your husband at
home?"

I told him that I had no husband, and he wondered at my temerity in living alone in such a terrible
neighborhood. But I assured him that I had faithful servants and was not afraid. As he expressed
his relief I excused myself and went out of the
room to give Mildred instructions that I was not
to be disturbed.

When I returned to my sitting-room I found that
the preacher had evidently been looking over my
books. He had picked up a copy of *Voices of Doubt*

and Trust and was holding it open at the poem beginning:

> All the world over, I wonder,
>   In lands that I never have trod,
> Are the people eternally seeking
>   For the signs and the steps of a God?
> Westward across the ocean
>   And northward ayont the snow,
> Do they still stand gazing as ever?
>   And what do the wisest know?

In a moment we were in a deep discussion of the theme suggested by these verses. The man, an earnest, educated fanatic, with an eloquence which thrilled me, talked on, with never a thought that he had entered this house with the avowed purpose of bringing a prostitute to her knees.

For an hour we discussed this subject on equal terms, he with no idea that I was the notorious woman that he had come to excoriate and I, oblivious of the fact that I was a harlot and a drunkard, who, in the very nature of things, was not supposed to know nor to think of those things which pertain to the Spirit.

When we ended the discussion the man arose and told me that he had come into the neighborhood for the purpose of denouncing to her face a terrible woman named Madeleine Blair. Inadvertently he had come into my house, thinking it was the place he sought, but as soon as he had seen me he knew his mistake. He was holding services at the First

Presbyterian Church, and hoped to see me there on the following Sunday. I gave an equivocal answer, and he went away after a gracious acknowledgment of a pleasant hour spent in my society.

After the man had gone I sat still for a long time trying to analyze my own soul. Why had I talked with this man about the things that I hardly dared think of?

I had been drunk last night, and in all probability I would be drunk again to-night, since I seldom went to bed sober. I was at war with society, and every man's hand was against me.

The Chief of Police had vowed that he would "set me afoot," and that when he had finished with me I would be glad to walk out of town. My enemy in the Mounted Police had left no stone unturned to injure me. He was fighting me from ambush, and only the fear of what I might tell the commandant had kept him from attacking me openly.

There was not a girl in the house who would not have given me "the double cross." And of all those who had sung my praises and professed friendship two years before only three remained faithful. There were Mildred and Fawn Kee who could not be swerved from their allegiance, and the young doctor was still my friend, though he was smarting from what he considered my interference in his affairs with the girls.

I was an outcast in my own house, for there were many men who would not come when they knew that I was at home. My absence from the house meant a great increase in business, for Mildred was now as popular as I had once been.

Paul had gone completely out of my life, and no one had or could take his place. I had nothing to look forward to, for I was on the down grade. Alcohol had me in its clutch, and, though I fought and prayed for release, its hold upon me was being tightened every day. Yet here was I, forgetting all this for an hour, to discuss "the signs and the steps of a God" with a man whose avowed purpose had been to flay me.

I walked over and looked at my own face in the mirror, searching for the signs of vice and dissipation which should have been there. My eyes looked very weary, and in repose my face was so inexpressibly sad that it was a subject of much comment, but it did not bear the scarlet brand.

CHAPTER IX

ONE night when I was drunk, as usual, I was writing to Paul, heaping reproaches upon myself for my dissolute mode of life, when suddenly one of the girls went through the hall singing a ribald song at the top of her voice. My transom was open, and the words came to me distinctly, also the admonition of Mildred to the girl, "You had better not let Miss Madeleine hear you singing that dirty song or you will catch it."

I looked down at my letter, and then my mood changed. Going to the door I called to the girl, "That's a fine song you are singing, Alice. Sing it again; I want to hear it."

After she had finished I incorporated the loathsome thing in my letter to Paul. I wanted to hurt and shock him by showing myself in my full depravity. After I had finished the letter I called Mildred in and read it to her, mouthing hideous words that I had never before used nor permitted in my presence without a protest.

Mildred tried to take the letter from me, but I turned on her in a rage, and would have struck her if she had not gotten out of the way. I mailed the letter myself to make sure that Mildred would not destroy it, and then went to bed.

I was not blessed with that convenient memory which forgets the scandalous actions committed while under the influence of liquor. I always awoke to a thousand scorpion stings of remembrance. As every outraged nerve in my body cried for alleviation, so my tortured mind shrieked for surcease from the accusing memory of the things I had said and done while under the influence of alcohol.

The morning after I had written the obscene letter to Paul I awoke to a full realization of my iniquity, with the horrible words that I had written dancing before my eyes. I closed my eyes again, trying to persuade myself that I was still dreaming. O God, it could not be true that I, who had loathed obscenity with all the force of my intellect, had fallen so low! I cared little what Paul might think of such a letter, but I cared much that my own inner, deeply rooted sense of decency had been outraged and draggled in the mire. Throughout the bitter years one idea had been uppermost in my mind, that some day, and somehow, I would take my place among those who walked in the sunlight; until that day came I would so control my thoughts and my words that I should not be unfit to associate with decent people.

During the years when my body had been subjected to every indignity and every possible violation my mind had thrown up defenses to keep out the filth. Even during the two years that I had been drinking myself into a beast the thought of another life had not died out of my consciousness. But, now that I had dipped my pen into filth, there was no hope for me; I was irretrievably lost.

Oh, well, what did it matter? Perhaps it was all for the best that I should realize the inevitableness of my fate. It would save me from further struggle.

I tried to get out of bed, for at that moment I wanted a drink of whisky more than I wanted my soul's salvation. My head was buzzing like a top and my feet refused their office. I sank back on the bed and rang the bell, but when Fawn Kee came I hesitated. Somehow I could never order a drink from Fawn with a good grace. He always looked too hurt. But what business was it of his if I drank my fool self to death? Why should my servant look mournfully at my disintegration? He could easily get another job when I went on the rocks.

If I chose to go to the devil, I didn't purpose to be annoyed by the interference of my servants. So I gave my order. "A big drink of Scotch, Fawn," I commanded, shortly.

Fawn's face was resolute and unsmiling. "I not bling you Scotchee," he said. "I bling you nice blekfast."

I was furious at his refusal. "You will bring me whatever I order," I screamed, "and do it quickly."

"No, not Scotchee; I bling blekfast," Fawn answered, and, dodging the slipper which I threw at his head, he went out of the room.

He returned in a short time with a tray containing my breakfast, and then, since I could not get up, I tried another tack. "Send the housekeeper to

308

me," I ordered, for I knew that I could manage Mildred.

Fawn shook his head. "Miss Mildled gone out; nobody got keys to wine-closet but me. You not need dlink. Here's stlong coffee; you dlink him. I tellee man bling you horsee; you go for long lide. Maybe so hab some sense when you come back."

I was too sick to dispute with him, so I drank the coffee and choked down a mouthful of food. I knew Fawn Kee of old. If he had decided not to give me a drink I could not get it from him by fair means or foul.

After a while I managed to arise and get into my riding-togs. I went triumphantly down the hall to the wine-closet, intending to break the lock, but I changed my mind and went out.

When I was in the saddle I reeled with the pain in my head and could not sit erect, but I crouched in the saddle and turned my horse's head toward the open prairie. When I was far from the town I dismounted, for I was racked with pain and with a soul sickness that was greater than the physical suffering.

I never knew how long I sat looking across the prairies without seeing anything, for my mind was seeking a pathway and I forgot the flight of time. I made a great resolution. I was going to quit drinking, and the little devils that danced before my eyes leered into my face, saying, "Of course you are going to quit drinking—when you are dead."

And the voice of reason whispered: "Every drunkard is going to quit drinking. That is not a

new resolution. You've made it every day for the
past two years. Stop making resolutions that you
do not intend to keep."

From out of Nowhere there came to me a line
from an old hymn:

> The arm of flesh will fail you,
> You dare not trust your own.

No, I could not trust my own; that was self-
evident. If I ever stopped drinking it would have
to be through a Power that I could not reach. I
wanted to pray. I had so often wanted to pray for
deliverance from the evils which had encompassed
my pathway, but I did not know how. I closed my
eyes, and before them still flitted the human wrecks
that I had known, and the wrecks that I had helped
to make, and the evil influences that had wrecked
me, and I begged of Something to deliver me from
the sight.

Then I attempted to plead not guilty of my sins,
but more especially the sin of drunkenness. I could
not help drinking; my father had been a drunkard,
and I had inherited the desire. As for selling liquor
to others, if I did not sell them booze, somebody
else would. If I closed my house to-morrow some
one else would open it again the next day.

Then the voice of conscience began to thunder in
my ear. "You are the most unmitigated liar in
Canada," it said. "You have no inherited taste for
alcohol. Your father did not drink until long after

you were born. And you are a coward as well as a liar, for if others sell whisky, it does not excuse you. You have too much intelligence successfully to lie to yourself. If you cannot be anything else, at least be square with yourself and recognize yourself for what you are."

I lay back on the sod, weary from the struggle, and after a while a great light broke. Again I repeated the words:

> "The arm of flesh will fail you,
> You dare not trust your own."

When I reached home Mildred, who opened the door for me, told me that the chief of police was waiting to see me.

"Tell him I cannot see him now; I am going out again. Ring for a cab." I brushed past her and into my own room, but she followed me, protesting. "For Heaven's sake, Madeleine," she entreated, "go in and talk to the chief. You can conciliate him, if you try. You know you can wrap him round your little finger, if you want to. But if you continue to antagonize him he will break you as sure as you live."

I was getting into a plain, gray street gown, but I paused to say, "Mildred, I am going in town to see a priest, for I am going to take the pledge."

"You are going crazy," she answered. "Do you remember how you sneered when Gertrude took the pledge? You remember you told her it was all superstition, going to a priest. If she would not keep her word with herself she would not keep it with a priest."

"But she has kept it," I protested; "she has not taken a drink for six months."

Mildred gave up the argument, saying: "You had better see the chief first. You can see a priest any time."

Fawn Kee came in to say that the cab was waiting for me, and I went out, leaving poor, troubled Mildred to square matters with the chief

CHAPTER X

ONE block from the church I got out of the cab and dismissed the driver. I was not sure how I should proceed, so I went into the church and sat down for the purpose of collecting my thoughts.

The evening service was in progress, and no one paid any attention to my entrance. I sat down in a pew near the door, but as I knew nothing of the ritual I kept my seat, though every one else was kneeling.

I tried to see the face of the priest, for he was a man of whom I had heard much from various sources. His piety and the largeness of his charity made him beloved alike by Protestants and Catholics. But the light on the altar was dim and I could only see that he was a tall man.

I picked up a prayer-book which lay beside me on the seat and opened it at random. I was disappointed to find it printed in Latin, but, turning over a page, I came across a familiar psalm, printed in English, and I read it with a responsive thrill in my heart.

Have mercy on me, O God, according to Thy great mercy. And according to the multitude of Thy tender mercies, blot out my iniquity.

MADELEINE

Thou shalt sprinkle me with hyssop, and I shall be cleansed:
Thou shalt wash me, and I shall be made whiter than snow.

I had forgotten that I had been taught to believe
that the Catholic service was "pure mummery,"
for I was reading a plain, unmistakable message.

A sacrifice to God is an afflicted spirit: a humble and
contrite heart, O God, Thou wilt not despise.

At the close of the service I asked a woman where
I should find the priest. She pointed out his house
to me, and, calling up all the strength of my will,
I went up and rang the bell. I waited some little
time, but my ring was not answered, and my resolution began to waver, for it seemed to me an unspeakable thing that I should go to this man of
God and declare myself a harlot and a drunkard.

I made a half-turn to leave the door-step, and then
the words I had so recently read flitted through my
mind:

A sacrifice to God is an afflicted spirit: a humble and contrite
heart, O God, Thou wilt not despise.

I rang again, and this time my ring was answered
by the priest himself. As I saw him closely under
the hall light he appeared more like a medieval monk,
a Bernard of Clairvaux, than a twentieth-century
clergyman.

"What can I do for you, my child?" he asked, and
the soothing, musical voice broke down all my
defenses.

"I want to take the pledge, sir," I blurted out, without ceremony.

"You do not look like a girl who needs to take the pledge; but come into my study, child, and tell me about whatever is troubling you."

Sitting opposite me in the study, he again said, "You do not look like a girl who needs the pledge."

I was facing my old difficulty of being taken for a good woman, and of being compelled either to lie or to confess that I was outside the pale. And for the first time in my life I confessed the truth to one who had met me outside the market-place and had been struck by my appearance of purity.

I told him that I was not a girl, but a woman of thirty-four, that I had not been sober half a dozen times in the past year, and that for two years I had been drinking heavily.

He then asked me where I lived, and I gave the name of my house, which was known as the Windsor Club. He nodded his head gravely, and told me that he had heard of this notorious place and of the iniquitous woman who kept it, but he could not credit that I was that kind of a person.

I looked him squarely in the face and told him that the keeper of that house was not so black as she was painted; that I was the iniquitous woman to whom he had referred.

If I had announced that I was the Prince of Darkness he could not have looked more astounded. But he asked, kindly: "Why did you come to me, my child? Are you a Catholic?"

I told him that I was not, but that I had come to the place where I could no longer help myself; that unless a higher Power could rescue me from alcohol, I was lost indeed. I had heard of him and of his kindliness to those who sought his aid, and so I had ventured to believe that he would not refuse it, though I was not a Catholic.

"You did right to come, my child," he said, gently. "It makes no difference that you are not of our faith."

Then, for half an hour, he talked to me as a mother might have talked to a sick child, soothing, healing, strength-giving words, that bore no resemblance to preaching. Then, before giving me the pledge, he exacted a promise the fulfilment of which would leave me almost a pauper, but I gave it unhesitatingly.

After I had made the promise he handed me a crucifix and, bidding me kneel down and repeat the words after him, he gave me the same pledge that I had signed as a little girl when I had joined the Band of Hope, except that he added, "To abstain from the use of liquor for one year from this date, and to avoid the occasion of temptation."

Then he knelt down beside me and asked me to say the Lord's Prayer with him. It was all so simple that I wondered that I had not thought it out for myself long before.

When we arose from our knees I asked him why he had said one year.

"My child," he said, "there are times when our Lord, seeing that we can no longer go on alone, takes us in His arms and carries us for a part of the way as a mother carries the child who has grown too weary to walk. But He will not always carry us. After a while He puts us down, then we must rely on our own strength and walk alone, for God would not have us weaklings. Trust Him and do not fear. You will be able to walk alone at the expiration of the year."

As he bade me good night he admonished me, "Remember what you are to do, and that you are to do it to-morrow."

"Yes, Fa—" I hesitated over the word. "Yes, Father, I shall do it to-morrow."

When I reached my house I ordered Fawn Kee to bring up all of my trunks, and in answer to his questioning I told him that I was leaving the house for good. He asked me if I had sold out, and when he found out that I had not he understood, for my "heathen Chinee" comprehended many things that it is not given to every man to understand.

I spent the remainder of the night in packing my street clothes, my books, and my favorite pictures. I instructed Mildred how to dispose of my evening clothes, and to all of her questions I could only answer: "I am going away, Mildred, but I do not know where. I am going to take the first train that comes through after I am ready to go."

Mildred became exasperated with such a vague answer. "You are going crazy," she expostulated, "that's where you are going. Why don't you say what your plans are? Are you going to Paul?"

But I told her that I had no plans and that I never expected to see Paul again; that I was going forth to work out my own salvation.

Mildred looked up quickly at the word "salvation." "Is that it?" she asked. "Have you got religion?"

When I answered that I hadn't "got religion," but that I was seeking the way to it, she gave it up in despair and went back to her first theory—"You are going crazy."

When we had gone over the books together I found that it would take a large part of my collection of cherished jewels to pay my debts.

Mildred stood looking on with the tears in her eyes. "For two years," she said, "I have kept your business afloat, while you have done all in your power to wreck it. I have taken in money with one hand and you have thrown it away with both. It's all very well for you to reform, if you like, but what about the girls and me? Will you rent me your house?"

"No, Mildred," I answered, "I am going to give it to you. If I rented it to you, some day when I found the struggle too hard I would come back. Come with me to my solicitors in the morning and we will have the transfer made."

"You are going crazy," she reiterated for the hundredth time. "I will not let you give me the house. If you lose it, you will be broke, excepting for what you can raise on your diamonds. If you will stay out of the way for seven or eight months,

AN AUTOBIOGRAPHY

I can save ten thousand dollars for you. But I
can't save money while you are spending it faster
than I can take it in."

All of my arguments were unavailing. She would
not be a party to the transfer. We left the matter
open, but I never went back; and before the expiration of the year I walked alone.

AFTERWORD

NOT long since a woman who devotes much time to social uplift — and whose activities are as wide as her ignorance is deep — wasted a perfectly good evening in trying to enlist my aid in a social-purity campaign in which she is gaining fame and earning a comfortable living. She reproached me for my selfishness and my indifference to present-day social conditions, and insisted that I was a dreamer, who by keeping aloof from the world was enabled to preserve my youth and retain my illusions, but who knew nothing of real life.

After endeavoring to impart to my benighted mind some understanding of the roots and ramifications of the white-slave traffic, the ravages made by drink, and the general feeble-mindedness and incorrigibility of the children of the poor, she advised me to wake up, acquire a first-hand knowledge of these conditions (taking her as teacher and guide), and then assume my share of the world's work.

All of which reminds me that, after many years spent in studying the conditions of which the lady reformer drew such a misleading picture, I still cherished many illusions. After a few years spent in close touch with the uplifters I have none, though I still possess an abiding faith in the eternal justice of God and in the underlying goodness of every human heart.

But there are times when the Lord, knowing that I am tempted to utter words that would place me in the pillory of public obloquy and forever nullify the small measure of usefulness that I now possess, bestows upon me the gift of silence. If the supreme gift of patience is not given me, it is because I am unworthy of it.

I may liken my state of mind to that of a physician who has spent years in the dissecting-room, in the hospitals, and beside the couch of pain, who loves his fellow-men, and who would gladly devote his life to their service; but who, for a sufficient reason, is forced to conceal his knowledge and remain silent, while those who never saw a dissecting-room, and whose hospital experience is confined to a case of measles, endeavor to teach him the science of medicine.

I do not know anything about the so-called white-slave trade, for the simple reason that no such thing exists. I know all there is to be known about prostitution. I know it in all its hideousness; and I know it to be one of the greatest plagues that afflict mankind. But well as I know the underworld, I know more of the hearts and the lives of the individual women of which it is comprised.

Society has decreed for them punishment more cruel than it has decreed for the greatest criminals. It has taken no account of the suffering and atonement of their daily lives; with one breath it softly whispers, "We are followers of the Crucified One; let us teach you the way to Him; let us help you to come back." With the next breath it shrieks in demoniacal fury, "We must have a victim for the sacrifice, and you shall pay! pay! pay!"

Through the countless ages, and on down into our own times, the scarlet woman has been looked upon as one who in sheer wantonness had chosen her evil mode of life. "Very well," said society, "she has made her bed, now let her lie in it." That countless thousands of its fairest and best came to lie in it also matters not at all.

It was left for the enlightened twentieth century to create the Great American Myth. "White slavery is abroad in our land! Our daughters are being trapped and violated and held prisoners and sold for fabulous sums (a flattering unction, this), and no woman is safe."

And forthwith any woman or man who had a financial motive for spreading this myth proceeded to spread it. From stage and pulpit, from press and platform, they hastened to promulgate it, until every silly girl or woman who gets herself into a scrape uses it as a defense measure; and not infrequently is it employed as a weapon of blackmail and revenge. This clamor of the ignorant, the mendacious and self-aggrandizing, and the reformers for revenue only, fills the market-place, until even the ears of the little children are assailed and sullied by it; and only within the last month have I witnessed the sad

AN AUTOBIOGRAPHY

spectacle of a young woman who came from a remote region to a large city, being driven insane through fear of white-slavers.

The letters of this girl's mother, evidently a woman of considerable intelligence, were an eloquent commentary on the havoc which a belief in this pernicious myth plays with the higher instincts. There was expressed in them the natural anxiety of a mother for her girl alone in a great city, followed by explicit directions for her guidance.

She was to read a certain book dealing with the activities of the white-slave ring; and she was to see a certain lascivious photo-play which had been indorsed by social workers, women's clubs, and ministers, and which was supposed to possess great educational value, especially for the young. She was to avoid all strangers; to question the integrity of any man to whom she applied for employment; and to look upon all women, not indorsed by the pastor to whom she had been referred, as being possible white-slavers. The trend of all these letters was to call the girl's attention to her physical desirability and her marketable value.

Nothing was said about her own conduct; there was no appeal to self-respect, nor mention of those qualities of heart and mind which might reasonably be supposed to keep a girl in the straight path; from first to last, these letters were conducive to pruriency, and voiced an appeal to the basest of all human emotions, fear. When the mind broke down under this strain the heartbroken mother, who arrived in response to a telegram, was forced to listen to incoherent babblings about imaginary white-slavers who had attempted to lure her daughter to ruin. Yet the poor mother herself, no less than the daughter, was a victim of this unspeakable myth.

In the great city in which I live it is almost impossible to pick up a daily paper without seeing, in glaring head-lines, the announcement that some girl has disappeared and is supposed to be held by white-slavers. Oftentimes a brief item in an obscure part of a later issue states that the girl has been found to have gone here or there of her own free will; but those who read the first article seldom see the second, and so the belief in this myth has become a fixed delusion in the minds of many otherwise sane persons.

Above the tumult of the white-slave myth promulgators the voice of pseudo-science is striving to make itself heard. "These poor creatures are feebleminded, they are the ripe and noxious product of poverty and ignorance, of alcohol and disease and degeneracy; this is the fertile and only soil in which they are produced. We must build institutions, that they may neither contaminate our own pure offspring nor propagate their kind."

But sinner or sufferer, victim or fool, or an amalgamation of these elements, the position of the woman who would come back to a life of usefulness has not changed a particle. The present-day Judah who shares her guilt still says with the Judah of old, "Bring her forth and let her be burned."

324

And the multitude still cries, "Let her be stoned." Frequently the woman whose own sins are the blackest casts the first stone.

There are rare and earnest men and women to whom all life is not presented in "stark and rigid outline"; these seek to get under the facts, as well as to get at them; but theirs is the voice crying in the wilderness. The voice of the self-advertising fills the world.

The one person who might reasonably be supposed to know something about the question, the intelligent woman who has lived the life for twenty-four hours a day through several years, who has gone down into the depths of hell and fought her way up again, fighting often in the dark, but always upward; who has returned to a life of decency and usefulness, not through any assistance given her by society, but despite every obstacle that society would place in her path, has not, heretofore, been heard from. On the stage she calls for applause and the tender tear of sympathy. In real life she is crucified.

It is true that occasionally some hystero-religious society picks up a poor derelict whom they induce to pose as a horrible example of depravity, saved by their particular brand of religion. If, by a miracle, such a woman is again made whole and seeks to use her dearly bought knowledge for the benefit of others, these same good Christians will have none of her. She may serve them in a lowly capacity, as long as she submits to being exploited by them, but the moment she seeks to serve in a constructive way she is told, in unequivocal terms, that her services are not needed. If she foolishly persists, she is cast out and every infamy which lying tongues can bring forth is attributed to her.

The result of such an experience either drives a woman to suicide or back into the depths from which she has come. And in this last event the good brethren piously fold their hands and say: "You can do nothing for them; they always go back. They love the life and do not want to leave it."

"A lie that is half a truth is ever the blackest of lies." This lie, that they love the life, that they always go back, is the blackest invention of the Father of Lies. Few women, indeed, love the life, but many love the ease and luxury, the power over men, the idleness and freedom from responsibility, which they enjoy. If they pay for these with their souls, they differ in only one respect from the women who sell themselves into unloved and often loathsome marriage—they do not cheat in the delivery of the merchandise for which they are paid.

But there are thousands of women who hate the life with such bitter loathing that nothing that money procures can compensate them for their suffering. They are the ones who strive to prove to themselves that a woman with a past is not a woman without a future. Many of these women do leave the life, and many never return to it. Many make good marriages to men they really care for, and, contrary to the usual belief, these marriages

AN AUTOBIOGRAPHY

are often happy, and few indeed are the wives who prove unfaithful.

The woman who marries well has few difficulties placed in her path by society. A husband is a visible means of support and covers a multitude of dead sins. It is the woman who goes forth alone to fight for her soul who finds every hand against her and every door of opportunity closed in her face. She is cut off from the world she knew; and the larger world, outside the door of the brothel, seeks to drive her back, as if she were a wild beast who had strayed from her cage.

I remember, vividly, indeed, a woman of means and position who hounded me from one boarding-place to another, and from one employment to another, until there seemed to be no corner where I could find refuge from her. When I called on her to ask the reason for her persecution, to say that I did not know her and could not possibly have injured her, that all I asked was the God-given right to earn a decent living and to be left in peace, she declared that she knew all about my former life and that I had no right and no place among decent people; that my place was in the red-light district, and that she would fulfil her duty to society by seeing that I returned to it.

She had reckoned without her woman, however; for she found herself face to face with a spirit that has always refused to be crushed. The fact that she did not succeed only increased the malevolence with which she pursued me. Finally she encountered a big-hearted man who informed her that he, too, knew all about my former life, that his wife also knew, and that I was not only a valued employee, but an honored friend of the family. Her chagrin knew no bounds. She told him he was a libertine who had duped his poor wife into shielding me; she predicted that the end would be a broken home for him.

She proved a false prophet, however, and by her very malevolence raised up friends for me, after she had succeeded in making my life a hell as black as the one from which I had come. I am no longer in this man's employ, but I am still an honored friend of the family and am looked upon as a second mother by the children.

This woman is no exception; the world is filled with women like her. The beautiful wife of my former employer is the exception, for very few women possess her understanding heart and her great loving-kindness.

At the present time, wherever two or three club-women are gathered together the chief topic of conversation is "soldiers and vampires." It has been decreed that, while prostitution must go, the "vampires" must be kept outside the pale. A most peculiar logic this and one which I am utterly unable to grasp—decrying a sin and yet condemning a fellow-woman to follow it for the term of her natural life.

"Surely, my dear," said a noted club president to me recently—"surely you would not have us condone? If we forgive them and take them back again into decent society, *where* will the family be? What will become of our social fabric?"

"Madam," I answered, "*where* is the family *now*? If the present social fabric is only a moth-eaten piece of cloth, patched up on the under side where the patches will not show, then it is high time we began weaving a clean, strong, new fabric wherein the warp shall consist of the fittest we have and the woof be made up of the broken fragments of life."

THE END